UNIVERSITY OF NEVADA PRESS | *Reno & Las Vegas*

GARBAGE

Leonard Dominic Stefanelli   THE SAGA OF A BOSS SCAVENGER IN SAN FRANCISCO

University of Nevada Press | Reno, Nevada 89557 USA
www.unpress.nevada.edu
All photographs courtesy of the author unless otherwise noted.
Cover design by Martyn Schmoll
Book design by Virginia M. Fontana

LIBRARY OF CONGRESS CATALOGING-IN-PUBLICATION DATA
Names: Stefanelli, Leonard Dominic, 1934- author.
Title: Garbage : the saga of a boss scavenger in San Francisco / Leonard Dominic Stefanelli.
Description: Reno & Las Vegas : University of Nevada Press, 2017.
Identifiers: LCCN 2017006307 (print) | LCCN 2017039587 (e-book) | ISBN 978-1-943859-39-9
    (paperback) | ISBN 978-0-87417-559-2 (e-book)
Subjects: LCSH: Stefanelli, Leonard Dominic, 1934- | Sanitation workers—California—
    San Francisco—Biography. | Sunset Scavenger Company—History. | Sunset Scavenger
    Company—Biography. | BISAC: BIOGRAPHY & AUTOBIOGRAPHY / Personal Memoirs. |
    HISTORY / United States / State & Local / West (AK, CA, CO, HI, ID, MT, NV, UT, WY). | NATURE
    / Environmental Conservation & Protection.
Classification: LCC HD8039.S2572 U666 2017 (print) | LCC HD8039.S2572 (e-book) | DDC
    338.7/628442092 [B] —dc23
LC record available at https://lccn.loc.gov/2017006307

FIRST PRINTING

Manufactured in the United States of America

Cover photo: Pasquale Fontana coming up a driveway from a backyard collection site on Cole
Street, San Francisco, 1972.

Contents

Illustrations follow page 118

Preface

There should be no rhyme or reason that anyone would want to write about, let alone share a man's life in, the "garbage business." But I have realized that, after sixty years of being intimately involved with it in San Francisco (and other municipalities in Northern California), where I helped to create one of the most comprehensive and cost-effective solid-waste management programs in the world, my story is in fact worth sharing.

However, it is important to note that this waste-management program would not have been possible if not for the efforts and contributions of so many northern Italians who migrated to America in the late 1800s to seek a better life.

Garbage is dedicated to those who made that voyage.

In this memoir, I have attempted to include the personal story of my good days and my worst possible bad days, in both the garbage business and my personal life. I have learned through personal experience that in order to respect the good things in life, you really need to experience the bad things. So it is important for me to include both.

I have attempted to share that philosophy and experience, as well as the 100-year history of the scavengers in San Francisco. I hope you will enjoy, and learn from the experience, just as I have.

—LEONARD DOMINIC STEFANELLI

Leonard Stefanelli, at the Sunset Scavenger Corporate Headquarters, 1980.

Acknowledgments

Many people had a direct influence on my career in the garbage business, starting with my Uncle Pasquale and the entire Fontana Family, my wife Virginia, her family, Benny Anselmo, Richard Granzella, Dewey Vittori, and many other scavengers I worked with over so many years. No words can ever say how much they have meant to me and to the success I have been able to achieve in my career.

Regarding my later years, I must express special gratitude to my former chief financial officer, now president of Recology Inc., Michael Sangiacomo, and his board of directors. They provided me the opportunity to return to my roots, which took hold on a Scavenger truck more than sixty years ago.

In doing so, Michael Sangiacomo has provided me the opportunity to continue to participate in the growth of Recology, and be involved in its continuing contributions toward resolving the problems of waste production for the world by way of second- and third- generation advanced technologies.

Also, I'd like to especially acknowledge the late Kevin Starr, whose encouragement, support, and guidance made this book possible. My association with Kevin goes back thirty-five years, to when he was a reporter for the *San Francisco Progress*, and he interviewed me regarding a waste-to-energy project we were proposing. When everyone thought our proposal was off the wall, he endorsed it, demonstrating his ability to cut to the chase, typical of his strong skills in addressing a range of issues, especially ones that were controversial.

There are not enough words in this world to express what this gentleman did for me personally—but not just for me—for the City of San Francisco, the State of California and its history, politics, and religion. In short, its people.

Few will ever know, appreciate, or respect Mr. Starr's contributions the way I have. But I had the opportunity to know him well, which is odd when one considers the vast differences in our personal and intellectual backgrounds. It's all still a bit of a mystery, but it happened.

However it happened, though, Kevin Starr was the one who encouraged me to write this book. I am indeed saddened over his passing, not just because of the loss of a friend, but in cherishing his never-ending contributions to the California literary community.

Introduction:

A Historical Summary of Garbage

The garbage business is what most people historically assume to be the lowest rung on the social ladder of life. Few of the so-called educated, elite, and blue collar—let alone white collar—workers would ever have any desire to be associated with garbage.

Despite that longstanding attitude, garbage is truly the common dominator of all people in the world. Whether white, black, brown, rich, poor, Communist, or capitalist, we all generate garbage. Until recent times, few people openly acknowledged that fact. Historically, few people have admitted that they produce garbage—and, worse yet—that they pay to get rid of it.

In San Francisco, where this saga takes place, filling the San Francisco Bay with anything—especially garbage—resulted in a huge outcry and controversy. Somehow, me and the company I managed were the villains, hell-bent on the ultimate destruction of the bay, while others were reclaiming tidelands 500 acres at a time with no outcry.

San Francisco, since before the turn of the twentieth century, has never missed regularly scheduled garbage collection services, except on April 18, 1906, the day of the Great Earthquake and resulting fire.

Other than that one day, garbage collection has continued un-interrupted. I know that the primary reason for such continuous service is that there has always been someplace to dispose of the garbage collected by the scavengers. That place was once San Francisco Bay, unfortunately the dumping ground shared by every community surrounding it.

Prior to this, as well as when the earthquake and fire hit San Francisco in 1906, the city fathers realized that dumping garbage in the bay and within the city limits could potentially be a serious health hazard to the people of San Francisco.

To minimize that potential disaster, the city concluded that all garbage should be transported out of the city, and it contracted with Southern Pacific Railroad to have it receive the garbage from the horse-and-wagon scavengers and transport it to a site located at 16th and 3rd Streets in San Francisco. The garbage would then be dumped into gondola cars—open-topped carts similar to those that miners used for coal transport—and hauled some five miles south on Southern Pacific's mainline, which paralleled the bay.

Once the garbage passed over the San Francisco/San Mateo county line, it somehow lost its health hazard. In fact, at the turn of the twentieth century, filling the bay with anything—including garbage—was acceptable and considered to be a form of "reclamation" for those "stinking mudflats."

This, of course, was long before we knew or heard the terms *ecology, environment, environmentalist, preservation, reuse, recycle,* and *environmental impact reports.*

As years passed, it seemed that all people, reluctantly, began to admit that they were the ones creating the garbage that was threatening the environment.

I recall a presentation at an environmental hearing in the 1970s where new environmentalists suggested that something had to be done immediately with San Francisco garbage. Since these people were demanding immediate solutions, I responded with a simple but logical question: "When did garbage begin?"

While the audience was pondering the question, I answered it myself:

> Read the Scriptures. Refer to when Adam and Eve were in the Garden of Eden and ate the proverbial apple. Didn't God create mankind, among others, affecting the world we know today? But what the Scriptures failed to mention was what Adam and Eve did with the apple core.
>
> Ladies and Gentlemen, that is when garbage began and realistically, how can anyone expect to solve a problem that has been with us since man first walked on the earth—a problem that we have just admitted that we ourselves create?

That response brought some reality to the newly created environmental movement. Environmental issues were now coming to the attention of the general public, as well as to people and businesses on the higher rungs of the social ladder. They had never envisioned themselves being associated with garbage, but now they realized that it was in fact a multibillion-dollar industry, with trucks, facilities, property, landfills, databases, and so much more, offering great opportunities.

All of a sudden, the so-called elite, who would never have been associated with garbage in the past, acknowledged the potential of the garbage business. While they realized that no one could change the product, they felt a name change was in order, so *garbage* became *solid waste*.

Thanks to this growing awareness, filling the bay with anything, least of all garbage, was being phased out. Beginning in 1906, when the earthquake changed many things, almost every square mile of the city was covered with housing, roads, and people. The city had no physical or legal space for anything, least of all for the disposal of its waste.

As the city grew and the means of disposal through the Southern Pacific Railroad became outdated, it was common knowledge that San Francisco lacked adequate space to dispose of the one million tons of waste it generated annually, that it was facing a serious crisis.

Even though there were no truly experienced and professional people in the field except the scavengers, our proven record was overlooked in favor of the newly found "experts" in solid-waste management: those people whose expertise was limited to putting out their garbage cans on collection day. After years of delays, the scavengers' professionalism and commitment finally prevailed, and we were able to demonstrate to the public that our knowledge and extensive experience could meet the long-term needs of the City of San Francisco.

San Francisco is the seventh-largest largest city in the United States and produces one million tons of waste a year, but by 1970 it had no physical or legal space within its forty-eight square miles for its disposal. Now, thanks to its scavengers, the City of San Francisco enjoys the most comprehensive, cost-effective solid-waste management program in the world.

Because of my achievements in the waste management industry, I was invited to President Jimmy Carter's White House, along with thirty-nine other guests. Tom Peters, an inspirational speaker for business and the author of *In Search of Excellence,* compared me to the presidents of IBM, Wal-Mart, American Express, and others.

I was also invited, in 1972, to travel to the Soviet Union under President Nixon's technology exchange program that had been established between the world powers. On one special occasion, I even had dinner in the Kremlin!

My life as a scavenger has been an extraordinary voyage, filled with memories and experiences that defy description. None of my achievements would have been possible without those Italians who came to this country seeking a better life. Many did not speak the language and could not find any work, except collecting garbage. Here was an industry that began because of discrimination. Because of the struggles these Italian immigrants endured, I have had great opportunities and many memorable experiences.

This book is dedicated to those Italian wayfarers who came before me. Their sacrifices paved the way for my personal success. I hope you will enjoy reading about my remarkable American journey.

GARBAGE

1

A Personal History

As a third-generation San Franciscan, I still reside here with my wife after almost eighty years. We have seen many changes in lifestyles, environment, and political infrastructure—and have been blessed with amazing views of hills, a magnificent bay and its bridges, extraordinary dining, and a population made up of every ethnicity in the world. This is a rare and unique city in every aspect, and I am proud to be able to say, "I am a native son."

As part of living so many years in San Francisco, I read *The Argonaut*, a journal published by the San Francisco Museum and Historical Society. *The Argonaut* prints many fine historical articles that are especially valuable to those of us who have resided here for a long time and can relate to that wonderful history. I especially enjoyed Ken Sproul's excellent article, "Growing Up in San Francisco: Boyhood Recollections from the 1940s and 1950s," published in the spring 2012 issue.

While *The Argonaut* has covered almost every aspect of San Francisco's unique and special history, it has never referenced the city's waste-collection services, possibly because it's not a glamorous or exciting subject, or maybe because no one pays much attention to this service.

After reading about Ken Sproul's experiences in San Francisco, I felt the need to share my experiences. My article, "Everything You Wanted to Know about Garbage and Were Afraid to Ask," was published in the summer 2014 issue of *The Argonaut*. But there is more to my story, and in this book I will share what I have experienced and the respect I have for all the men and women who made it all possible.

Childhood Memories

I was born in the Haight-Ashbury District on May 6, 1934, at 1822 Fell Street. When I was three, I moved in with my grandparents, Lenora and Harry Corbelli, who lived in a grand, three-story Victorian home at 117 Cole Street. My grandfather worked for the Southern Pacific Railroad.

My uncle, Pasquale "Pas" Fontana, lived around the corner at 2122 Grove Street. He was a scavenger who would play an extraordinary part in my future life, starting when he gave me the task of "Collecting the Book" when I was seven years old.

Every scavenger was responsible for "Collecting the Book"—collecting the fees for picking up the garbage. At night, a scavenger would ring a customer's doorbell and when the door opened, he would say "Garbage bill!" and be paid accordingly. At that time, the fee was $1.10 for two months' service. When I was seven, Uncle Pasquale taught me how to ring the doorbells and make change—probably giving me a better math education than I could have had in school.

Around the corner from my grandparents' house was Andrew Jackson School, where I attended elementary school. My teachers were Ms. Shea (kindergarten—a young woman), Miss Anderson (first grade—also a young woman), Mrs. Wendell (third grade—she acted like a mom), Mrs. Daniels (fourth grade), Miss Sanders (fifth grade—she had a wedding band), and Mrs. Walsh (sixth grade—she also had a wedding ring). I have no idea why I remember all these names and details at this stage in life, but I do, especially Mrs. Walsh, who had the worst case of body odor anyone could imagine.

Most of us tried not to ask Mrs. Walsh too many questions because when she would come to our desk and look over our shoulder to respond to a question, the odor was severe. It was better not to ask for help.

Myrtle B. Ozer was the school's principal. I got to know her because I was sent to see her more times than I want to admit, because of "problems" over the years with my teachers (or because of my teachers' problems with me). I remember a little wooden stool that I would be told to sit on in the corner, awaiting the call to come into her office, anticipating and dreading the stern warning of impending disaster if I did not get my life in order.

In his article, Ken Sproul referred to building wooden coasters to ride down a hill. We made ours with a long flat board and two 2 x 4 pieces of wood. We nailed one 2 x 4 on the rear, which extended outside the board; and we would cut a hole in the center of the other 2 x 4 and another hole in the long board.

We would connect the two with a long nut and bolt, using several washers, to allow the front 2 x 4 to swivel. Then we would take roller skates (the ones that, with a skate key, you could make longer or shorter depending on shoe size). By taking the skates apart using the skate key, we now had four sets of wheels, which we would nail onto the extended 2 x 4s now mounted on the board. We now had a coaster that would roll down a hill. We were able to steer the coaster by putting our feet on the front 2 x 4.

We dragged our coasters up to the top of a steep hill at Cole and Fulton Streets, across from the former entrance to the University of San Francisco, where we would "mount up" and let them be powered by gravity. We reached a speed of at least twenty-five miles per hour, streaking across the intersection of Grove and Cole Streets, oblivious to oncoming traffic, and down the street to the intersection of Cole and Hayes, where the Market Street Railway Route 21 could be arriving, once again oblivious to us.

Approaching the intersection, we would swing far to the left and then make a sharp right turn onto Hayes Street, missing the railroad tracks in case a streetcar was arriving, thus preventing injury or death. We had no fear. Looking back, I often wonder why no one was killed or maimed by auto or, worse yet, by sliding under a moving streetcar.

We played games against the stairs with tennis balls—olly olly oxen free, kick the can, hide-and-seek, basketball, stickball. We played until dark and went home, where no one ever locked the front door. If you did, the key was under the floor mat.

We played in the "Big Lot," which was land owned by the University of San Francisco. On the top level, a magnificently maintained garden was directly across the street, in front of the church that is now the site of USF Law School. If our play activities in the Big Lot would overflow into the USF gardens, the Italian gardener would run us off with a big machete.

We climbed trees, dug caves in the clay soil on the side of the hill, which occasionally caved in on us, and did other crazy antics that make me wonder why we are still alive today.

I recall that, while digging in the soils of the Big Lot, we would find seashells and wonder where they could have come from. Now I realize that these properties, eons ago, were no doubt under water. We also joined the Cub Scouts and the Boy Scouts. (I never was smart enough to join the Eagle Scouts.)

Cecil Briones owned the Park Pharmacy. Aside from selling medical supplies, the Park Pharmacy had a magazine rack that included comic books. I always enjoyed Walt Disney's Donald Duck and his three nephews, Huey, Dewey, and Louie. I also liked Uncle Scrooge, who had a swimming pool that he swam in, but instead of water, it held money.

One day I did not have the five cents necessary to purchase the new edition, so I thought it would be cool to pick up the comic book and walk out the door without paying. Cecil Briones promptly caught me. This was the most embarrassing experience in my short life, and it resulted in a lesson I would always remember, one that made me a better man. As life went by, Cecil and I became friends.

The Park Pharmacy also sold books. One day we heard of a very racy book called *Catcher in the Rye*. Allegedly, on one page of the book—in bold print—the dreaded "four letter word (f--k)" appeared. When no one was looking, we would pick up the book at the Park Pharmacy. After some lengthy reading, we found it, in bold and brassy print. Wow!

When I graduated from Andrew Jackson, many of my friends and I went to junior high and then seventh through ninth grades at Dudley Stone School at Masonic and Haight Streets, some seven blocks from my home. During my two years there, I never did learn who Dudley Stone was. My friends and I attended Saturday movie matinees at the Haight Theatre. We sat in the back row and had our first exposure to the opposite sex. We ate donuts at Metz's Donuts next door and played touch football in Golden Gate Park's Panhandle, long before people slept there.

When we graduated from Dudley Stone, some boys went to St. Ignatius or Lowell, either because their families had money to pay for the private school education that St. Ignatius offered or because the kids were smart enough to get into Lowell, a free public school with elite academic standards.

Others, including Don Streltzoff and me, went to Polytechnic High School, across the street from Kezar Stadium. I thought I wanted to be an auto mechanic, and Poly High had great auto mechanics, woodworking, and metal shop classes. It also had an excellent football team under the leadership of the famous coach Milt Axt.

At fourteen years old, I thought I had the world in my hands. I made lots of new friends—and met girls. I had some great times and some bad times as well. Poly High School had a reputation for having some resident Muns ("bad-asses"). Because I was short, I was initially picked on—in today's terms, bullied—on a regular basis.

My grandparents were getting on in years, and I had a long leash. As a result, I started to become a badass as well. I wore Levi's jeans with the cuffs rolled up and black shirts with white buttons tucked into my pants, a chain for a belt (also a defensive weapon), and a flattop haircut with fenders combed into a duck's ass. Boy, was I a mean badass! *Nobody* screwed around with me!

I got in a few fights, drank a lot of beer, chased women (did not catch many), and had fun, fun, and more fun. My first term report card reflected that attitude: five Fs and one D (in gym).

At the time, I had to take my report card to each individual instructor, who would write my grades by hand and initial them. I then took a pen and made each *F* look like a *B* or an *A*. I did this to satisfy my grandmother, Noni Lenora, who for some reason thought I was special.

Noni was getting older, and I convinced her that she needed someone to drive her around in my grandparents' 1941 Plymouth sedan. She signed a "need and necessity" form, which allowed me to apply for and receive a learner's permit at age thirteen-and-a-half. At fourteen, I got my driver's license.

Once I had my license, I put fender skirts and musical horns on the car to bring status to my driving skills and make people realize I was the cock of the walk. Few kids had driver's licenses, let alone access to a car. Having both resources at my disposal was a great social advantage, but not necessarily conducive to getting a good education.

After such a dismal report card for my first semester in high school, one would assume that I would have attempted to improve the following year. As the record will show, to mitigate that problem, I "applied myself." In my second term, I was the proud recipient of—count 'em—*six* Fs. This time, I flunked gym.

However, it was something of a turning point in my simple life, because all the people I started school with were now one year ahead of me in the school's curriculum.

For the first time, I realized that life might be passing me by. I tried to apply myself, but I surely was not at the head of my class.

I did finally graduate four years later, but only after the dean of boys, Paul Hungerford, who for some reason or another took a liking to me, allowed me to take the civics test four times. I finally passed the course and acquired the sufficient credits to earn a diploma.

As graduation day neared, after spending five years in a four-year curriculum, I was called into Dean Hungerford's office. He sat me down (he was a football coach before becoming the dean) to give me some fatherly and brutally frank advice, evidently because, for some reason, as I have noted, he liked me.

After a bit of a lecture, he pointed his finger at me and then out the window at Kezar Stadium, philosophically stating in a commanding voice: "Stefanelli, I know you have some f - - -ing brains, but if you go outside in that world, and f - -k around like you f - -ked around in this school, you will end up picking up garbage!"

And that is exactly what I did. At age nineteen, I went to work at Sunset Scavenger Company, driving my Uncle Pasquale's Truck 3, serving the neighborhood and the people I had lived and played with since I was born.

As time went by, I realized what Dean Hungerford was suggesting. Simply put, he was reflecting the opinion of most educated people—that the last choice in life for anyone who had to work for a living was to collect someone else's garbage. In other words, being a garbage collector represented the lowest possible rung on the social ladder.

I did not realize the impact of that statement until later years. What he was saying is this: "Anyone can be a garbage man, that is, have a strong back, a weak mind, and do the work of an Italian." I didn't realize that Dean Hungerford was not deliberately or consciously discriminating against garbage collectors. His statement simply reflected what the average person thought about the men who provided this service.

Looking back at the way the scavenger company was founded and still operated in the 1950s and early 1960s, I see that I did not have much opportunity for advancement compared to the way today's modern waste collection companies are run. Although education was clearly an important tool, there were not many areas within the company where a higher education would be an asset or a resource for advancement. I also knew that oftentimes the "old ways" were in fact the "best ways" to do business, and unless something changed, that would be the order of the day.

In other words, when you became a shareholder (a Boss Scavenger), you did the same job as you did yesterday—and more. You collected the garbage but, as a shareholder, you also collected the book, ringing the doorbells of all individual accounts.

Working on the old open trucks was clearly a backbreaking job. You used a hook that hung off your shoulder to pick up small garbage cans, dumped them into a larger 75-gallon aluminum container, and took the load to the garbage truck. Once there, you carried those 100-plus pounds of weight up seven stairs and into the truck's open body. You dragged or walked the contents over the existing garbage and shook the bags open to recover rags, bottles, newspaper, and cardboard for recycling. Then you jumped on the waste to compact it in the truck.

The job was extremely hard, especially when compared to today's scavengers using contemporary equipment. My experience collecting trash for ten years in the Fillmore District can be summarized by this description: I carried a can up the stairs and into the open truck on a hot day, dripping with sweat, wiping off my neck the live maggots that fell out of the top of the can and onto my back. The scavengers often referred to this experience as the "seven stairs to heaven" because you saw stars when you got to the top of the truck.

One day I happened to see a black man on a stairway, staring hard at me. I yelled down to him, "Hey man, you got a problem?"

"Stay cool man," he replied.

"Then what in the hell you looking at?" I yelled back.

His response overwhelmed me. He said, "I just never saw any man work like that. I thought Lincoln freed the slaves."

As long as I live, I will never forget that comment and how right he was. Unless you were there you cannot possibly understand how brutal our job assignments were, especially compared to a scavenger's job today, in the age of modern compaction equipment.

But that was the way scavengers had done business since before 1900. The only real thing that had changed was that now we had a gas engine instead of a horse.

In 1962, as an employee/shareholder of Sunset Scavenger Company, you were a scavenger, a mechanic, or one of three so-called "executives" who worked in the office. There was little opportunity for advancement.

Our job was simple: drive to the route, collect the garbage, dump the truck, ring the doorbells to collect the money, deposit the collections into a company account, go home, eat dinner, and go to sleep. Then get up and go to work again.

I actually loved working on the truck. I was proud of being a scavenger, and I had a great crew: Louis Bertone, my godfather Pete Guaraglia, and Booker T. Day. We worked together like a well-oiled, coordinated, and finely calibrated piece of machinery.

In simpler terms, a crew—a good crew—is made up of people who work in conjunction with—not against—one another in perfect liaison. Our crew worked well and as a result, we finished a scheduled eight-hour day in five (and got paid for eight). That was the benefit of working on the trucks. In addition to working in the open air, we got a beer or a coffee royal at every bar on our route—not many, but sufficient to feed a thirst.

Because the job was tough, especially on the older members, back, leg, and hip injuries were commonplace. I was only twenty-eight years old at the time but, looking into the future, I knew that there was little opportunity for advancement. I did not see myself carrying garbage until I was fifty-five, the earliest I could retire.

Thinking ahead, I realized that it might be beneficial if I went to college somewhere and learned something. I attended night school at the University of San Francisco three times a week, for three semesters over an eighteen-month period, studying corporate law and accounting and business administration. The latter was taught by a salesman at the Emporium Store. I always thought this a bit strange—his being an instructor while holding a modest sales position.

He made a profound statement on the first night of the course, which I will always remember, where he introduced himself and told us where he worked. He then complimented the class for being "special." It was his opinion that because we were there, we were seeking something more in life than "an 8-to-5 job, going home to drink a cold beer, have dinner, to bounce the kids on your lap, to watch TV, and to go to bed and start the routine over. . ."

I never forgot that. Unfortunately, all the courses I wanted to take were full, and because I had no way to apply what I was learning, it became almost a repetition of my high school days.

In later years, I often made fun of the fact that I went to USF twice a day—once to get an education and the other to pick up the garbage.

I then went to Golden Gate College and obtained an agent's license from the State of California to sell general insurance with a friend of mine, Joe Picetti. Joe's dad encouraged me in this, saying that I was a "natural born salesman." Joe and I used a split commission arrangement. Selling insurance on the side, I found that in three years I was making more money in insurance than working at Sunset as a scavenger.

In 1965, I was planning to leave the garbage business for a full-time job in the insurance business, when something unique happened at Sunset Scavenger Company and changed my life. I found myself as Second Boss on Truck 27, on Friday, August 27, 1965, and president of Sunset Scavenger on August 28. At age thirty-one, I was president of a three-million-dollar-a-year business.

It would have been a traumatic experience for anyone, but I believe that I survived it because of the little bit of education I had gotten at USF. I had nothing to apply my education to as a garbage man but, without that education, I would have failed as president. Because of my classes at USF, I could read and understand income statements, balance sheets, and the like, and I could comprehend corporate law and business philosophy.

I began to realize the history and contributions that the Italian community had brought to the overall welfare and reputation of the city. Many members of my family were scavengers, and I married into a family that came from a long line of scavengers, where everybody worked hard and played hard and had fun doing it. We all had a strong work ethic and contributed greatly to the efficiency of the service we provided.

To this day, I recall memories of the "old-timers." We asked questions like what part of Northern Italy they came from. In the United States, they lived in boarding houses, where as many as six scavengers would live in a single home, sometimes sharing a bedroom. An Italian woman would cook and wash their clothes. On weekends, they would make and drink wine and play bocce ball, horseshoes, and Pedro. All week they worked and saved their money so that they could bring their families from Italy and eventually buy a home here.

There is a rich history about the San Francisco scavenger companies after the turn of the twentieth century. I remember listening to a bunch of old-timers sitting around a table drinking wine and talking about driving in a car, going deer hunting, or having a holiday dinner. Then they would begin talking about the old days, saying, "Remember Mingo Ballestrasse on Truck 31 in the Mission . . .?"

2

The Birth of Sunset Scavenger Company

As best I can determine, Emilio Rattaro arrived from Italy in 1904 and, as was typical, could not find work. He ran a small farm at 12th Avenue and Judah Street in the Sunset District. Like his colleagues before him, Emilio purchased a horse and wagon and became a scavenger to supplement his income.

He called his company the *Sunset Scavenger Company* because he lived in the Sunset District. One of his claims to fame was that his was one of the first scavenger companies to serve what is now known as St. Frances Wood, when the first house was built in the sand dunes.

He told his family that it took a long time to drive a wagon from 12th and Judah to service just one account, but he envisioned that if there were one customer, then someday there would be two, and so on. . .and he was right.

As the Sunset District began to grow, more scavengers (horse, wagon, and Italian) came into the area, competing for the growing business. The only way they could compete was to offer the service at a lower rate than the competition. But as a result, no one was making any money.

Emilio Rattaro had a vision in 1912, which was to create a new entity by joining together some five companies (remember a "company" was a horse, a wagon, and an Italian). He knew that by consolidating the five companies into a single entity, each company could be assigned to a specific service area and could eliminate the competition in that area. Also, it would allow each scavenger to raise his rates so he could make a profit.

As an added incentive for these companies to merge into this arrangement, each worker could garage his horse and wagon in a central location, purchase hay and other needs in volume, and reduce his expenses. All revenue collected would be pooled together (or "placed on the table").

After bills were paid, all funds still on the table would be split equally by the five partners. Today, this form of operation could be challenged as a violation of antitrust laws. On the other hand, it might be defined as socialistic—or, worse yet, communistic.

Nonetheless, for the Italian immigrant it was a means of survival. I sometimes referred to that concept facetiously as a "quasi-communistic, capitalistic organization. Capitalist in theory, but communist in reality, where everybody shared equally the fruits of the combined labor."

The arrangement was defined; the concept caught on. From 1912 to 1920, ninety-two scavengers merged under the roof of the Sunset Scavenger Company. As the company grew, Sunset Scavenger Company joined forces with the Bank of Italy (now the Bank of America), whose president was A. P. Giannini (a Genovese, of course). The new company was made up of ninety-two Genovese Italians, and it was only natural that they did business with a Genovese banker.

Mr. Giannini recommended that Sunset Scavenger Company become a corporation. Sunset Scavenger retained the services of an attorney, Angelo Devencenzi, who also recommended that the partnership incorporate.

Articles of Incorporation and corporate bylaws were drafted in English and Italian (the Italian was a Zeneize dialect). Each partner signed the Articles of Incorporation by hand. As I have seen and now preserved, that signed document notes that, of the ninety-two signatures, seven were signed with an "X" and witnessed by the company's attorney, Angelo Devencenzi. The bylaws, which were written in Italian, stated in part:

> Every Boss Scavenger [term for shareholder] shall be treated absolutely equal and alike, regardless of office, position or responsibility. . . and shall be compensated equally, shall have one vote on matters requiring the Shareholder/Boss Scavenger vote on corporate matters, such as elections for the Board of Directors. . . and other matters where it was deemed legally necessary for shareholder/Boss Scavenger approval.

The merging of these ninety-two companies resulted in a more secure income source. It also created higher efficiency in the collection of the waste. There were fewer horses and wagons and, rather than one man and one wagon, the crew concept was created where two and possibly three men worked on a wagon. The size of the wagon was doubled, with two horses instead of one, resulting in a more cost-effective means of providing services.

Each partner or Boss Scavenger working on a specific route was required to ring the doorbell at night and collect money for the services provided during the previous month. Conceptually, the money was still "placed on the table." Bills were paid, and what was left over the partners shared equally—except now, the partners were all paid a fixed wage, incorporating this basic law: All partners shall be compensated equally, regardless of office, position, or responsibility. . .including the president and all officers.

If at the end of the year the company made money or had a positive cash flow, a dividend would be paid; each shareholder was given the same amount—no bonuses, no exceptions.

Prior to the incorporation of the Sunset Scavenger Company, the other dominant company in the greater San Francisco area was the Scavenger's Protective Association. In 1970, this group changed its name to Golden Gate Disposal and formed itself around the same concepts as Sunset Scavenger Company. The majority of Scavenger's Protective Association's business was concentrated in the downtown area and northern portions of San Francisco, while Sunset's base was in the southern and western portions of the city. Some smaller companies, including many "one-horse" entities, still operated as well.

As history indicates, Scavenger's Protective Association and Sunset Scavenger Company were not necessarily friendly. Each entity always felt, even into the mid-1980s, that its own company was superior to the other. Ironically, both companies were incorporated on the same day, September 20, 1920; and the same attorney (Angelo Devencenzi) legally incorporated all those companies. But I could never find out why this coincidence occurred.

To cloak this event in even more mystery, the Oakland Scavenger Company formed under the same concept as Emilio Rattaro's Sunset Scavenger Company and was also incorporated on the same day as both of the San Francisco companies and by the same attorney.

The Boss Scavengers of all three entities had another common ground of sorts. Most of the original members came from the same general area of the Province of Genova, near and around Fontanarossa.

The bylaws of Sunset Scavenger Company established an eleven-member board of directors and mandated that meetings of the shareholders (Boss Scavengers)' be held on the third Wednesday of each month. The election of the directors and officers was held on the third Wednesday each December.

An election was held at the first meeting of the Boss Scavengers, and two of the eleven members who were nominated to the board of directors were Emilio Rattaro and Giuseppe Fontana. (Giuseppe Fontana was the brother of Dominic Fontana, my yet-to-be-born uncle and his yet-to-be-born brothers, Pasquale, Dominic, and Alfredo.)

At first, Emilio Rattaro was the "Boss" of the Sunset Scavenger Company. After Sunset Scavenger became incorporated on September 20, 1920, he became president.

Three months later, at the scheduled annual elections for the board of directors, he was reelected to the board; but Emilio Rattaro opted to step down as president and become vice president. Giuseppe Fontana became president and remained in that capacity for forty-two years, until he passed away at age seventy-four during a trip to Italy in 1952.

When Emilio Rattaro stepped down, in lieu of working on the garbage wagons, his job was sorting rags at the Joseph Petigera Company, the salvage (recycling) arm of Sunset Scavenger Company. (The people collecting the garbage recovered the bottles, newspaper, cardboard, and rags. Then they brought these items to the company for segregation and further processing for sale.)

Also in 1920, Antonio Fagliano became secretary (and ran the office). Francisco Brandi became the dispatcher, and the balance of the board of directors collected garbage. Emilio Rattaro retired in 1937 and moved to Santa Rosa, where he passed away in 1970 at age 84.

Unfortunately, after Sunset Scavenger was incorporated, the business did not have professional advice or sophisticated accounting procedures. It continued to operate as a partnership in concept, but it failed to put aside funds for corporate taxes. As a result, some twelve years after incorporation, the federal and state tax collectors filed claims against the company for unpaid corporate taxes and failure to file tax returns, while still operating as a partnership.

Several auditors concluded that the failure was not an effort to intentionally defraud the agencies but was due to a lack of oversight. The IRS applied a levee against the company for some

$250,000 in back taxes and interest, a significant amount of money at that time.

To pay this penalty, the company offered to sell shares to employees who were not part of the original shareholders when the company incorporated in 1920. During this period of time, my uncles Pasquale, Dominic, and Freddy became Boss Scavengers.

The need to sell additional shares in the company came at a good time because San Francisco was experiencing substantial growth and generating more garbage. The need was for more scavengers to collect refuse and fees from over 125,000 individual accounts. To meet that demand, the number of shareholders grew to 320 in 1955.

As an interesting side note, my future father-in-law became a Boss Scavenger the year I was born. He married Jennie Rattaro in 1938, daughter of Emilio Rattaro, founder and first president of Sunset Scavenger Company. A year later, Jennie gave birth to their first daughter, Virginia, who was to become my wife in 1959.

Aside from incorporation, 1920 was another milestone for Sunset Scavenger Company when it purchased its first gasoline engine garbage truck, a 1920 White Motor Car frame and a wood body (from the forerunner to Garwood Industries) designed with seven stairs. In lieu of stepping on the spokes of the wooden wheels in order to gain precarious access to the dump body, the scavenger now climbed actual steps. This allowed the scavenger to walk up the steps with the barrel on his back, making the task substantially easier than with the old horse and wagons.

This was the first step—no pun intended—in many over a ten-year period that replaced horsepower with gasoline power. Sunset Scavenger Company was eventually located on Hampshire Street in the Mission District, where horses and gasoline trucks were housed in the mid-1920s. During the process of converting from horse and wagons to gasoline-driven collection vehicles, horse and wagons were still used to collect refuse located nearest to the "barn" (closest to the headquarters), while gas trucks were utilized for areas farthest from the barn.

3

Sunset Scavenger during the 1940s and 1950s

When Japan bombed Pearl Harbor on December 7, 1941, the United States government declared that the services scavengers provided throughout the Bay Area were "essential services." Scavengers were exempt from military service during the war.

My research suggests that some scavengers opted to join the service during the war, but I can confirm only four cases. Eugene De Martini joined the United States Marines, fought in the Pacific Theatre, and returned with Battle Combat Stars and a Purple Heart. Benny Anselmo Sr. had a similar record in the Pacific, participating in the invasion of Iwo Jima and its infamous battle on Mount Fujiyama. After the war, he returned to the garbage trucks, eventually taking over the P. G. Torre Company, the salvage arm of the Scavenger's Protective Association/Golden Gate Disposal, and was eventually appointed to the board of directors.

Emilio Rattaro, my wife's grandfather, had four children: Jennie, Virginia (my mother-in-law), Serafino, and Giovanni "John" Rattaro. John opted to join the US Navy and was assigned to a destroyer called the *USS Hull*, one of the ships under the command of Admiral William "Bull" Halsey.

This ship was involved in major sea battles but was unfortunately also caught up in a hurricane's perfect storm when many ships in the fleet were sunk, including the *USS Hull*. John Rattaro was lost at sea and never heard from again. According to my mother-in-law, Emilio never got over the loss. John's brother, Serafino "Fing," became a scavenger.

On the other side of the street, Uncle Freddy went to war, but under a somewhat different circumstance. Before I explain how that occurred, I should explain that Alfredo (or "Freddy") was the youngest of five siblings: Dominic "Mingo" Pasquale, "Paul" Florence, Inez, and Alfredo. Uncle Freddy was the youngest of them and, as I was to learn in the years to come, the most unpredictable.

He was a loose cannon, fun to be with, and someone who could "let the badger loose" at the drop of a hat. His brother-in-law, Guillermo "Willie" Damonte, was as wild as Freddy. When together, they were a "pair to draw to," but that's another story for a later day.

At a Sunset Scavenger shareholders meeting, president Fontana (Freddy's uncle) announced to the shareholders that the company was donating $2,500 to Italy for the war effort. According to Freddy, there was some grumbling, but he was the only one who openly opposed the decision. Freddy's argument was simple and logical. "Let me ask a question, Mr. President, and tell me if I am wrong. The last time I checked, Italy had declared war against America; and if they did, why in the hell is the company sending money to the enemy?"

That comment brought similar protests from many of the Boss Scavengers, resulting in a rare public disagreement from the floor, questioning a management decision.

As noted, men working in the garbage business were provided deferments from military service because they provided an "essential service." However, because Uncle Freddy challenged the decision and authority of the company president (and his blood uncle) and the board of directors in a public forum of the shareholders, he was called to duty. He was drafted into the United States Army less than a week after the challenge to his uncle. Giuseppe Fontana, president of Sunset Scavenger Company, was also a member of the draft board.

Everyone knew that Freddy got called up because he pissed off his uncle. No one ever again mentioned the contribution to Italy's war effort nor openly challenged any decision by the president or the board of directors.

After boot camp, Uncle Freddy was trained in the Sherman Tank Corp and was eventually assigned to Italy because he spoke Italian. After the war, he returned to Dago Alley (Oakwood Street) to a huge reception as an Italian hero with a Purple Heart, a Bronze Star, and a boatload of stories expressing his experiences in vivid detail.

Some stories were funny and others were about horrible incidents, like pulling the gold teeth out of German soldiers killed in action. I do not know whether there was any truth in these stories, but who was to know?

During the years that followed, Freddy would get serious about his experiences, saying that he did not like the thought of killing Italians, but when he realized they were trying to kill him—

"Italians, Germans, whatever—I wanted to come home, and I shot back."

I am sure that other scavengers volunteered. One example was Natale "Ned" Biaoni, who served in the Army and brought back a war trophy of a magnificent German Luger, which was given to me in later years.

Although scavengers were not mandated to go to war, they did in fact contribute greatly to the war effort. For example, on Sundays they volunteered their own labor and trucks to go to every intersection in the city. Residents were instructed to wash and flatten all tin cans and other metals and place them on the street corners, along with nylon, silk stockings, bacon fat, and other grease byproducts that were collected and reused for the war effort. The companies and the Boss Scavengers did this without compensation other than replacement of fuel, which was rationed during the war.

The Loss of the President, Giuseppe Fontana

Giuseppe "Joe" Fontana became the second president of Sunset Scavenger Company on January 1, 1921.

Giuseppe and his brother, Dominic Fontana, were born in Suzzi, the Italian province of Genova. Dominic and Joe, like so many others, made the trip to the United States by walking to Genoa, getting on a ship, landing on Ellis Island, riding a train to San Francisco, and eventually ending up in the garbage business and sending for their families.

For many years, I did not know much about Pas, Mingo, and Freddy's uncle, Giuseppe, other than his being the president of Sunset Scavenger Company. I knew that he lived with his wife in a set of flats on Funston Avenue. He had no children, while his brother Dominic had five, living and raising them on Dago Alley. He ran his garbage route (with others, including their horses) from that location.

I met Giuseppe only twice: once on that day when I was working on Uncle Pasquale's truck and once when I visited him to help Uncle Pas lift a huge safe with jacks, placing a 2 x 4 under it to distribute the weight on the closet floor underneath. I asked Pas why anyone needed a safe so big, and he said it was full of cash. (I was never able to confirm that.)

Giuseppe left for Italy in the summer of 1952 with his wife Maria. He passed away in Genova and was buried there. After

Giuseppe's death, Joseph Dominic Molinari, Sunset Scavenger's vice president and a member of the board of directors, was elected to the presidency, a post he held until August 27, 1965.

Giuseppe's wife, Maria, came back to the United States, settled their affairs, and sold their property. Then she moved back to Genoa where she had family. She passed away in 1980 at the age of 90.

4

Disposal of San Francisco Waste, 1906–1966

There is a basic rule of thumb in this business: If you cannot dump the truck that you collected garbage with, then you cannot collect any more garbage. Prior to the earthquake in 1906, the primary place for the city's waste, regardless of who collected it, was anyplace close by and in the bay. After the 1906 earthquake and resulting fires, there was chaos, people living in the streets, and serious concerns about health issues in San Francisco.

The city fathers sought means to minimize the health threats from garbage and contracted with the Southern Pacific Railroad to build a crude transfer station in the general area of 16th and 3rd Streets. This is where the scavengers, with their horses and wagons, delivered their loads of garbage and dumped the waste into standard gondola cars designed for gravel hauling. Once a unit train of at least twenty cars was loaded, the train was transported to the San Francisco/San Mateo County border along the railroad's mainline, which had been constructed thirty years earlier. After San Francisco's garbage passed into San Mateo County, the health hazard it had posed for the City of San Francisco mysteriously disappeared. Onsite, the waste was unloaded with clamshells and dumped into the bay; San Francisco used this method to dispose of its waste from 1906 through 1966.

As the horses and wagons were replaced with gasoline trucks, the scavengers drove those trucks directly to the future garbage transfer station located in the Southern Pacific train yards, in the vicinity of 16th and 3rd Streets.

At this point, the refuse wagon would be backed up to the ramp, where the refuse would be shoved down the ramp by hand into waiting gondola cars and then rail-transported to the future City of Brisbane in San Mateo County. There the untreated garbage would be unceremoniously dumped by clamshell into San Francisco Bay but beyond the San Francisco city limits of San Francisco Bay. Once gasoline engines and trucks were adopted, the transfer station at 16th and 3rd Streets was phased out.

This means of dumping garbage in the bay with no environmental controls was a practice followed by virtually every city that bordered the bay, and the practice of waste disposal was considered to be "reclamation" of property from those "stinking mudflats."

At the time, most cities dumped raw sewage into the bay. When the tide went out, the residuals were exposed, creating offensive odors—thus the term "stinking and useless mudflats." Covering them with garbage was considered an acceptable option.

As sad as it was, there were few efforts to contain the severe water pollution created by dumping raw garbage into saltwater. The only attempt to minimize pollution was to float a series of telephone poles, linked together with cables, in front of the raw garbage going directly into the bay waters. The only pollution control, if you want to call it that, was that a majority of float waste did not get out into the bay.

Aside from water pollution, there was also air pollution. In addition to burning certain forms of trash and the resulting contamination, there were also severe odor problems. Mixing newsprint and other paper products with saltwater creates hydrogen sulfide gas. Sometimes the smell was so bad that some said it would "gag a maggot."

Fortunately, the predominant westerly winds that historically flowed down Visitacion Valley blew the pungent odor out across the vacant bay, so the smell offended only an occasional boater passing by.

That would soon change. In 1952, when U.S. Highway 101 cut across the bay from Sierra Point and north past and through Candlestick Hill, the drivers on the new freeway could not help noticing the horrible rotten-egg odor. As a Band-Aid cure, an engineer was hired to design a fifteen-foot-high metal fence.

This was not to hide the garbage dump. The westerly wind velocity averaged seventeen miles per hour. Using that factor, it was concluded that, with a fence at a fifteen-foot elevation, the odor would be lifted up and over the automobiles. This solution was marginally successful, but when the wind velocity was below seventeen miles per hour, the odor was present more than ever; and when the wind exceeded seventeen miles per hour, it started to blow the fence down.

Although covered with brush and trees for landscaping, part of the fence is still present on the right side of Highway 101 South, crossing the San Francisco County line and ending at the City of Brisbane off-ramp.

The odor problem was totally eliminated when Sunset Scavenger created a disposal company called Sanitary Fill Company, which assumed responsibility of disposal operations from the railroad in 1952.

Sanitary Fill Company purchased Candlestick Hill and built a dike in the bay. The company pumped the water out of the diked areas and created a sanitary landfill for the disposal of San Francisco's waste without dumping it in the bay or burning it. Instead, Sanitary Fill Company covered the waste with soil—a new technology at that time.

It is ironic that when Sunset Scavenger and Scavenger's Protective Association formed a joint venture called Sanitary Fill Company and took over the disposal operations in the early 1950s, the environmental laws that would eventually govern and regulate activities of this type were nonexistent. Yet the scavengers were adopting polices that would minimize the negative impact on the environment by covering the waste with clean soil every day—a practice now known as *sanitary landfill*.

Around 1960 the Southern Pacific Land Company, owners of the sanitary landfill site that the city had utilized since 1906, advised the scavengers that use of the site would not be extended beyond 1966. Some ten years later, an investor from Taiwan paid $110 million to the Southern Pacific Land Company for 1,100 acres of garbage-filled properties and 100 acres of submerged land that included 450 acres of former bay lands filled with garbage, demonstrating that even bay fills had substantial commercial value.

Scavengers advised San Francisco of this dilemma, and the city directed the scavengers to secure additional tidelands to make sure that San Francisco had a disposal facility for the next twenty-five years.

The only site available for that purpose was on the east side of State Highway 101. The scavengers needed enough land for twenty-five years; 260 acres of this land would fill that need. The cost of purchasing and developing the property was estimated to be $2.1 million. The scavengers, who seldom used credit to purchase anything (it was the historical Genovese philosophy to pay cash) and as a result had no credit history, were faced with the difficult chore of financing this unexpected demand.

Even though the scavengers had fifty years of experience with

Bank of America, the bank would not lend them the funds; it was willing to lend only $600,000 for the project. Eventually the balance (approximately $1.5 million) was secured from the Occidental Life Insurance Company, with an outrageous interest rate of 7 percent and very restrictive controls on the waste companies.

The scavengers purchased the land from the Crocker Land Company and filed permit applications. Right at this time there was a huge hue and cry to save San Francisco Bay from any kind of fill, especially garbage. Environmental groups singled out this site as a model for future opposition to bay fills of any kind.

While that battle was going on, other projects (including one that involved Utah construction, which was filling in 600 acres for residential development) were *unopposed*. The Scavengers' permits were finally approved for health and safety reasons, because the City of San Francisco had no place to dispose of the millions of tons of waste generated annually.

Even with the approvals received, the City of Brisbane, where we had been dumping refuse for sixty-five years, attempted to re-zone the new site to prohibit the dumping of garbage, while dumping was allowed to continue across the freeway at the old site. The Scavengers appealed that decision and lost. At noon on August 27, 1966, we terminated the old disposal site and moved operations to the new, disputed site in Brisbane.

This effort on August 27, 1966 was a well-executed event, comparable to a well-planned aggressive military invasion. Before the City of Brisbane was aware that the landfill operations were being moved to the new site, the city police placed a barricade across the road to the disposal site, stopping some eighty garbage trucks from dumping their loads.

What I didn't know was that our attorney had obtained a temporary restraining order (TRO) from the court. Because the press was at the police barricade, our attorney Angelo Scampini told me to get in the driver's seat of the lead truck. He stood on the outside of the truck and told me in Italian to drive ahead and mow down the barriers. That could have been an easy task except that police officers were present, including Bud Dyer, the chief of the five-man department.

When I was about six inches from the barrier, the chief commanded me to stop; but Angelo Scampini yelled, "Give it the gas!" Then Bud Dyer pulled out his revolver, pointed it directly at me, and screamed, "Damn you, Lenny, please stop! Otherwise I'm going to have to shoot you!"

Needless to say, I was getting nervous. The TV and cameras were going. Before anything more happened, Angelo jumped off the truck and handed the TRO to the chief. Talk about drama! But the effort was worth it because it brought the matter to the public's attention.

After several months of battling the City of Brisbane and after several ugly court battles, we were issued an order to operate the landfill. But instead of the twenty-five years we had planned on, we were able to use the newly developed Sierra Point site for only five years (until 1970), and we lost the use of 160 acres of submerged lands at $5,000 per acre. All told, an $800,000 loss.

Eventually, the scavengers working with the City of San Francisco developed a long-term program, which I will detail later in this book. But nothing was easy.

Upgrading the Collection of San Francisco's Wastes

Even though Sunset Scavenger Company and Scavenger's Protective Association were the dominant collectors of waste throughout San Francisco, a significant number of independent scavenger companies were still collecting garbage throughout the city, competing with the two larger companies.

As a result, the standard of service declined, creating problems for the city in how to create a minimum standard of services and how to charge customers consistently. For example, if garbage were left on the street, the city would file a complaint to Giuseppe, who would deny that he had failed to provide that service. He would point the finger at Pietro for the failure, and the problem would persist with no resolution.

This created problems for the city to establish and maintain minimum standards of service, complicated by the fact that it had no real means to enforce standards because of its inability to identify and penalize the person or firm providing the substandard service.

To correct that problem, the 1932 Initiative Ordinance amended the City Charter to divide the City and County of San Francisco into ninety-two independent districts. The ordinance dictated that only licensed refuse collectors were authorized to operate in these defined districts.

If the minimum standards of service declined, the city knew exactly who to blame, and if the problems were not corrected, the city had the option to cancel the license to operate and issue it to another firm.

Sunset Scavenger and Scavenger's Protective Association covered most of the ninety-two districts, but at least twenty-five of the permits were issued to other, smaller companies. From 1932 to 1942, Sunset Scavenger and Scavenger's Protective eventually acquired the other permits by purchase or merger. Sunset Scavenger acquired the last independent company, the Mission Scavenger Company, in 1942.

Rate Adjustments

San Francisco's 1932 Initiative Ordinance included a maximum rate for garbage-collection services. Any rate increase required filing an application and receiving approval from the San Francisco Board of Supervisors. This process was cumbersome and expensive, especially when an elected official was required to vote to increase costs for his own constituents. To mitigate this problem, the scavengers proposed in 1952 an amendment to the 1932 ordinance that would create a Scavenger's Rate Control Board (Proposition I). It was defeated.

Undaunted, the scavengers went back to the voters in 1953 with Proposition C, which had the slogan "C is the key for better garbage service." We won that vote. The program assured a net return of 5 percent after taxes, based upon approved costs of doing business. The process was modeled after the trucking industry because it was labor intensive as compared to capital intensive. In other words, our company invested in labor and not capital (such as equipment).

That philosophy was appropriate at that time because the scavengers purchased used trucks from the US Post Office, rebuilt the power trains, mounted them with new 20-cubic-yard bodies, and sent them to work spending less than $2,000, apparently following their (economical) Genovese Heritage. Today, one truck costs more than $275,000. Yes, the industry has become "capital intensive."

Getting Involved at Dago Alley

The corporate headquarters of Sunset Scavenger Company was located on Hampshire and 19th Streets in San Francisco's Mission

District; but prior to that, many of the horse-and-wagon components of the company were garaged in private homes throughout the city.

One such location was the dead-end street called Oakwood, just east of Dolores and 18th Streets, where my Uncles Pasquale, Mingo, and Freddy were born and raised. The garbage wagons sat there every night and left from there every morning until they were replaced with gasoline trucks.

Many of Sunset Scavenger's Boss Scavengers lived on this street. They had names like Campi, Fontana, Chiosso, Borghello, Onarato, Moscone, Leonardini, Guaraglia, Scolari, Salvi, and Musante. In fact, so many Genovese Italians lived there that Oakwood Street was it was referred to as Dago Alley.

Eventually, the city cut through 19th Street, creating a thoroughfare, and the informal family atmosphere that had existed for so many years began to change. The old boarding houses where scavengers resided and the horses and wagons had been housed were slowly phased out, and Oakwood became a typical nondescript San Francisco street.

5

How I Became a Scavenger

One person who had a tremendous impact on me as a mentor was a distant cousin, Benny Anselmo Sr., who was on the board of the Scavenger's Protective Association and in my opinion one of the most forward-thinking people in the solid-waste business. His son, Benny Jr., is now vice president in charge of equipment acquisition at Recology Inc. and is certainly a result of his dad's influence, love, and respect for the garbage business.

Benny Sr., like most garbage men, was a hunter. Italians love to hunt. When I was sixteen year old, we were driving back to San Francisco after a successful hunt at Grizzly Island. As we were driving across the Bay Bridge, just coming out of the Yerba Buena Island tunnel and looking at the broad horizon of the city, Benny said philosophically, "Look at that city, Lenny. The garbage men are like the city's asshole. If we don't go to work every day, the city will shut down like you and I would if our assholes didn't function. It's our responsibility to the city for allowing us to continue in our chosen business."

I never forgot that. I was not actively employed by the company at the time, but later I did go to work for Sunset and became a Boss Scavenger. How could anyone envision that I would someday be in charge of the entire system?

Meeting the President of Sunset Scavenger Company, 1951

In 1951, once the trucks were all out on the street, the company president would drive throughout the city, looking around corners to see if the crews were working as mandated by company rules. Never knowing when the boss was looking at them left an air of paranoia in the crews' minds, but it was good because the services were always maintained at the highest possible standards.

On the rare occasion when the boss caught a crew failing to provide the standard of service expected, the crew might receive a monetary fine or suspension of employment (or possibly both), depending on the severity of the violation.

What was interesting is that drinking on the job—that is, stopping for a beer or a couple of drinks at a bar on the route—was *not* a violation of the rules. It was considered public relations because we spent money on our route customers. It was not uncommon to see a garbage truck double-parked on a street in front of a bar for a half hour at a time. Scavengers typically loved to stop for a drink. If there were no bars on the route, there was always plan B: buying beer from a grocery store.

In fact, one of the posted rules in the company stated, "If for any reason the driver of the truck is determined to be drunk, it shall be the responsibility of the Boss of the truck to bring the truck to the barn [garage]."

Once an individual became a Boss Scavenger, he and the company were "bonded at the hip" for the rest of the man's working career unless he was caught stealing money or committing some other similar violation. If you could not fire a Boss Scavenger, the only means of maintaining discipline was through fines and suspension of employment, thus hitting the worker's pocketbook.

The only real day that I encountered this policy and actually spoke with the company president was when I was about seventeen years old. One of my friends and I were working with Uncle Pasquale on Truck 3 at the intersection of McAllister and Stanyan Streets when the company president, Giuseppe Fontana, drove up in his 1951 green Chevrolet coupe. He immediately asked who I was. Uncle Pas explained, adding, "You know him. He is training to be a scavenger."

Fontana responded in Italian, "*Troppo piccolo*"—I was too small to work in garbage.

(As an aside, he was half-right because I only weighed 145 pounds when I worked for the company at age nineteen. But the training I had with Uncle Pasquale after the boss showed up enabled me to pass the test. When I actually became employed, I'd lost ten pounds, becoming a skinny 135. After six months, I weighed in at 170 pounds—not an ounce of fat.)

When Giuseppe Fontana drove off in his Chevrolet, Uncle Pasquale called him "Snuffy" after a Katzenjammers' cartoon character in the Sunday newspaper. Fontana said that all the partners referred to Fontana as Snuffy. He was short and stubby, wore old clothes, and had a mustache. Of course, no one in his right mind would ever call him Snuffy in his presence, for fear of receiving the "Wrath of God."

Never would I see Giuseppe "Joe" Fontana (Snuffy) again until his funeral in 1952. I officially became employed by Sunset Scavenger in 1953.

Becoming a Scavenger

Many people, including Uncle Pasquale, told me that I did not have the physical strength to become a scavenger.

In 1953, after graduating from Polytechnic High School, I had a job stocking shelves and delivering groceries at the Hill View Market, around the corner from where I lived on Cole Street.

All my uncles and other relatives were avid deer hunters. In early 1954, they leased some property to hunt deer in Mendocino County, and they asked if I wanted to join them. I had to pay $150 to be included in the hunt. I paid the $150 in May of that year, and then I was told that the man whom I had replaced at Hill View Market had been drafted into the military. According to the union contract, the man could have his job back upon discharge—and he did want it back.

As a consequence, I gave up my job as a grocery clerk; and because I had invested $150 in a deer hunt, it was not possible for me to look for another job. If I could find one, I would have to ask for ten days off to shoot deer after only a few months on the job. Recognizing that would not happen, I could not just sit around and do nothing. I got up every morning and worked on Uncle Pasquale's truck, meeting him at his house around the corner at 2122 Grove Street at 4 AM

We would get into his Jeep and, with his dog Duffy, drive to Jerry's Donuts at Fulton and Divisadero for coffee with the scavengers of surrounding truck routes, discussing what was wrong with the company and politics in general and how tough their individual routes were, complaining that other guys' routes were the easy ones.

Uncle Pas and I would drive back to Ashbury and Hayes Streets. Gisberto "Hoppe" Nardi (Gisberto had a slight limp, thus the nickname) and Salvatore "Sal" Cresenti would pull out the carrying cans, the *cuvertas* (burlap blankets), and other tools of the trade, awaiting the garbage truck to show up at 5:30 AM

I was sort of the fifth wheel on a crew of four. The crewmembers chipped in and paid me $12 a day to work on the truck with them. I figured that I was being compensated at a rate of $1.50 per hour (minimum wage then was 75 cents).

August finally came, and we were off to Dos Rios (two rivers) on the Eel River (Mendocino County), where we met my uncles Pasquale, Mingo, and Freddy, plus six others, to set up camp for deer hunting. Camp, as such, was a stove set up on the tailgate of a pickup truck, tables and chairs, paper plates (all near a stream for water and washing needs), sleeping bags on the ground, and lots of food, beer, and Manhattans.

Everyone sort of went his own way to hunt, and I shot my first deer. My uncles showed me how to gut the animal by making a small incision in the abdominal area, allowing access to the internal organs. I was required to reach in the small hole and pull out the stomach, intestines, and more.

My uncles explained that the reason for making only a small opening was to minimize fly infestation. (I do not want to make the reader sick, but this was still another level of the many diverse learning experiences for me in the wonderful world of scavengers.)

On the fourth day of the hunt, we all came back for dinner. Uncle Pasquale, who always hunted without wearing a shirt, did not show up at camp. The sun was going down, and he was nowhere to be seen.

We took our Jeeps out, scanning the ridges, shining lights, hollering his name, and firing shots in the air (a common practice when someone was lost). Finally, we heard a rifle shot in response.

We located Uncle Pas way down in a deep canyon. He was alright; he'd gotten lost and had a fire going. He said he would walk out when the sun came up. Uncle Mingo suggested that we make some coffee royals, return to the ridge where we'd found Pasquale down the canyon, light a fire, and keep him company while he spent the night by himself.

It was then that Uncle Mingo, who knew I did not have a job and who happened to be a member of Sunset Scavenger Company's board of directors, asked me what I planned to do after the deer hunt. My response, of course, was, "Nothing."

"Why don't you come to work for Sunset?" he asked.

"Uncle Pas said I was too small to be a scavenger," I said.

"Bullshit," said Uncle Mingo. "I know what's going on. My brother likes you just where you are—collecting his book, being an extra man on his truck—and he wants to keep it that way . . . so that you keep doing his work."

The next day we got Uncle Pas out of the canyon (cold but

okay), had a good laugh, completed the deer hunt, and returned to San Francisco that Saturday. Much to the chagrin of Uncle Pas, I followed Uncle Mingo's advice. I applied for a job and told Pas that I was now an independent scavenger and going to work for the company.

First Day on the Job

I began work as a *garsun* (replacement worker) and reported to Sunset Scavenger Company Corporation at 4:30 AM on a Monday morning in late August 1953. The apprentice program at Sunset was direct and simple: the apprentice was assigned to whichever route among the 104 four-man routes was short a man. Depending on the situation, injury, emergency, and so forth, an apprentice could be assigned to as many as five different trucks with different crews in five days. The men facetiously referred to this as the "merry-go-round."

Once you proved your worth as an apprentice, it was suggested that you get a Class B driver's license, which meant that you were stepping up in the wonderful world of garbage and a step closer to becoming a Boss Scavenger (an equal partner) in Sunset Scavenger Company.

I received this promotion after about thirty days of my apprenticeship work. Even with my somewhat small stature, I proved to be a good scavenger and received my driver's license. Guess what truck I was assigned to? Truck 3, of course, with Uncle Pasquale. So now I would arrive at Sunset Scavenger at 4 AM, park my car, and walk in between the more than 100 White Motor Car trucks mounted with 20-cubic-yard bodies and seven steel stairs where the scavengers would carry their loaded cans up and into the truck.

Each driver was required to recover a bundle of what the old Italians called cuvertas for collecting and storing cardboard and then check the oil and water in the six-cylinder gasoline engine—always an exciting experience because, more often than not, cats or rats would be sleeping on the warm engine blocks and scare hell out of you.

Once that chore was completed, the driver went into the dispatch office where coffee was provided for ten cents per cup; then he would check his box for complaints about service the day before or other instructions.

If an extra man were assigned to your route, the dispatcher

would call you into his office by way of a loudspeaker in the yard or office. Virtually all the scavengers had nicknames. The dispatcher was Louis "The Crow" Crosetti.

The Crow was a no-nonsense, dictatorial individual who never took shit from anyone. He was feared and rightfully so because he was a member of the Sunset Scavenger Company board of directors and the board's vice president. Simply put, the Crow was the most powerful individual in the Sunset Scavenger Company, a fact that I was to learn more about in the years to come.

For many years, the dispatcher was a member of the board of directors and always got more votes than any of the other ten members, including the president. The reason was twofold: first, he was in contact with the Boss Scavengers (voters) on an ongoing basis (even at Sunset, politics came into play for elected officials); and second, the dispatcher could do favors for the partners, such as providing extra men when they were available, priority for days off, vacations, and other amenities.

Experiencing the departures of 100 trucks was an unbelievable and memorable adventure. You had to be there to realize what a coordinated and controlled event it was. At 5 AM sharp, the Crow would blow a Bosun's pipe over the loudspeaker, indicating that drivers should start their engines. No one was allowed to start the truck engines until the Crow blew that pipe.

If your engine did not start (usually because of a dead battery), two mechanics were on standby to correct the problem. This was necessary because one stalled truck could screw up the entire process. At precisely 5:15 AM, the Crow would blow the Bosun's pipe again (those of us in the front of the dispatch office could see him looking at his watch), and the mechanic directed one row of trucks after another onto Beatty Road with a flashlight, starting on the south side of the yard.

This process was clearly similar to launching airplanes from an aircraft carrier at sea. (Maybe the Crow once had had a naval tour of duty.)

From there the trucks turned right (in front of the offices), drove west to Tunnel Avenue, turned right again, drove north, and passed in front of two city blocks of single family homes. Although only one side of the street had homes, I often thanked the good Lord I did not live there, especially every morning from 5:20 AM to at least 5:45 AM, six days a week, except Christmas and New

Year (and they were replaced with three Sundays), when 104 garbage trucks took off with roaring engines and banging metal rear doors. It must have been a nightmare for the people who lived in those houses.

The trucks all came back around 9:30 AM and went back up Tunnel Avenue for their second loads, returning around noon.

Driving an open garbage truck was always an experience. The driver had only a steel seat, usually enhanced by a cushion that was found in the garbage. The driver was exposed to the elements, and cold wind was a daily experience.

When I first worked on a truck, I noticed that the windshield wipers were on both sides of the glass and, at first, I thought that was unusual. But when the first rains came, I realized then that it rained on both sides of the windshield. In addition, the company did not provide rain gear. Wow! What a learning experience for me.

Driving up to Ashbury and Fell, I would again start the routine that I'd started with Uncle Pas, Gisberto "Hoppe" Nardi, and Salvatore "Sal" Cresenti, except my assignment was to stop and service 1600 Fell Street, a twenty-four-unit apartment building that required daily service.

From there, I rode for two blocks to Ashbury Street where my first stop was Lowell High School. The garbage was kept indoors on all four floors of the school. We had to collect the waste in burlap sacks, tying the four corners together with a square knot and shoving the sacks out the windows. When the sacks hit the ground, spillage was minimal because of the unique means the two men used to compress the waste when tying the square knots. This was an efficient means of compressing waste to minimize spilling it on the ground.

Once the blankets hit the ground, we picked them up, carried them up the seven stairs to the truck, untied the knots, and dumped the waste into the open body. We also recovered any cardboard that might be found in that portion of the waste. Recovering material from the waste stream was part of the job. A worker would hang a cuverta in one corner inside the open-body truck, and garbage collectors would place all loose pieces of cardboard inside. Once the cuverta was full, a worker tied the four corners together and hung it off the back of the truck. Then he replaced it with another sack, and the process was repeated.

As I mentioned earlier, I began "collecting book" at a young age. Now working with Uncle Pasquale on Truck 3, I might as well have been a Sunset Scavenger partner because I was still collecting his book.

When I indicated to Uncle Pas my desire to become a Boss Scavenger, he always said, "Wait, I will get you a better price" (for a share). He always claimed that he could save me $500 on the potential share purchase because he knew someone who was going to retire soon and could get the share for a reduced price, but this was BS. In reality, he wanted to keep me as his driver and to keep collecting his book.

Uncle Mingo argued to the contrary, saying that no shares were available at a reduced rate and adding that, with three $150 monthly payments, I would more than make up the purported savings. Much to the chagrin of Uncle Pas, I renewed my efforts to become a Boss Scavenger.

Becoming a Boss Scavenger

How does an employee become a shareholder, a Boss Scavenger? You have to demonstrate that you have the physical ability to provide the work, and you must have the mental ability to follow orders and work well with others.

Obviously, the first step is to get a job being a garbage collector. I served as an apprentice to Sunset Scavenger for one year, but then I was drafted, and I had to do a stint in the US Navy Submarine Service. I returned to Sunset in 1956. Because I had already served my apprenticeship, I reminded the company of my desire to become a partner, a Boss Scavenger.

My father-in-law, Guido, purchased his share the year I was born (1934) and paid $10,200 for it. So there was much potential for appreciation.

Antonio Fagliano, the corporate secretary, told me that when a share was available, he would advise me and give me a name and phone number, with instructions to contact the individual to see if I could make a deal.

Actually, the board of directors set the deal (price) for the share—at that time, $14,500. I was to find out later that the reason for establishing this value was to assure that, with the increased wages once a person became a shareholder, the added income would be sufficient not only to pay the principal on the note but also to pay the interest on the unpaid balance.

The point of this exercise was to make sure in purchasing a share, the standard of living of the incoming shareholder would remain unchanged because the income he was receiving prior to becoming a shareholder would remain unchanged. From the day he became a shareholder, during the next eight years or so to pay down the note, increases in wages, dividends, and other benefits would offset inflationary trends.

The down payment and interest rate on the balance due was negotiable between the seller, Luigi Varni, and the buyer, me. I met him at his home on Florida Street and, after some discussion, we agreed that the price of the share was $14,500. I made a deposit of $500, leaving a balance of $14,000, secured by a note that would accrue interest at a negotiated rate of 2 percent. I agreed to pay $150 per month.

After we negotiated the deal (interest and down payment), Luigi invited me to have a glass of his homemade wine, a tradition that old-timers brought from Italy. Each old-timer had his own formula to make "vino"— sweet, white, red, dry, and so forth, with variable alcohol content.

Some wine was referred to as *paint* because it was so thick and powerful that it would stain marble. This best described Luigi's wine, which was enhanced by very high alcohol content. We sat down at the kitchen table, and he poured me a glass of the Varni Custom Red from a *demijohn* (gallon glass container). Thank God the glasses were small.

The wine was so bad that it surely fell into the category of paint. After I drank one glass, he automatically filled it again, telling me, "You cannot walk on one leg." I did not want offend him—after all, thanks to him I was on the way to becoming a Boss Scavenger. So I drank it and told him that I had a date with a lady friend and had to leave.

We shook hands and I left. In about ten minutes, I realized that I was drunk as hell. I barely made it home, turned on my Hoffman TV—with a green screen—and promptly fell asleep. Fortunately, I had set the alarm clock. When I woke up at 4 AM, I had a monumental hangover. When I bent over to pick up my first can of garbage, I felt that I had a bowling ball banging in my brain.

It was a memorable and learning experience for a multitude

of reasons, one of which is you cannot drink and pick up garbage without severe, painful consequences. God bless Luigi, but he can keep his vino.

This was how it worked. I went into debt for $14,000. The note was secured by the share certificate, thirty-two shares of Sunset Scavenger Company, in my name, and held in trust by the Bank of America. From that point on, my wages went up some $200 a month as a shareholder.

The first check of each month was delivered directly to the Bank of America at Divisadero and Hayes Streets. I signed the payroll check, and the bank deposited $150, plus the interest of 2 percent on the unpaid balance due on the note, into a special account in the name of Luigi Varni. So for each month, I ended up with a positive cash flow of about $15 while making a payment of $150 on a note that would eventually become my full paid equity in the company of at least $14,500. It took me about seven years to pay off the note.

An interesting aside is that the company's policy required shareholders to cash their payroll checks only at the Bank of America. Failure to do so would result in a penalty, a fine to be deducted from the person's paycheck. The theory behind this policy was that the company did not want anyone to know its business.

I reported to the corporate secretary, Antonio Fagliano, that I had come to an agreement with Luigi Varni. I was then brought before the board of directors of Sunset Scavenger Company. Company president Joseph Molinari presented me with a copy of the bylaws, written in Italian and English, and provided me with an oral overview of what was expected of me as an equal shareholder in the company.

He added that the company had a few assets in the form of trucks and property, but the real advantage of becoming a shareholder was that I had a job for the rest of my life, "or as long as you wanted and were capable of working. . .and so long as you don't punch me in the nose."

I was a young man, and it meant a lot to me to have the security of a job for the rest of my life. It is ironic and to some degree sad, as you will read later on, that I did more than "punch him in the nose."

Introduction to Truck 27

As soon as I became a shareholder, I was assigned as Boss #3 to Truck Route 27 in the Fillmore District, a predominantly black area of San Francisco. At one time in the 1920s the dominant ethnicity group was wealthy Jewish, but by the 1960s it was almost a slum area, predominantly black and filled with hippies caught in the early stages of drug abuse.

The majority of company shareholders considered the Fillmore District to be the worst area because most of the garbage cans were inside, in backyards, or up flights of stairs. Many of the apartments needed daily service and the use of cuvertas. All of this was compounded by the filthy conditions of the area in general.

Despite Mayor George Christopher claiming that there was no prostitution in the city, I had seven whorehouses on my route. The garbage man knows more about the people he serves than the people themselves.

I was the third Boss Scavenger on Truck 27. Boss Scavenger #1 was Louie Bertone, pronounced "Bertoni." I mention this because he was one of the few "high-tone" scavengers. He invested in income properties and resided in a high-end part of the city. He always drove into the garage without getting out of the car, not wanting his neighbors to see him in his garbage clothes.

When meeting people for the first time, he made his name with an "e" at the end so that he appeared to be a Frenchman, and his vocation was a "sanitary engineer." This somewhat bothered me because I was proud to be a scavenger and he seemed to be ashamed.

But setting that aside, Louie, although short in stature (5'6", weighing 150 pounds soaking wet), was one helluva garbage man and carried more than his share of a day's work.

The second Boss Scavenger on Truck 27 was Peter Guaraglia. Peter's family came from Fontanarossa, and he was my godfather. It was chance that I was assigned to his truck. Peter was as tough as they come. As noted, we worked in a predominantly black part of the city. If anybody gave Peter any shit, he would start a fight at the drop of a hat.

When I was assigned to Truck 27, our driver was one of only three black employees in the company. His name was Booker T. Day, after Booker T. Washington, and he was the only black man working on the garbage trucks. Booker T. and I developed a strong friendship working together, and he proved to be an extraordinary resource to me working with the customer base, teaching me the language of black culture. Bertone, Guaraglia, Stefanelli, and Day sounded like a law firm, except we picked up garbage.

Truck 27 served an old part of San Francisco made up of flats, two- and three-story buildings with up to six residential units, apartments, and commercial businesses. Serving these customers was brutal because the garbage cans were located up the stairs and inside the buildings—not like today when most of the garbage cans are outside and near the curb for easy access.

The scavenger then had to walk up three flights of stairs to collect the garbage. In those days, the customer paid a paltry seventy-five cents more per month to get that service. There was no financial incentive for the customer to bring the garbage down to ground level. For just seventy-five cents a month, it was more convenient to put the garbage outside the door and let the scavenger company pick it up. This was to change in later years after I became president.

We serviced many apartment buildings that had large containers at the bottom of chutes. A large metal tube ran down from the top floors, and people would place their garbage in paper grocery bags (most of the time) and drop the bags down the chutes into large metal containers commonly referred to as "chute cans," typically a 200-gallon container. We would gather the garbage by spreading the six-by-six-foot burlap cuverta on the floor. One of the crew would hold two ends while the other "humped" the large barrel, causing the waste to flow into the cuverta.

Placing the container back under the chute, the "humper" would grab the two remaining corners of the blanket, handing them one at a time to his partner, who would secure the cuverta by gathering three of the corners together and wrapping the fourth around those three. Then he would pick it up, throw it over his shoulder, and haul it to the truck.

At that time, the use of the cuverta was the only means of collecting and transporting large volumes of waste that could not be transported in the regular carrying can, the primary tool of the scavengers. This method had its risks; broken glass and razor-blades posed an ongoing hazard, and anything liquid would flow through the burlap sack and down the crack of your fanny—not a very comfortable situation, but part of the job.

6

Work, Courtship, and Marriage

Guido Campi, my future father-in-law, lived with his family at 57 Oakwood Street, next door to Uncle Mingo, who lived at 61 Oakwood with his fourteen-year-old daughter, Virginia. We were working on a small house trailer that we planned to sleep in during the duck season. That day Virginia Campi happened to walk by. Uncle Freddy knew her and introduced me to this beautiful young girl. After a brief conversation with us, she walked up the street to her home.

I said to Freddy, "What a nice looking gal!"

"That was Guido Campi's daughter," he responded. "She is too young for you, so forget about her."

In time that all changed. A few years later, I happened by Uncle Mingo's home during the hunting season. I spotted Guido Campi, whom I'd gotten to know through the garbage business. His garage door was open, and he was picking ducks with his daughter Virginia. I thought to myself, "If I ever get married, she would be the ideal wife."

A few weeks later, I was again at Uncle Mingo's house, and Virginia came over to visit Mingo's daughter. I told Virginia that I had two tickets to the movie *Around the World in Eighty Days* and asked if she would like to go with me.

To my surprise, she agreed to go, even though she had a boyfriend who had just joined the Army. His plan was to marry Virginia when she was eighteen, after he returned from the service. I assumed that she was bored waiting for her boyfriend to come home, but for whatever reason she agreed to go out with me.

I was twenty-one; Virginia, sixteen. She told me later that she had brought money with her to take a cab home if I got out of order. That was fifty-nine years ago, but let me add with my tongue firmly in cheek that "she has not picked a duck since then." Funny how fast things change after a ring is on the finger, but I would not trade her for reasons you shall read.

After working for Sunset Scavenger Company for a year and demonstrating that I had the physical and mental ability to become a shareholder (a Boss Scavenger), I was allowed to purchase a share in 1954 and was assigned to Truck 27 in the Fillmore District.

Some years later, when my future father-in-law Guido was president of the Sanitary Truck Drivers Teamster's Union Local 350, we attended a ten-dollar-a-plate dinner at the Fairmont Hotel honoring James "Jimmy" Hoffa—I actually shook hands with him. After the event was over, Guido and I stopped for a couple of adult beverages, as scavengers usually did.

When we came home to Oakwood Street, it was pouring rain. I was boarding with Uncle Mingo in a room over the old stables at 61 Oakwood Street, next door to Guido. While Guido and I were sitting in the car, discussing adult beverages and the fact that both of us had to go to work in five hours in the pouring rain, I found enough courage to pop the question.

"Guido, I would like permission to marry your daughter."

His response was simple: "Ma and I figured that out already, and I respect your decision to ask me first. But let me add this: If you are marrying my daughter for my money, forget about it because I have none. People who have money don't spend it. I spend my money, and I don't have any because of that." He added, "I have a roof on my house, food on the table, and no one trying to take it away from me. What else does a man need in his life?"

I responded that it was never my intent to go after his money, and he agreed to accept me as his pending son-in-law. At 4 AM, with heavy heads from booze and cigarettes, Guido and I left to work in the garbage business. He walked to his route, and I drove to the company, picked up my truck, and drove to my route in the still-pouring rain.

After many years had passed, I realized and respected what a profound philosophical and simple logistical response that was. Simply put, money should not be the goal of any man, especially an immigrant coming to this country seeking a better life. What does any family-oriented man need to complete his obligation to his family? As I matured, I realized and respected what Guido shared with me.

When my future mother-in-law, Jennie Campi (the daughter of Emilio Rattaro, the founder and first president of Sunset Scavenger Company), heard of my plan to marry her daughter, her initial response, "Damn! My father was a scavenger; my brothers were scavengers; I married a scavenger; my cousins are in the garbage business, and now my daughter is going to marry a scavenger! I'll never get out of the garbage business!"

After three years of courting and my brief stint in the United States Submarine Service, Virginia and I were married on September 5, 1959. We have been married going on fifty-eight years.

We had our son Joseph almost exactly a year after we were married. The need for paternal responsibility became evident to me, along with the importance of long-range planning, and I concluded that I had to somehow improve my potential—whatever that may be.

I decided to return to USF for two years of night school, where I studied accounting, corporate law, and business administration. Our beautiful daughter Gina came into our life, and I thought that I might someday want to do something different, possibly even work my way up the corporate ladder at Sunset Scavenger Company. However, as in high school, I had no place to apply the learning I was getting at USF. I became bored. What I was being taught seemed foreign.

For me, the ultimate educational experience would be to go to school for four hours in the morning, have lunch, and then work in the business I was learning about on the same day. I wanted to apply what I was learning in school to my actual field of interest. What an outstanding educational process that would be!

I knew that using what I was learning on the same day I learned it would eliminate the boredom of school and mitigate the feeling of repetition associated with reading and oral instruction over an eight-hour period.

7

The Art of Scavenging and Recycling

The Man in the Box

A twenty-yard open truck and a four-man crew serviced each of the 104 garbage routes in 1956. A person unfamiliar with the process might assume that all four men collected the garbage and dumped it into the open truck. Actually, one of the four-man crew at any given time had to take a turn "in the box" (in the truck).

The primary reason for this was that the garbage collector carried the garbage up the truck's seven stairs and dumped the first load by leaning over and placing the carrying handle onto the front of the open box. The garbage would fall out by gravity, but eventually that area would fill up. To dump his carry barrel, the scavenger had to walk onto the garbage in front, lay down his barrel, and dump the garbage into the sloped void at the rear of the box.

Once that person was there, one of the three men still out collecting garbage would show up and lay down his barrel. The man inside the truck would automatically drag in that container, dump it, and return it to the man who had just brought it up.

In the interim, the man in the box shook all the paper bags in which the combined wastes were typically stored before putting it into the garbage can to be collected. During that shaking, all bottles, cans, metals, rags, nylon stockings, bras, girdles, and so forth would be thrown into one of the two stucco barrels.

When a bunch of relatively clean newsprint was found by shaking the bags, it would also be put into the second stucco barrel. When either barrel was filled up, the man in the box would dump the contents in the cuverta, tie the four corners with the traditional square knots, and hang the cuverta off the hooks on the back doors of the truck.

Since the early years, the company had always encouraged customers to set aside newsprint, tie it into bundles, and place the bundles alongside the garbage can on collection day. The scavenger, once he had his carrying can on his shoulder, would pick up the bundle and carry it to the truck, where racks were installed to store the newsprint.

During this process, aside from sorting and recovering rags, bottles, newsprint, and virtually every piece of cardboard/corrugated material found during the day's collection, the man in the truck would also jump on the garbage in the truck to compact and create space inside for additional garbage. We facetiously referred to this process as "Italian Power." In those days, hydraulic power did not exist to compact garbage.

As the day went by and garbage filled up to the top of the truck's steel body, we improvised a system that increased the capacity of the truck through a combination of sideboards and fences. The sideboards were two 4 x 8-feet pieces of ½-inch plywood panel with holes cut in them; they were hung inside of the box. As the garbage filled the inside of the body, the man in the truck would systematically pull up the plywood panels. They were eventually some three feet above the side of the truck and held in the garbage.

The "fence" was a cardboard container that at one time housed a refrigerator. This cardboard was placed inside and around the back of the truck connected to the sideboards, and it was supported by four 2 x 4s, each eight feet long. By incorporating this bit of imagination, the crew was able to increase the hauling capacity of the truck by almost 70 percent.

One might assume that this strategy was a mandate of the company as a means to increase capacity. On the contrary, it was the crew. On any given route, the work assignment was based upon revenue production. Some days any given route could make three loads instead of two, meaning more time on the job. By utilizing sideboards and fences, the day's route was cut to two loads, which meant going home earlier.

This part of the job was implemented from the very first day a scavenger operated on the streets of San Francisco. The primary reason was not to "Save the Earth's Resources"—which is the cry today—but to subsidize the actual cost of providing garbage collection, because early on that service was highly competitive.

Day's End

After the day's work was completed, we put a canvas cover over the top of the truck and tied it down with ropes to minimize refuse flowing out into the streets. Then we drove the truck to the landfill site for disposal.

Scavenged materials brought to the company for further process in preparation for resale had two distinct economic advantages:

1. Over time, recycling became a profitable enterprise because the actual cost of recovering the material was zero. While collecting the garbage, scavengers recovered these materials and gave them to the processing center free of charge. What was sold brought in almost 75 percent profit.
2. Every ton of the secondary materials recovered in this manner resulted in additional savings for the company at lower disposal expenses.

Secondary Processing

We dropped off all the materials recovered for recycling—cardboard, newsprint, and "stucco" (rags, bottles, and metals)—before passing through the truck scales, where each truck was weighed and charged a fee based on weight.

As noted, the recovered materials were broken down into three basic categories:

1. Corrugated/cardboard fibers
2. Clean newsprint
3. Stucco (rags, bottles, and metals)

The first stop prior to passing through the scales was the flat-bed cardboard truck. The driver would pull back the cover on the open truck and offload the cuvertas holding the cardboard. At the second stop, the driver would throw all the cuvertas holding the scavenged newsprint and the tied bundled paper onto a large open truck. The third stop was inside a building. The cuvertas holding stucco were thrown off to a waiting man who would stockpile them until he could place them on a simple conveyor belt. Eight individuals were typically on the sort line, and each individual would recover a specific component.

- Rags were picked and dropped down a chute, which dumped the items to another picking table where each rag was segregated by grade—cotton, wool, etc. For whatever reason, women conducted this chore. Benny Anselmo once referenced this operation as working with *pegurggi* (fleas) because the work environment was infested with them. The women, as bad as it was, seemed to accept it as a way of life and part of the job. Once graded, the rags were baled by grade, sold to be washed, and then used for a multitude of purposes. I was told that nylon and rayon were processed for reuse, and that other rags were ground up and integrated with plastic to make covers for radios.

- Metals were recovered by hand, dropped down chutes into containers by type, and then taken to another area, where they were segregated by type and eventually sold for recycling.

- Glass containers were separated by type. Glass bottles like those for soft drinks were typically custom-designed, while those for beer, wine, and milk were of standard design. Virtually all wineries used the same standard, dark green, hollow-bottom bottles. We washed and sanitized them, put them in boxes, and sold them for twelve cents each to various wineries for reuse.

- Champagne bottles were all the same standard size; once washed and sanitized, they were sold back to the champagne makers for fifty cents each. When we came across those bottles, it was like finding gold in the garbage. Most dairies utilized a standard-sized bottle. All bleach bottles, such as Sani-Clor, Clorox, and Purex, used the same standard-design glass container. All breweries used a standard bottle that we washed, sanitized, and sold to the multitude of breweries in the Bay Area. Soda containers, because of their special design, were accumulated over a period of time. When we had collected a commercial quantity from a specific company (for example, Hires Root Beer), we washed and sanitized the bottles and invited the soda manufacturer to come, pick its containers, and pay for the recovery and processing. Whiskey bottles had no value primarily because federal law prohibited the reuse of this type of container, a law adopted after the end of Prohibition. The law made no sense, but why question the government?

All other materials were taken to the landfill for disposal. As time went by, the glass container manufacturing companies embarked on an advertising blitz with whiskey, wine, beer, milk, and other entities that used glass for their products, offering custom-designed containers to make the product attractive to the consumer.

As a result, the standard glass container no longer existed, and there was no need or incentive for anyone to wash and reuse glass containers. To complicate the matter, when "packer" compaction garbage trucks replaced the old open trucks, the materials that were historically part of the scavenger's daily work were no longer available.

The era of real reuse and true recycling ended. The purveyors of consumer goods and the way they packaged those goods were at least partially to blame for the change in disposal.

Working on Route 27

Some years back, the TV series *Naked City* had a memorable opening statement: "New York City: Eight million souls and eight million stories."

The same philosophical explanation could be applied to any garbage collection route, though not necessarily by today's methods. Today no one sees, let alone comes in intimate contact with, the product.

In my day, every can of the customer's garbage was picked up and dumped into the scavenger's carrying can and was to some degree observed as it was transferred from one container to another as well as when it was dumped and sorted.

Typically, people stored waste under sinks, placed it into paper bags, and lined small trash containers to collect all wastes such as cans, bottles, and whatever else was stored. When the trash container was filled up, people placed it in the regular garbage can along with the waste generated earlier.

Every residential service unit was made up of mansions, apartment houses, single residential houses, but mostly two- and three-story flats. Traditionally these structures stored their garbage cans upstairs on the back landings. In 1954, we would climb those three flights of stairs for an extra seventy-five cents per month.

Eventually that was to change but, at the time, it was only seventy-five cents a month more to walk out the door, dump your waste, and go back inside, rather than have to walk down three flights of stairs to dump your garbage and then have to walk back up the stairs. Seventy-five cents a month was a bargain.

We also had a key service, which was a complimentary service offered by the company. At one time, we estimated that we had almost 22,000 keys to apartments, residences, and businesses. (It was somewhat facetiously noted that the public trusted the scavengers as much, if not more, than the police department.)

A Few Unusual Experiences in the Fillmore District

Every time we found a woman's purse our automatic process was to check the interior, since women would often leave coins and other cash in the little coin pocket inside the purse. I once found a small diamond ring in a coin purse.

Another time, while dumping the barrel on the third floor of a house, I found a coin purse chockfull of cash. Not wanting anyone to see me, I waited until I went downstairs and into the basement to open the purse. I counted out seventy-two one-dollar bills, a substantial find in those days.

For whatever reason, we often found cash on the streets walking to and from the truck. Not anything of great value—but one, five, and ten-dollar bills were the norm. I never understood why we found money like that. On a more negative side of the garbage man's day, we found premature babies twice while shaking bags. Sometimes I wonder how many we may have missed.

During and after World War II, properties were often not maintained. Drug dealing was commonplace, as was open prostitution—streetwalkers looking for "quickies" in a car or a dark doorway. As we went to work at four in the morning, it was amazing to see so many people on Fillmore Street, from Fulton to Geary, a strip of some ten city blocks.

We learned that many of the bars that were supposed to close up at 2 AM only turned off their exterior lights and remained open until the sun came up. For whatever reason, the cops and others just looked the other way.

One such bar was the Blue Mirror, where the more expensive hookers hung out. Once a woman connected with a client, all she had to do was walk across the street to Earl Hotel, a six-story complex that made a great source of revenue from the "hot sheets" clientele.

The rock band Jefferson Airplane lived on Steiner Street between McAllister and Fulton. When not performing, they were up all night and slept all day. There was a permanent odor of marijuana whenever we went near the place. Another unusual event there was in a ten-story apartment building on the corner. On the third floor, a man was masturbating in the window. My driver threw oranges at him.

Serving customers in the dark hours had its downside too. Without the use of a flashlight to service certain customers, it was potentially dangerous for a new man on the route. Carrying a flashlight wasn't helpful when collecting garbage, though, because it was always in the way.

After you became familiar with the layout of a structure on your route, you could find your way in and out of a customer location almost blindfolded; but there were inherent problems when it was dark. One such issue was a long, dark, narrow alley with a wooden floor. Homeless people would sleep on the wooden floor for warmth on cold nights. If someone was sleeping on the floor, you could walk down the alley and fall over the sleeping body—which scared the living hell out of you. To compensate for that potential problem, we would roll a beer bottle down the alley. If it did not stop and went into the room, we knew that we were safe from that form of hazard.

Another situation came up when we had a garbage chute to service. A string would hang from the center of the room. When we pulled the string, a light would come on and illuminate the room. Upon entering the room, you would wave your hand until you found the string. In this particular case, I lightly touched something while looking for the string, but I still found the string and pulled the light on. The something I had touched was a man who had hanged himself in the garbage room. I never forgot that experience!

One of our customers was a halfway house for alcoholic priests. We were told at one time that there were as many as a dozen men being treated there. Being a Catholic, I was sad because when we picked up the garbage we would always find a Mickey or an Old Crow whiskey container. Somebody was smuggling booze to the priests who lived there.

Down the street, an Italian man named Santino made wine in his basement. It wasn't traditional red wine but a semisweet white wine. When we went to serve his home, he would always invite us in for a glass. The wine was unique, with a sweet taste that camouflaged the alcohol content; after two glasses, you could really feel it. It reminded me of my godfather, Pete Guaraglia, who would always break a raw egg into the glass of wine and suck the egg down with the wine. I could never do that.

On Page Street, there was a two-story, four-unit building with a tunnel-style entrance to the four separate apartment doors, each with a clear glass door usually covered with a curtain for privacy.

While collecting the garbage bills, I had to keep coming back to apartment #3 because no one was ever there.

I recalled that his garbage can on the second floor had been empty, and there was a horrible stench in the entranceway when I came back a week later to collect the money due. I wondered why no one had complained. On further inspection, I noticed a dark stain on the curtain of the glass door and saw ants moving around. When I peered through the curtain, I noticed something large leaning against the door and realized it was a big man pressed up against the glass door.

I knocked on the next door down and explained to the woman who answered that I believed the man was dead against the doorstop. At first, she refused to believe me, but she called the police anyway, especially since I brought to her attention the horrible odors.

When the police showed up, I explained who I was and that the police could gain access through the backdoor, where the garbage cans were. When the officer entered the apartment, he pointed his flashlight down the stairs. Preacher Hall, who lived in the house, had shot himself, fallen down the stairs, and ended up against the door.

The officers asked me to stay, and I watched the coroner remove the body. The stench was overwhelming—I couldn't believe that no one had complained about it prior to my seeing, smelling, and reporting it.

Just another day on the job.

One night while collecting bills, I was approached by two men who knew who I was and demanded my money. Since they had no weapons, I ran up the street into a dark alley that I was familiar with because I collected the garbage there. I ran down the alley, jumped over the fence, and ran down other familiar alleys. My pursuers got lost. After that experience, I thought it would be prudent to carry a firearm for protection, even though it was illegal.

One night about six months later, I saw a police officer stopping people on the street and asking questions. As I walked up to him with my collection book, he asked me who I was.

I looked at him and said, "I'm a scavenger collecting for garbage service."

He said that he had a report that a man was seen carrying a firearm.

"Well, I'm the man. I have a gun on my back belt."

The police officer took away my gun and put me in handcuffs, put me in a police car, and drove to the police station in Golden Gate Park.

As it turned out, I knew the booking officer at the SFPD Park Station. The arresting officers insisted that a report be filed, so I was transferred to the Hall of Justice on Kearny Street. A police officer was hanging off the back of the old paddy wagon with me inside, and everyone who drove up behind the paddy wagon tried to see what kind of criminal was inside. I was transferred from the vehicle to an elevator and placed into the tank, waiting to be processed. It was quite an experience being in an iron box with no window, bars on the roof, and a trench for a urinal.

When I finally got into the hearing room, I bailed myself out with the money I had collected that night from the garbage bills. (I was surprised that the judge gave the money back to me so I could bail myself out.) I went to trial and was exonerated, even though it was against the law to carry a concealed weapon in San Francisco. I never did again. It was quite an experience, my first—and last time—tangling with the law.

Historical Means of Managing Boss Scavengers

I have referred to Sunset Scavenger as a capitalistic communistic society. In theory, it was capitalist; in reality, it was also a communistic organization. The common goal was for everybody to own an equal share of equity as well as equal income and benefits, but a single person made the decisions. The final analysis was simple: it was a communistic society.

The bylaws of the company stated clearly that everyone was paid equally, "regardless of office position or responsibility." Everyone shared equally in any dividends or rewards at the end of each working cycle.

From the incorporation of Sunset Scavenger Company in 1920 until 1965, the company had to change some of its procedures to remain competitive. Although the communistic philosophy that the company was based on proved successful, the fact remained that it was dying on the vine. With the company's means of enforcing the rules and regulations and its methods for governing the so-called partners, the company could best be defined as a dictatorship. The workers voted for the board of directors and the board of directors elected the president, but the president was the supreme commander.

As demonstrated in the board minutes, the president, Giuseppe Fontana, made all the policy, and the board of directors formally approved whatever decisions he made. The board appeared to select decision-makers, such as dispatcher and corporate secretary, but the decision-maker was always the president.

On the rare occasion that a stockholder ever questioned the decisions of the president, or when an employee violated a standard rule, he was reprimanded by a fine or other means, assuring that the shareholders would always be in total agreement with the president's policies.

As dictatorial as it was, the company functioned well. The garbage was picked up every day. The scavengers had a mutually beneficial relationship with the City and County of San Francisco and kept a low profile. The company was successful, even though it was operated as a dictatorship.

Over these many years, very little changed in how the company ran. Men still had to carry the waste from people's backyards and stairways, climb up the truck's steps, and dump the waste into the truck. The process was the same in 1965 as it had been when Giuseppe Fontana took over the company in 1920. The only real change in work was that an engine ran in front of the truck where a horse used to be.

In 1952, Joseph Molinari, a member of the board of directors and vice president of the Sunset Scavenger Company, became president, and he carried on for all practical purposes the same basic company policies that were followed under Giuseppe Fontana.

I became a shareholder of Sunset Scavenger Company in 1956. During one of my first shareholder meetings, someone asked why Sunset Scavenger Company was not buying the packer trucks that would eliminate the need for the "seven stairs to heaven" and make the job substantially easier for the men on the truck.

President Molinari responded, "Sunset Scavenger Company is primarily in the scavenger (recycling) business." That was his opinion and, as long as he was president, this was his policy: "Collection of garbage is secondary, and we are going to build even bigger trucks to allow that to continue. If we use packer trucks, we would not have access to the materials that we are presently recovering and reselling for profit."

I believe that President Molinari's statement exemplified the lack of imagination by company management. He was obviously trained in the old ways of doing business, and he was continuing the traditional means of conducting the business, i.e., "collect the garbage, collect the money for the services provided, recycle, keep our business private, and do as we have done for sixty years, following and perpetuating the proven, successful means of doing business."

It was my opinion that a continuation of that philosophy would surely result in a profit loss, and that the company would suffer if management refused to adopt new directions or did not respond to the rapidly changing world of solid-waste management—as will be demonstrated later on in this book.

It is true that the recycling arm of the company, Joseph Petigera Company, always showed a profit—therefore justifying its existence. But in reality, the cost of the raw material was zero because it was recovered by and paid for by the Boss Scavengers working on the trucks. If the Joseph Petigera Company would have had to pay for the raw material or reimburse Sunset Scavenger Company for the cost of recovering these materials, the Joseph Petigera Company would have lost money. But that was the way the companies had operated fifty years earlier, and Molinari saw no reason to change.

The Boss Scavenger's Task: Collecting the Book

When you became a shareholder in the Sunset Scavenger Company, you took on a second responsibility in addition to collecting garbage. After collecting the garbage and sorting the material, you went home, took a shower and a nap, and then drove back to your route in the evening and rang doorbells to collect revenues for the service you had provided during the month. You recorded your collections for a six-month period in "the book," a 4 x 9-inch softcover notebook.

The book was simple. You listed the street or avenue at the top of the page. The address of the account (but not the name) went below that and, next, the rate being charged. Six columns on the following page covered the six months of collection for your particular account.

We usually collected for two months at a time, one for service already provided in the previous month and one for the coming month. For example, if the rate were $2 a month, you wrote $4 in one column for the month of December. Then you wrote "P" (paid) for the month of January, indicating that you had collected two months at $2 per month. On the first of the next month, the book would be available for you to start your collecting again.

The company also provided a book of receipts. You would handwrite a receipt, give the copy to your customer, and keep the original for your records. Using the book and that receipt book, you rang the doorbells at night and said, "Garbage bill!" Your customer would ask, "How much?" You responded with the amount, wrote that amount in your receipt book, took the money, and gave a copy of the receipt to the customer.

The company required that you make an initial deposit of the money you had collected from the first of the month by the eighth of each month. This deposit indicated that you were collecting or least attempting to collect your accounts on or before the first of the month, thus assuring the company that you were doing your job properly. If you failed to make a deposit by the eighth, the company fined you.

By the twenty-seventh of the month, you had to make the final monthly deposit. At that point, you added up all the money you had collected that month. After making your last deposit for the month, you took your book down to the company, where the staff transferred the information in your book into a general ledger that you were required to reproduce once a year for the company.

You added up the dollars that you had recorded in the book at the end of each month, and hopefully that total would equal the amount of money of your two deposits. If you were short, you had to make it up at the meeting on the third Wednesday, where all the Boss Scavengers would raise their eyebrows; being short was considered living beyond your means.

In other words, if you were short in last month's deposits, you were using the current month's collections to pay for last month's shortages. In some cases, this was an accurate assessment, because there were incidents where Boss Scavengers had to go to the bank to bring their book current.

Garbage men always had a facetious comment about the period between the eighth and the twenty-seventh of the month. We all acted and looked like millionaires who had an abundance of cash in our wallets. But sometimes the twenty-seventh was the moment of truth. We found out how much of a good time we had had during the month, and we had to make up the difference out of our own pockets. The twenty-seventh always made "honest Christians" out of us all. Then we would start this ritual all over again on the first of the next month.

8

The Board of Directors and How It Governed

To better understand how Sunset Scavenger Company was managed, we have to go back again to the Articles of Incorporation dated September 20, 1920. In 1920, the corporation's bylaws required that the board of directors be elected on the third Wednesday of December of each year.

Stockholders would vote for eleven directors or confirm the existing board. The original board of directors in 1920 was not elected, though, but appointed by Emilio Rattaro. All were partners in the original Sunset Scavengers before incorporation, and included my wife's grandfather, Emilio Rattaro, and Giuseppe "Joe" Fontana, the uncle of my future father-in-law.

Seldom did anyone run for the board without fear of retaliation. This was the way it was until 1952, when president Fontana passed away in Italy, and for all practical purposes that was still the way the company was run until 1965.

Since 1921, the president and the board of directors could best be defined as dictatorial—the supreme authority of the corporation. No one in his right mind would ever protest what the president and board did; if you did, you would eventually be sorry for doing so.

It is also interesting to note that no Boss Scavenger ever signed up for the board of directors. Such an effort would always be seen as a gross expression of disrespect—somehow, somewhere, or sometime, such an effort would result in something bad happening against the individual.

When a current board member needed to be replaced because of illness or death, the board would make an appointment that was acceptable to the president and compatible with the president's recommendations for the company's needs and goals. I hesitate to use the term "Black Hand," as in the Cosa Nostra, because these men were Genovese, not Sicilians; but the fact remains that the company is and was ruled by an "iron hand." No one argued against company policies, whether they were good or bad. Once, my uncle Freddy, my godfather Pete Guaraglia, and I went out golfing. We had a few cocktails (referred to as "road shorteners").

Those days—being a scavenger—playing golf and having a few drinks was part of the job, working your ass off and playing hard, just having a good time. Anyway, we arrived late for the shareholders meeting, as when we got there, the meeting was just getting underway. Joe Molinari, who was on the rostrum, sort of looked down on us and criticized us for being late.

The meeting was typical and boring and went on as usual, talking about garbage trucks, collecting the moneys, and so forth. The meeting was more for propaganda, telling us how well the board was taking care of our interests. But they were also saying that, if you did not go to a meeting, you would be fined ten dollars— no small amount of money at that time—for being absent.

After the meeting was over, for whatever reason (stupidity), Freddy, Pete, and I thought it would be funny to throw a couple of boxes of fluorescent tubes that were in the alcove into the back of the pickup truck, even though we had no use for them and had no intention of selling them. I later took them back to the company and apologized. Nothing much was said about it until I got a call telling me that I was going to have my book audited.

This was the typical means of enforcing company rules, to put paranoia and fear in Boss Scavengers. Having your book audited meant that you would sit down with a professional CPA to go item by item in your book. Some people may have fudged and actually spent some job money in the bar.

There was always room for error in your book because everything was written and transposed by hand. This was an archaic method of doing business, but it was the way things had been done since 1920, and that was still the way they were being done in 1962 when my books were audited.

An error found by the audit could result in a substantial monetary fine and/or suspension of employment, if not termination. It all depended on how pissed off the board was at your infraction and how much money was involved. In any case, a fine or suspension would cost you money and embarrassment.

Everyone panicked if an audit was being conducted. These audits were not regularly scheduled and only occurred when you screwed up. As a result, you kept your mind and thoughts to yourself and did not question anything the board of directors did.

As an example, my uncle Freddy, who was working on the Route 37 Haight-Ashbury District in 1964, was rattling the cages with then-president Joe Molinari. In response, the company did an audit on Freddy's books and on his route. They set him up, with some customer paying Freddy twenty dollars cash for "extra work" after the day's normal workday.

Freddy and the other Boss Scavengers on the route spent the twenty dollars in a bar. Then the company suspended him for stealing company money and forced him to sell his share in Sunset Scavenger Company. He ended up working for Golden Gate Disposal Company without holding company shares. It was the ultimate punitive action.

Ironically, what Freddy did was in fact a common practice throughout the company. The "rules" indicated the money should be turned in (although the rule was never enforced unless you challenged the board authority), but to terminate Freddy's livelihood, rather than require a fine or suspension of employment, was outrageous and an abuse of power. This was yet another example of the power the board and the president held over the partners.

For the record, when I completed the audit of my book, I could not account for ten cents. And, after I became president, I brought Uncle Freddy back home to the company.

9

The Revolution

Preamble to the Revolution

As noted earlier, Joseph D. Molinari became president of Sunset Scavenger in 1952. Like all board members, Molinari worked on the trucks and became a Boss Scavenger in 1930.

In 1934, he was assigned to Truck 44 in the Richmond District, on the route where he and his family lived at 12th Avenue and Balboa Street. From what I have been told by the few people who are still around, Joseph Molinari was born in 1918 and went to work for Sunset at age sixteen in 1934, the same year my father-in-law Guido became a Boss Scavenger.

Nicknamed "JD" and "Nin," Molinari was appointed to the board of directors in 1940 because of the retirement of one of the board members.

When the company officially relocated its corporate offices to 412 Hampshire Street in the Mission District in 1926, the board of directors' room was located on the top floor. When any Boss Scavenger was called before the board, he often said, "Shit, I am being called to the thirteen steps." There were exactly thirteen steps from the main office to the dreaded and infamous boardroom.

Clouds Gather for the Revolution

As history dictates, communistic societies are subject to revolution. Since Sunset Scavenger Company did in fact operate like a communistic society, it was surely eligible for such an event after 50 years. The company's record at first was commendable. Over the years, the company's management refused to recognize the need to change, and it was just a matter of time before an incident would occur to trigger some kind of revolution.

The board of directors and the corporation bylaws governed the company. One key and unique component of the bylaws was that everybody was paid "absolutely alike, regardless of office position or responsibility." Whether you were a truck boss, driver, mechanic, officer, or light-duty worker, you made the same amount of money as everyone else.

At the end of the year (barring some extraordinary overtime or unused vacation pay), the base compensation of roughly $9,200 a year in 1965 was uniform and consistent throughout the company. The president had some perks, such as a company car (a 1962 Ford) and a minimal expense account, but otherwise even the president made the same amount of money.

As I have noted, in my early years at Sunset Scavenger I embarked upon two ventures aside from the garbage business. I took classes at the University of San Francisco, and I attended Golden Gate College, applying for and receiving a license to sell comprehensive general liability auto insurance.

My initial efforts in sales were slow. After all, I had no reputation and I was a scavenger, not an insurance agent. But in less than two years my insurance business began to grow. In addition to my connection with the scavengers, I began picking up some commercial accounts. In 1965, I was making as much money in insurance—even on a split-commission basis—as I was making as a Boss Scavenger at Sunset Scavenger.

In May of 1965, I attended an Elks State Convention in San Diego with my close friend and insurance man, Joe Picetti. At that time, Joe suggested that I quit the garbage business and work for him fulltime on a salary basis (plus commission), which would have put me in the area of $25,000 a year, a significant offer and worthy of consideration.

The decision clearly made logistical and economic sense, especially because I was only thirty-one years old, and it would almost triple what I made as a scavenger. Plus, I would no longer have to carry garbage.

After some thought and serious consideration, I reluctantly accepted the offer. I decided that, as soon as I got home and back on the job, I would prepare to sell my Sunset Scavenger Company shares.

But as fate would have it, I picked up the *San Francisco News* when I arrived at the airport for the return home. On the front page, in a section at the bottom, a headline read: "Scavenger President Increases Salary 200%." The article went on to quote Gal Campi, my wife's cousin and the corporation's secretary, who said the company was removing the president from the garbage-collector ranks, placing him into the prestigious rank of executive officers, and setting his compensation at $30,000 a year.

From my personal knowledge of the company bylaws and my limited education in corporate law, I immediately realized that the president or board could not do that without an amendment to the corporate bylaws. I assumed that the change had already been made that would allow him or the board to approve such an action.

Back in San Francisco, I was overwhelmed by phone calls at home telling me what had happened. Apparently, while I was away, the board had sent out word notifying the shareholders of the change in policy but did not mention anything about amendments to bylaws. The written announcement just said:

After due consideration and study, the board of directors has determined that the executive branch of the corporation is under-compensated for their services, and as a result, the board of directors has approved the following annual compensation to the following offices:

President	$30,000
Vice President	$25,000
Secretary	$23,000
All Directors	$3,000

This added compensation for being a board member was clearly a break from the traditional means of doing business within the corporation. To say the partners (shareholders) were upset would be an understatement. Many came to me, maybe because I was selling insurance to them and because most of them thought I was educated and a businessman of sorts.

Some other shareholders were so upset that they began talking about "cement shoes" and "walking in the bay," threatening bodily harm to the president and all members of the board of directors. I hoped that these were idle threats, but who could know?

The Challenge

Unlikely as the decision was, it was done. Surely the board knew there would be anger, but board members might have assumed that, based upon past experience, such responses would be unorganized anger among the troops. The decision demonstrated the power the president and the board of directors felt that they had over the shareholders—virtually ignoring the existence of any organized effort to challenge a decision of the board.

And they surely would have gotten away with it unless someone legitimately challenged that decision.

On Wednesday, June 21, at the regularly scheduled monthly Sunset Scavengers shareholders meeting, the minutes of the May meeting were read, approving the new compensation schedule for executives of the Sunset Scavenger Company. Following that announcement people began screaming, hollering, and making threats.

The president tried to calm down the shareholders. After several comments from the floor—all of which were in gross opposition to the change in policy—I asked the president for permission to speak.

When I did stand up, I was surprised that everybody shut up. My statement was straightforward:

> Mr. President, I personally have no problems about the senior management of the company making more money than I do working on the garbage truck, but I do have complaints about the lack of future thinking and needs of the company by you and the board of directors.
>
> For example, the Scavenger's Protective Association is acquiring packer trucks to provide better working conditions for the garbage collectors. Sunset Scavenger Company is buying bigger open trucks, and the reason you give us is because we are primarily in the salvage business and secondarily in the garbage collection business, where you claim if we used packer trucks, we would no longer have access to materials that could be sold, which makes no physical or economic sense.
>
> Mr. President, in my opinion—and I'm sure all the stockholders in this room believe—this is not the type of management that needs to lead this company into the future. Therefore, in theory, they are not qualified to be the recipients of these new compensation schedules.
>
> But that's not the point of my personal concerns at the present time. The question here now is how could you provide yourself a significant increase in compensation without amending the bylaws? Point being also that I did not hear anything in the minutes since the last stockholders meeting from the board about amending the bylaws to allow for the increase or change in compensation to happen or that this was ever considered or adopted. Could you tell us when the board approved this amendment?

The result was a blank look on President Molinari's face. He looked at the board members and then immediately called for a temporary adjournment of the shareholders meeting, indicating the need for a board of directors meeting. He promised to return with a response. As the board left the room, I went into the main office with a few of my peers. On the telephone switchboard, I noticed a light on the line marked "directors' room."

In those days, our company was still somewhat backward. We still used the "wire-in" phone connection system. When someone called, the operator grabbed a wire and connected the call to the appropriate person or office by plugging the wire into a slot. In this case, the board of directors' room was lit up, so I took the earphones out and plugged them into the slot that was lit up.

When I heard the conversation, I was surprised to hear that it was President Joe Molinari on the phone with the company's attorney, Gregory Harrison, of the prominent law firm of Brobeck, Phleger & Harrison. Harrison, the principal partner in the law firm, questioned how the board could make such a move without consulting its legal advisors.

In a rapid effort to correct the problem, Harrison told the president to call for a special meeting of the board of directors to adopt an amendment to the bylaws of the corporation. He dictated the amendment over the phone. Hearing that, I immediately disconnected the phone and discussed what I had heard with a few of the shareholders. The board returned in about twenty minutes. The president reconvened the meeting and read the revised board minutes, allowing for the differential in compensation for the executives of the company.

At this moment, they read the minutes of the special meeting just held, indicating that the board had adopted and approved an amendment to the bylaws providing for the differential in wages. To add insult to injury, they made the compensation schedule retroactive to January 1, 1965, which pissed off the partners even more.

Based upon my limited knowledge of corporate law (limited, but knowledge nonetheless) from my education at the University of San Francisco, I again asked for the floor and asked the following: "Sir, I know that the board of directors has the authority to amend existing bylaws and create new bylaws within the corporate structure. However, unless laws have been changed in California, I do believe that before such changes can be formally and/

or legally adopted and placed into effect, they have to be ratified by the shareholders either by oral or written vote!"

I added, "Did any one of you shareholders vote to approve this amendment?"

The response was a loud and resounding "NO!" From that moment on, the so-called revolution was born. The president adjourned the meeting, then he and the entire board of directors walked out.

In doing what I did—challenging a board decision—I had violated the traditional rule of keeping my mouth shut and never challenging the board of directors on anything, let alone a matter of this magnitude.

I was certain that I had crucified myself, so I concluded there was no going back. I had broken the cardinal rule of the company. Even though I believed I was right (and I knew I had the insurance job as a backup), the fact was that Sunset Scavenger Company was my life.

The following day, my wife's cousin, Gal Campi, the corporate secretary, asked me, "What the hell are you doing—trying to wreck the company?" He added that I should rescind my accusation, as it would surely destroy the company. Then he enhanced his direct threats by suggesting that if I kept my mouth shut and supported the board, there might be new and better things for me in the future.

I listened to what he had to say without committing to anything, but I realized that his coming to me with that proposal meant that I had surely gotten the board's attention. I indicated that I would get back to him after I spoke to some of my fellow partners.

In the meantime, many of the shareholders contacted me and asked me to take a leadership role and develop a plan to stop the president and the board from what they were doing. I realized that there was a great degree of interest, so I organized a group of partners to discuss options, plans, and how to coordinate our efforts to take on the board.

At our first series of meetings, we decided that the first step was to send a formal letter on behalf of the class of shareholders, demanding that the board rescind the compensation amendment and reimburse the corporation for the retroactive pay from January

1965. We sent the letter on behalf of concerned shareholders via registered mail on or about June 20, 1965.

When we received no response in five days, we sent a follow-up letter, saying that we expected a response within 48 hours and that if no response were forthcoming, additional steps would be taken to ensure that our demands were addressed.

The 48-hour period of demand came and went with no response. Clearly the board was ignoring us. After further consideration, we concluded that the only real option we had was to charge the board with a breach of fiduciary responsibility by adopting a policy contrary to the company bylaws without shareholder approval. I had learned that charge from my USF law book.

Reviewing my text on corporate law and what I'd learned at the University of San Francisco, I drew up a document summarizing the board's infractions and demanding the immediate resignation of all the board members of the Sunset Scavenger Company for a breach of fiduciary responsibility and failure to respond to shareholder demands.

The document was circulated among the shareholders. In less than three days, 268 of the 320 shareholders signed it. We submitted the document to the board of directors and they again refused to acknowledge it. However, company attorney Gregory Harrison of Brobeck, Phleger & Harrison (and several other attorneys) called a meeting of our committee of garbage collectors to explain that what we were attempting to do was wrong.

At this meeting, I argued that it was the attorneys' opinion that was wrong. I added that the board could not make the compensation changes prior to an amendment to the bylaws. I added (what I knew by listening to the telephone conversation) that the bylaws were changed under the president's direction, long after the change in compensation was made and then made retroactive.

I also said that the shareholders never even had a chance to vote on the amendment, that the board refused to acknowledge the demands. All of this provided sufficient cause to demand the present board's resignation and call for a special election. The attorneys adjourned the meeting, indicating that they were scheduled to meet with senior management to discuss the matter and would get back to us shortly with the company's response.

I must have done a reasonably good job in this meeting, as they reluctantly agreed that they had to call for a special election.

I found this out later from Gal Campi, the corporate secretary, who in my opinion was an extremely smart and educated man. I had worked with him for one week on Truck 70 when he was #1 Boss before he became the corporate secretary.

After further consideration, Gregory Harrison and other attorneys appeared before the board of directors, stating that the members had no choice but to tender their resignations and call for a special election to elect a new board, which could be made up of the same men, a completely new board, or a combination of new members and incumbents.

Our group developed a slate of eleven directors, including myself and others, who represented a broad base of the shareholders— young, old, different districts, and so forth. The meeting was scheduled for August 27.

Altogether, twenty-two shareholders signed the book of candidates—eleven incumbents and eleven new candidates—all working Boss Scavengers.

We sent letters of support to the new group. As part of that effort, we also incorporated a slogan similar to the Avis Car Rental slogan. Ours was, "We Will Do More and Do It Better," and we promoted it in many languages, including Italian: *Faremo di Piú Emeglio*. We got hold of these little metal badges and, by bending the tips, we could attach them to any shirt collar. In no time, it seemed as if the whole company was wearing them. It was quite a well-organized campaign.

The board members came down on our efforts with everything they could and were especially critical of me. They claimed that I did not care about the pending terminal damage to the company, their personal equity if they lost their positions, and added that, as the leader, I had nothing to lose because I had a second job in the insurance business. It got really ugly.

The plan was that, if we did in fact win the election with eleven new members to the board of directors, there was nothing in the bylaws saying that the executive officers of the corporation had to be members of the board of directors. We were not looking for glory—only to bring the company into the modern age, especially a company of this size. The company was one of the largest and oldest privately owned garbage companies in California, yet in reality it still operated as if it were in the Stone Age.

In many ways the company had been one of the most backward,

operating on the same basic philosophy that once allowed it to succeed. All that had to change if we were to meet the demands of the future.

Assuming that we got eleven new members of the board, the plan was to elect J. D. Molinari president, me as vice president, and Gal Campi as secretary. Louie "the Crow" would remain as dispatcher but not a member of the board, because he commanded more power than anyone as a dispatcher.

The plan was simple. We would have a new board of directors with entrepreneurial thinking and with ideas to move the company from the horse-and-wagon days into the modern age, while maintaining the current service and not interrupting its day-to-day management.

The election was held and we had eleven new board members. It is interesting to note that, of the eleven new directors, I was dead last—clearly because of the concerted effort of the old board members to discredit me through negative personal attacks.

As soon as the election was over that night and the votes were counted, I contacted J. D. Molinari and said, "Let's get back to the boardroom with our new board of directors and have our organizational meeting."

As I said, our intent was to reelect him as president.

But his response surprised even me. Although I had a premonition of what was to occur, I really didn't think he would do it; but he looked me in the eye and announced that he, Lou Crosetti (the dispatcher), Gal Campi (the secretary), Willie Barone (the salvage company operator), and the balance of the board were taking two weeks' vacation. They all threw their keys on the table and walked out the door, leaving us high and dry.

I could see the panic in the eyes of the ten new directors. I felt the same way.

As I was largely the organizer of the coup, I clearly had to take command. The majority of the shareholders were still in the meeting hall, so I went back inside and told them of the old board's decision to go on vacation, which I presented as the old board's means of spreading fear and uncertainty about the new board's ability to run the company.

Some weeks later Gal Campi confirmed what I already knew: the board had followed the advice of the public relations people and the attorneys to walk out completely and leave the company to a bunch of "garbage men."

The attorney and the public relations people assured the board that, "In less than a week, they will be begging for you to come back and when they do, you will have regained absolute control of the company."

They might have succeeded, especially if the election had been held on a Monday, because in reality we had no knowledge of and no experience with the administrative affairs of the company, the crew requirements for the coming week, and ever so much more.

Fortunately, it was a Friday. The regular Saturday crews already knew their routes and the drivers were already assigned. Learning about the board throwing the keys on the table only enhanced the incentives for the partners to cooperate with the new board.

On Saturday morning, August 28, the new board met at the company to go over the business plan for the coming week. My personal friend and advisor, John "Jack" Ertola, was a member of the San Francisco Board of Supervisors and an attorney who followed our efforts. When I called him on August 27 to tell him we had won the election but the former management had immediately gone on vacation, he was surprised, to say the least.

As an elected official recognizing the important role the scavengers played in the city, Ertola offered to come to the company on Sunday and meet with the new board, bringing his law partners, including Angelo Scampini, a respected, crusty old Italian attorney from the "old school" who at one time represented A. P. Giannini of Bank of America fame.

We found that all the records—route books, payroll, and more—were in order. After some effort, we were satisfied and comfortable that we could commence work on Monday, with the added assurance that the vast majority of the shareholders would hold up their end of the program.

The Sunday meeting was a different story, as some of the eleven new board members were getting nervous—*very* nervous—and something needed to be done to mitigate that problem. We considered the previous plan to elect Joe Molinari president. It became clear to me that the new board members were beginning to lean toward bringing back the former executives while maintaining the new board.

Attorneys Jack Ertola and Angelo Scampini were present as

observers and advisors at this first official meeting of the newly elected board of directors. Scampini stated that bringing back the former executives would be a foolish move, suggesting that each of us—especially me as the "leader of the pack"—had taken significant risks to assume control of the company. He said that the new board had to assume that none of the people were coming back, and we could not start the business week without corporate officers.

Angelo took me aside and said, "Lenny, you started the coup and you called this meeting to order to elect the corporate officers for the balance of the year. Now, above everything else, you should place your name in nomination for the president of Sunset Scavenger."

The organizational meeting was called to order. In a matter of minutes I submitted a slate of officers, which after some discussion was unanimously approved:

President, Leonard D. Stefanelli
Vice President, Dino Quierolo
Secretary, Paul Cavagnaro
Chairman, Frank Brandi
Assistant Vice President/Dispatcher, John Armanini
Director, Camillo Borghello
Director, Donald Bongi
Director, Freddy Guaraglia
Director, Louis Bertone
Director, Eduardo Curotto
Director, George Campi

This all was an amazingly rapid sequence of events for me. On August 27, 1965, I was second boss on Truck 27, and on August 29, I was president of a multimillion-dollar-a-year enterprise. I knew nothing about running a garbage company, but I surely knew how to collect garbage. My meager education and limited business experience would prove to be significant resources in the years ahead.

10

My Role as the New President

After a somewhat sleepless night and finding a replacement for my position on Truck 27, I took a shower early in the morning and put on a suit and tie. The first order of business was to go to the Bank of America at Hayes and Divisadero Streets—ironically—one of my customers on Route 27.

All the company's business was conducted at this particular branch. Manager Peter Tarantino and assistant manager Bernie Katz were my friends. I had actually opened my first checking account with that bank with $10 when I was seventeen years old, so I had a personal relationship with the bank and the people who ran it.

The bank opened at 10 AM, but at 8:30 I was knocking on the door. Peter Tarantino came to the door and the first thing he said to me was, "Lenny, what are you doing here today? You picked up the garbage on Friday."

"Peter, do I look like I'm collecting garbage?" I responded.

"No, of course not."

I explained, "We have a situation that I have to sit down and discuss with you."

He directed me to his desk, and I proceeded to tell him what had happened at Sunset Scavenger. I thought he was going to have a heart attack! I soon learned one reason he was nervous was that the two garbage companies, Sunset Scavenger and Scavenger's Protective Association, had just borrowed $2.1 million to develop the potential Sierra Point disposal facility in Brisbane, a development that would extend the life of the current landfill an additional twenty-five years.

Peter was concerned about the $600,000 loan that Bank of America had given to the two companies. The companies' lack of credit experience had been a concern to both lenders (Bank of America and Occidental Life Insurance Company), but this concern was reduced because, when the companies applied for the loan, one of the statements was that the management of both companies was "permanent and stable."

And here I walk in, informing the bank that I, at the age of thirty-one, was the new president of Sunset Scavenger and that the entire board of directors had been "excommunicated" from the company after an internal revolution. Peter Tarantino assumed that the company had gone to hell in a handbasket.

Historically, the companies saved up cash and purchased equipment as needed. In the case of Sunset Scavenger Company, we purchased used US mail trucks, stripped off the bodies, rebuilt the engines and transmissions, put open truck bodies on the truck chassis, and used the trucks to pick up garbage.

Once Peter Tarantino understood what had happened, he contacted the bankers downtown, who contacted me later. I thanked Peter for his help, and we signed the new signature cards for payroll and other documents necessary to commence operations under Sunset Scavenger Company's new regime.

Once that was completed, I went to the Sunset Scavenger office and commenced my education, learning what had to be done and when. During the process, the shareholders and everyone else were very cooperative, and I was surprised to see that everything went extremely well in the conversion of management roles. That said, we began to review the books and to figure out what had to be done to commence and continue a normal line of doing business.

The balance of our work on Monday and Tuesday was to inform our certified public accountants of the company changes and sign a contract with the law firm Scampini, Mortara & Ertola. (Brobeck, Phleger & Harrison clearly had a conflict of interest in working for the new board and for me.)

We also had to inform our purveyors and contractors that we had taken over the company and that any future contacts had to be made through me as president. Part of that process was to inform Scavenger's Protective Association president John Moscone and his board that I was the new president of Sunset Scavenger Company and that all future dealings between them and Sunset were to be through me and me alone.

We also had to inform Sanitary Fill Company, the disposal company that was owned by both collection companies, that I was to be the new vice president of that company as well. Needless to say, that news shook up a few people there.

Late Tuesday evening, Benny Anselmo, senior board member of Scavenger's Protective Association, called and asked me to have lunch with him, John Moscone, and Al Arata, who represented the Leach Company, which sold packer garbage trucks. One of the new board's pledges was to convert our fleet of open collection trucks to compaction (packer) trucks. I had to speak with someone who sold this equipment and concluded that we should do this as soon as possible. Benny, John, and I met for lunch at Bertolucci's restaurant in South San Francisco.

Benny Anselmo was my mentor from an early age. He and I had spoken many times regarding specifications of trucks and equipment. He taught me more about the garbage business than any other person in my life. He had visions of what a garbage truck should look like, how it should operate, and how it should be designed. Regarding truck design, he said we should convert our fleet to packers with diesel engines and Allison Automatic Transmissions in lieu of the standard gasoline engines with standard transmissions. How ironic it is that this combination is standard protocol today!

As a result of that luncheon, I ordered four three-axle white trucks with diesel engines and Allison transmissions with 25-yard Leach Packer bodies, which at that time were the best-built trucks available. I sometimes look back and laugh because all four trucks, with tax and license, cost less than $125,000, whereas one garbage truck today costs almost $275,000.

This was truly a mindboggling situation. The biggest thing I had done up to that time was to purchase my first home for $32,000. I had never made a deal that big in my entire life, and I didn't have any means of paying for it yet. I assumed the bank would lend us the money, but this was the first step forward to show the shareholders that the board was not sitting around doing nothing, but was making positive steps to bring us into the future.

Later on in life, and especially while running the company, I realized that a good executive has to make decisions and not sit on his ass, especially when there is no time to communicate with colleagues. Also, I eventually realized that running a business was no different than running your household (with the exception of dealing with politicians), where decisions regarding income and expenditures must be made in a prudent manner.

The only real difference between running a household and

running the company was that there were more zeroes on the company's income statement. I had to make many decisions. Fortunately, over the twenty years I was president, the vast majority of those decisions were good ones.

I went home that night realizing that I had made a decision to buy new trucks without getting formal board approval. But it had to be done, and I was confident that I would figure out some way to pay for these trucks.

Another matter was the necessity to introduce myself to the professionals, purveyors, and colleagues working for the companies' interests and, of course, to deal with the City of San Francisco. There was so much to do and no time to do it!

On Thursday, I scheduled a meeting at my office with Tom Kunz, senior manager of John F. Forbes & Company, the company's auditors, and a prominent major CPA firm. Tom Kunz, like all others doing business with the company, was extremely apprehensive when he first met me, not knowing whether my current position was a long-term deal or if I would only be around until the old regime came back.

As a side note, Tom Kunz, now the managing partner of John F. Forbes & Company, was the same man who was assigned to audit my book when I got in trouble for stealing the fluorescent light some five years past.

During my brief meeting with Kunz, I was advised that interest of equipment financing was not an allowable expense for increasing service rates with the Rate Setting Board in San Francisco—I believed this was ludicrous.

Another problem was that buying and financing trucks on time typically required a down payment, and the company did not have significant surplus cash for that purpose. After some analysis and meeting with the Bank of America financing department, convincing them that I was not some wild-eyed idiot, I learned that leasing these vehicles was an allowable expense for setting rates.

No cash was required upfront, and the expense could be recovered through increased rates. Armed with that information and tentative approval from Bank of America, we formulated a two-year plan to acquire some sixty-five packer trucks that would involve a projected capital investment plan of $2.5 million.

Tom Kunz and I met with the Bank of America representative

that Thursday afternoon. I explained that one of our goals when I became president was to obtain the necessary financing to incorporate a more efficient waste-collection service throughout San Francisco, and that leasing the trucks would accomplish that goal. The bank agreed and provided me (the company) with a $2.5 million line of credit.

I was able to solve this problem in less than a week on the job. During that same week, we heard nothing from the executives who were "on vacation."

Jack Ertola called me and asked me to come to City Hall in the next few days for a face-to-face introduction to John Shelley, mayor of San Francisco; Thomas Mellon, chief administrative officer; and S. Myron Tatarian, director of public works.

Jack Ertola introduced me to the mayor in his office at around 4:30 PM While we were chatting, a woman came in and asked the mayor if he wanted his "afternoon tea." The mayor nodded affirmatively, and she returned a few minutes later with "tea" in a glass cup. It looked like tea; it was hot water, but the "tea" was clearly Irish whiskey. Let the fun begin.

All and all, considering that just days before I was second Boss Scavenger in the Fillmore District and now I was president of the company, I was able to accomplish the following in just one week:

- Being introduced to and having a drink with the mayor of San Francisco.
- Setting up a $2.5 million line of credit for the company to lease new equipment.
- Being introduced to banking, legal, and accounting firms to establish credibility with these primary professional entities.
- Learning San Francisco's ratemaking process and policies.
- Ordering four new trucks (packers), with a first-time-ever plan that the Sunset Scavenger Company might order sixty-five more.

I had made substantial progress, and I was pleased with the results. I was also somewhat proud of myself when I realized what we had accomplished in only one short week. Contrary to my thoughts when we initially got involved with this nightmare, after one week I was feeling comfortable and, more importantly, confident in my new job. I wondered what the future would offer.

After the First Week

After I became president, I realized that I could not continue to retain the services of Brobeck, Phleger & Harrison, the primary legal representatives of the Sunset Scavenger Company, because of their opposition to our shareholders' position regarding the "revolution."

As a result, I secured the firm of Scampini, Mortara & Ertola to be the company's in-house legal representative. This firm had assisted me from time to time during the period leading up to the revolution.

Contrary to the feelings of some board members, I concluded that that it would be foolish and self-destructive to terminate completely the legal services of Brobeck, Phleger & Harrison, because the firm was involved in some of the other programs of both Sunset and Scavenger's Protective and its associated Sanitary Fill Company.

One of the important projects that Brobeck was involved in was the pending new disposal facility at Sierra Point on the east side of State Highway 101 in the City of Brisbane. Because of that project and the firm's experience with San Francisco rate increases, I decided—and the board agreed—to keep and retain Brobeck, but with the stipulation that the firm would have nothing to do with the internal affairs of Sunset Scavenger Company unless it was so called upon.

On Wednesday, some ten days after the revolution, or "coup," I received a call from Clem Whitaker, principal of Whitaker and Baxter Inc.,[1] the public relations firm for both Sunset Scavenger Company and Scavenger's Protective Association. He asked to meet with me on a confidential basis. With some hesitation, because of the past relationships, I made an appointment for Whitaker and his vice president, Mike Abramson, to come to my office the next day at 2:30 PM

After a somewhat formal and difficult introduction, Whitaker and Abramson got right to the point, indicating that they were representing the senior management of the company—President J. D. Molinari, Vice President Louis Crosetti, Secretary Armando

---

1. Whitaker and Baxter was an active participant in drawing up the many mailings to the shareholders, crucifying me, through direct and personal attacks, for leading this effort to change company leadership. Because the executives of garbage companies never actively testified at hearings, this firm was the public face of the garbage companies.

"Gal" Campi, Willie Barone, and the others—stating that they were prepared to come back from vacation and assume their former positions.

My response was brief: "If they had come back a week ago or earlier, I may have been of the opinion to allow that to happen. But because they did not, the others and I have become comfortable and confident in our respective roles. To allow the president and vice president to return in those roles at this time would surely be counterproductive and detrimental to plans already implemented."

I also said that because they and they alone had elected to take a vacation without formal approval, they forfeited their right to return to their former positions without formal approval by the board of directors. I added, "I can assure you that will not happen."

I explained that the original plan had been to retain the senior management of the company, but before we could offer that option, they went on vacation, no doubt based upon a recommendation from Whitaker and Baxter, as well as the company attorneys. I suggested that they had underestimated the commitment, desire, and talent of the new board.

In summary, my response was direct and brutal: "The offices of president, vice president, and secretary are no longer available. If any of the eleven former board members want to return to work, the only openings available are the positions of Boss Scavenger on the trucks." I emphasized that this decision was the result of the former senior management's past policies and bad decisions.

The Final Results

J. D. Molinari opted not to return. He took early retirement and eventually took a job as dispatcher in a small waste-collection company in Marin County. Sunset Scavenger purchased his share for $14,500 in cash.

Louis Crosetti also opted not to return but, because he was only 54 years old, he lost his pension benefits. He eventually found employment with a local brewing company in San Francisco. Sunset Scavenger purchased his share for $14,500 as well.

Armando "Gal" Campi, because of his demonstrated administrative skills, returned to the company. Some on the new board and some of the shareholders opposed this move, charging me with nepotism, because I had married into the Campi family. But that had nothing to do with my decision.

I had worked with Gal on the trucks in past years, and he was damned good at what he did. He knew the garbage business, and he was truly a company man. He had been loyal to his president, and that's why he opted to do what he did. With that thought in mind, I went to Gal Campi's home, laid out my proposal, and offered him the position to come back to the company as chief administrative officer, a non-board-member position.

My proposal made this grown man cry, and I knew right then that I had made a good move. It was a sound and correct decision. I could never hope to have a more loyal and dedicated member of the executive team.

All other former board members, most of whom drove debris box trucks or worked on the routes, returned to their former positions. In the final analysis, only two people were hurt in the "revolution of 1965."

I believe that the decision to challenge the board was a correct one because the company grew and prospered; shareholder equity increased substantially; and, equally important, the scavengers created and sustained credibility and respect from the politicians and the general public, something that was long overdue.

I had my first interview and hit the third page of the *San Francisco Chronicle* with the headline: "Long Time Scavenger President Ousted in an Internal Coup by Shareholders."

By the way, during my term in office as president, people assumed that I held that position because I had married into the hierarchy of the scavenger world, having married the granddaughter of the founder of Sunset Scavenger Company, and because the former president was my uncle's uncle. Nothing could have been further from the truth.

11

Dirty Work, Pride in Ownership

In 1966, Dr. Stewart E. Perry, a professor of sociology at Boston University, came into my office and asked to interview the scavengers. Of course, I was a bit suspicious of this inquiry—and I was new to the job. Then Dr. Perry said that, in his opinion, the garbage men were happy and he wanted to compare them to others that he had observed throughout the United States during his career as a sociologist. I gave him permission to interview some of the scavengers—in particular, my uncle Freddy on Truck 37, who worked in the Haight-Ashbury District when it was booming for the hippie generation.

Dr. Perry initially concluded that the workers were happy because they were shareholders in the company. However, after further research over another year from grant money provided by the US Government, Dr. Perry interviewed other people within our company. Contrary to his initial analysis, Dr. Perry's final conclusion was that workers at Sunset Scavenger were happier because they were not ashamed to be garbage men.

On the contrary, we were all proud to be scavengers, and our work ethic was higher than that of our counterparts throughout the United States. If one thinks about it, it just makes sense.

In his initial research, observing garbage collectors around the nation, Dr. Perry found that waste collectors were depressed because somehow they felt they could not find employment in more socially acceptable work. Perry concluded that they were forced into a line of work that, from the average person's point of view, was the lowest rung on the social ladder. This comment was based upon my personal conversations with Dr. Perry.

After researching and gathering information for several years and interviewing our garbage men, Dr. Perry wrote a white paper to share what he had learned from Sunset Scavenger Company and how what he learned might be applied to other garbage collectors throughout the United States. I have no idea where the white paper went, but he used it as the basis for his book, *San Francisco Scavengers: Dirty Work and the Pride of Ownership* (University of California Press, 1976). Twenty years later, after following the growth of Sunset Scavenger, Dr. Perry republished the book with a new title, *Collecting Garbage: Dirty Work, Clean Jobs, Proud People* (Transaction Publishers, 1998). The newer book contained a foreword by Raymond Russell and an updated epilogue by Perry.

A simple summation of Dr. Perry's inspection, research, study, and conclusions can be summarized in the following: Ownership in the company was really secondary; garbage collecting was our chosen profession, and we were extremely proud of the services we provided.

I didn't realize that fact until he brought it to my attention. When he did, I recalled that, unlike my partner on Truck 27, I was in fact proud to say I was a scavenger and, clearly, that was the basic philosophical attitude of the vast majority of the personnel, whether they were Boss Scavengers or employees.

As part of Dr. Perry's research, he actually worked on the trucks—more specifically, on Uncle Freddy's truck in the Haight-Ashbury District. The descriptions of his activities and observations on the Truck 37 route are not only informative, but also put a face on the real life of a scavenger.

In that second book, he covers the company history, from birth and through its growth from 1906 through 2002, including my departure from the company in 1986 and the subsequent dramatic change in management. His publication is one of the many reasons I decided to write this book, in order to put a more detailed and personal history on what a great company Sunset Scavenger (now Recology Inc.) has become.

I have always suggested that, as conceived, implemented, and practiced since 1920, the company has had a quasi-capitalist/communist philosophy. Dr. Perry used a more politically sensitive term: a "cooperative corporation"; but the fact remains that the company was a society built upon a communistic philosophy.

In any case, whatever we were doing proved to be an extraordinary success. The company grew and prospered but, as time went on, things had to change, and that business model, internally and externally, had to change as well.

12

A Visit to Where the Boss Scavengers Were Born

My father-in-law, Guido Campi, once told a story about his dad, Giovanni, who migrated from a small village called Fontanarossa in the Province of Genova. He explained that his dad left there in 1904, came to the United States, and by 1921 had saved up enough money to bring his family to San Francisco.

As the story goes, after his family came to the United States, Giovanni alone went back to Italy in 1931 for a visit. He purchased lumber, corrugated metal, nails, and other materials in Genova, drove these items some seventy miles to the entrance of a four-mile dirt road that went up the steep mountain, and loaded them on burros to be transported to the town of Fontanarossa.

Once he got all the materials there, Giovanni built a roof over the spring-fed fountain in the small square. All of the residents used this fountain for their drinking and washing needs. Giovanni built the roof over the fountain so the women of the town would not get wet when it rained. His work demonstrated to me the great love and respect he held for the place he was born and all the people who have lived there over the centuries. According to my father-in-law, the town acknowledged the gift by putting a small marble plaque on the wall, stating "Dono di [donated], G. Campi, 1931."

Giovanni's son Guido never visited his father's town, but my wife and I did in May 1972 during my return from a technological exchange in the Soviet Union. I met up with my wife in Rome and we headed to Fontanarossa. Before we left on the trip, my Guido asked me to tell the people in Fontanarossa about his father's fountain roof. Guido also said to me, "When you get there, tell them that Virginia is the granddaughter of Zuwallo" (his dad's nickname).

What little Italian I do speak is a northern dialect, Zeneize. I felt that I would have one hell of a time communicating that much of a story to anyone, especially because I assumed that no one would ever remember the event that occurred so many years before.

In 1968, my wife and I visited Rome and thought it would be fun to pay a visit to Fontanarossa. I asked the *carabinieri* in

Italian where the city dumped its garbage. To my embarrassment, he couldn't understand a word I said.

As I was to learn, the proper word for garbage is *immondizia* and the Zeneize word is *rumenta*. (There are other words that have changed: for example, pencil is *matita* vs. *pensulo*.) I assumed that my attempts to communicate with the people in Fontanarossa would be an effort in futility, especially because I was sure that no one would remember Zuwallo, let alone understand the way I spoke Italian.

When we arrived in Genova I found that, even though my Italian was limited, we were able to rent a car, get a roadmap, and drive to Fontanarossa. We took the main highway, found the side road to our destination, and drove the sometimes-paved, four-mile, one-lane road to the town.

Prior to arriving in Fontanarossa, we passed by an old cemetery with markers that dated back more than 150 years. We saw names like Campi, Moscone, Duni, Mangini, Guaraglia, Fraguglia, Chiosso, and more—all names synonymous with San Francisco's garbage industry and with other garbage companies in California. After spending time in the cemetery, we drove through the narrow streets of Fontanarossa and passed *really* old homes. We eventually came into a small square with a small *trattoria* across from the town's church.

We parked the car, entered the church, lit a candle, and said a prayer. Then we walked across the square to the *trattoria* and went inside, noting three elderly men drinking wine. They looked up, and I heard one of them say, "*Turisti!*" referring to us. A nice lady by the name of Maria Toscanini came up and said, in somewhat shaky English, "I am sorry, but we are closed."

I responded by saying (in English), "I am sorry, but we came such a long way for *pasta con pesto*."

She asked me in Zeneize where I was from. I responded in my best Zeneize, "Stati Uniti."

"Si si, Stati Uniti, dove negli Stati Uniti?" (Where in the United States?)

"San Francisco," I said, and she asked me my name.

"Stefanelli," I answered.

"Presidente della Sunset Scavenger Company?"

I asked her if she knew me, and she answered that of course she didn't, but that they knew my name.

When the three old-timers in the corner heard the exchange, they came up to introduce themselves—followed by virtually the whole town. They treated us as if *Cristoforo Colombo* had come back to town. (Legend says his mother was born in Fontanarossa.) We were treated with the ultimate respect.

We explained our primary reason for coming to Fontanarossa, and they agreed to take us to the fountain. We then went to the house where the parents of John Moscone, late president of Golden Gate Disposal Company, were born. We went to Virginia's grandfather's house, now used as a chicken coop and manure storage, where we met a man in his nineties, Paolo Guaraglia. In my broken Italian, I mentioned to him that Virginia's grandparents were born in the house and casually mentioned (again in fractured Italian) that she was the granddaughter of Zuwallo.

With that, Paolo raised his hands to his face and declared, "Ma Cristo, Zuwallo!" He explained to me in great detail how he left Fontanarossa with Giovanni (Zuwallo), Campi, and three others in 1903. They walked to Genoa with a pack mule and their meager belongings. They sold the mule, boarded a ship to New York, were cleared on Ellis Island, boarded a train to San Francisco, and joined others who had preceded them looking for work, any work.

I had heard this story before, but now I was hearing it firsthand from an individual who had actually taken the trip to get a better life. He confirmed that because he had no education and could not speak English, he sought work in the general labor market, only to find that the *irlandesi* (Irish) had filled those labor positions and were given priority for jobs in the Bay Area, leaving little left for those who could not speak English.

Paolo described how he and his colleagues, to survive, picked up trash and scavenged—a forerunner of today's recycling programs—to feed and house themselves, typically in boarding houses or communal housing.

I asked when he had come back to Fontanarossa. He said 1906. When I asked why, after less than two years, he had returned, his response was *grande terremoto* (big earthquake). It scared him so bad that he got on the train, went to New York, sailed to Genova, walked to Fontanarossa, and never looked back.

I spoke with many people in the town and felt the respect they extended to me and my wife because I was president of Sunset Scavenger. Many of the people who left Fontanarossa had become associated with the garbage business as independent scavengers. "Independent" meant having a horse, a wagon, and an Italian, reflecting what Paolo Guaraglia told me when he arrived in San Francisco and could not find work, except to pick up garbage, a chore that no one else wanted to do. That is where Paolo, Giovanni, and others found work.

When I came home, I realized that, even though I was raised in the garbage business and had heard about the company history from my uncles Pasquale, Mingo, and Freddy, I did not really comprehend the real history of what I was now in charge of until my visit to Fontanarossa, meeting and speaking with people like Paolo Guaraglia.[2] After I heard of his and so many others' sacrifices to come to this country, I began to understand the magnificent opportunity that had been placed in my hands because of their guts in seeking a better life.

Still another Guaraglia who left Fontanarossa was Carlo "Charlie" Guaraglia, who immigrated to America and started in 1920 with Sunset Scavenger Company. He was assigned to work in the outer Richmond District, providing services to Playland-at-the-Beach, the Cliff House, and the Veterans Hospital. He and his wife, Maria, had a son, Giovanni ("John"), in 1925. At the age of fifteen, John began working with his dad. Between them, they provided services from 1920 through 2000, 80 years. When John formally retired, he had provided such a legendary degree of service that the famous Cliff House built a special area with a large marble plaque that read, "The John Guaraglia Room."

John and his dad were excellent examples of men who took pride in their work and provided the highest standards of service. As I write this book, John is going on 90 years of age and has been a great source of historical data for me.

I had found a new level of respect for what I was in charge of. I committed myself to never forgetting who made that possible: all the Zuwallos and their brothers, who made the trip to the United States, leaving their homes and family to seek a better life.

During our visit to Fontanarossa and speaking with Maria Toscanini, the owner of the *trattoria*, I learned that she was born in

2. As I understood from Paolo, my godfather and Peter Guaraglia's father, Italo, were born in Fontanarossa and left with his cousin Paolo to come to the United States. Paolo went back to Italy because of the paranoia experienced after the 1906 earthquake, but Italo stayed in San Francisco, got married, and had four boys: Pietro (Pete) my godfather, Romo, and (twins) Romeo and John.

the *paese* (town) called Suzzi, the same *paese* where Giuseppe and Giulia Fontana, the parents of my uncles Pas, Dominic, and Alfred, came from. This is also where Giuseppe Fontana, the man who became president of Sunset Scavenger Company on January 1, 1921, was born.

Maria Toscanini pointed out Suzzi's home to Virginia and me. Across a deep canyon, we saw some structures that were best described as a "rifle shot away" but a "two-day walk to get there." We didn't have the time to visit Suzzi, but Maria explained that there were a lot of Fontanas living there from my uncle's side.

Hanging around and being virtually raised by the Fontana family since I was three years old, I knew that the family had come from Suzzi, but I was unaware of precisely where. My uncle's dad, Dominic Fontana, left there after the 1906 earthquake and fire and founded the Fontana Scavenger Company, one of many scavenger companies in the Mission District of San Francisco that eventually merged with Sunset Scavenger Company.

To make this story even more personally relevant, my in-laws told me that another *paese*, Vegni, was a two-hour walk up the mountain from Fontanarossa. It turns out that this was the town where my wife Virginia's other grandfather, Emilio Rattaro, was born. He was the founder and first president of the Sunset Scavenger Company. (Emilio Rattaro came to San Francisco following the same route as Giovanni "Zuwallo" Campi and Paolo Guaraglia, but sometime after the great San Francisco earthquake and fire.)

Unfortunately, we did not have two hours (or more) to walk up to Vegni and see where Virginia's grandfather and my uncles came from, but it was clear that the general area had generated a multitude of scavengers. The experience was an extraordinary, once-in-a-lifetime opportunity that I will always cherish. It enhanced my personal respect for all these wonderful men who were the foundation of this great San Francisco company.

13

Sunset Scavenger, Catching Up in Time

In addition to starting an aggressive and complicated program to modernize and upgrade the Sunset Scavenger Company, another huge and controversial problem involved the proposed new bay landfill that the two garbage companies borrowed $2.1 million to develop.

This was an imminent and significant problem, not only for the companies but also for the City of San Francisco, because without the use of that site, the city and the scavengers would not have a facility in which to dispose of the collected garbage. This problem had to be resolved within eighteen months.

When I became president, I assumed that the attorneys and the PR people were the key players in handling that problem. In a very short time, I realized that this assumption was wrong and concluded that a more aggressive stance had to be adopted. Once again, I found myself taking an active role in that matter because of the lack of initiative shown by those bureaucratic entities.

At the time of the management change at Sunset Scavenger, approximately 104 open-body collection vehicles operated for waste-collection services. Each crew had four men; the entire company had an estimated waste-collection staff of 408. The first priority was to create a better work environment and a less-backbreaking means of collecting garbage in San Francisco.

Clearly, packer trucks would help resolve that problem. We had ordered four new truck units, but we needed to implement a strong, long-term plan to convert the entire fleet of 104 trucks to an efficient, cost-effective, waste-collection system. Converting the entire fleet to packer trucks would also create a substantially enhanced work environment, no longer requiring scavengers to climb the "seven stairs to heaven" and sort through the refuse to recover rags, bottles, cardboard, newspaper, and so forth.

I concluded that we no longer needed a four-man crew because a crew of three could do the same work more efficiently. As explained earlier, the fourth man of a four-man crew was required to station himself "inside the box," to sort and recover the materials and drag cans from the front of the truck, while the other three brought the garbage up and into the truck.

We calculated that not only could three men do the same work but that they could also be more productive. Using a packer truck with three men increased revenues, but also made the labor less strenuous with no appreciable increase in time on the daily route.

The decision to boost resources with a three-man crew, of course, was not greeted with enthusiasm by the partners. They felt I was increasing their workload without proportionate compensation, setting aside the fact that both their productivity and personal income would be increased because of the proposed innovations.

For a while, workers talked about another revolution because, in their opinion, I was making them work harder. But, as the new plan was phased in, those grumbling crews that were cut from four to three came to appreciate the wisdom of the new program. They found that the workday actually became considerably easier and, in many cases, shorter. The new organizational model became widely accepted.

While the workers did not openly embrace the new plan (they never completely stopped griping), they eventually admitted that the changes were not only acceptable but also successful. The physical work environment for the men on the truck was significantly improved, and work productivity was enhanced.

After almost four years of planning and implementation, we had purchased new, custom-designed, waste-collection equipment, including front-end loaders, commercial-waste containerization, roll-off units, and packer trucks, and had consolidated work assignments.

Before the revolution, we had some 104 open trucks and approximately 416 men to provide waste-collection services. By 1969, after the upgrading of equipment and improved working conditions, we were collecting the same volume of waste but with sixty-three packers, using eighteen pieces of specialized equipment—front-end loaders, roll-off units, etc.—and with fewer than 275 waste collectors and scavengers.

With the new and more sophisticated equipment, we had to expand substantially our fleet maintenance programs, personnel, and other job opportunities for the partners within the company, including long-haul drivers and management positions in the yet-to-be-implemented transfer station and related business acquisitions.

In other words, we had pared down the labor force to collect garbage, had adopted significantly improved working conditions for the men, and were providing high-quality services to get the company out of the shadows and into the public's eye.

Over time, the public began to recognize and respect us for the complexity of the services we provided. Sunset Scavenger employees were happier as well. Through organized schedules and approved rate increases, we were able to pay for our new equipment; and through the reduction in manpower, we could increase benefits for all employees—not just the partners—in the form of wages, pension benefits, and health benefits.

Updating Our System for Collecting Fees

Although we were upgrading many of Sunset Scavenger's services, the age-old method of hand-collecting close to 136,000 individual accounts was still the responsibility of company partners and Boss Scavengers. Many longtime residents expected the scavenger to ring the doorbell on the first of the month to be paid for his services, but the fact remained that our customers didn't necessarily like anyone coming by at five or six o'clock, during dinnertime, ringing the doorbell, and announcing "Garbage bill!"

Clearly, a modern-day company would not collect for its services this way. Even newspaper boys didn't ring doorbells at night. Sunset Scavenger Company had to do something to create a more efficient means of collecting revenues. At one time, collecting for garbage services had been a great public relations tool. It put a face, a personal touch on our services.

However, the means of being paid for our services had to be upgraded because Boss Scavengers didn't want to do it anymore. The "friendly garbage man" no longer existed.

I can remember hearing the story of an old-timer who went collecting with his son (Gal Campi, the former corporate secretary and my new CAO). Some customer chewed out his father for leaving the lid off the can or some other "Mickey Mouse" problem. Gal was frustrated and embarrassed that his dad took such abuse from this person. But Gal said his dad responded by saying, "Yes, I was hurt somewhat; but she paid me and that's all that counts."

This incident was an accurate assessment of the general public's attitude toward scavengers. If I had anything to say about it, that had to change. Another matter was the fact that people who worked on the garbage truck would probably prefer to stay home in the evening with their families, or do whatever they wanted, without this added responsibility.

Some form of computerized billing was clearly in order and long overdue. That alone brought us a new challenge, because no one in the garbage company had any experience in database or computerized billing of this magnitude.

To meet that need we contacted International Business Machines (IBM). Representatives provided a series of programs on how to convert a billing system from hand-collection to automated billing.

This was an extraordinary challenge for many reasons. For example, the scavengers provided *specialized* services, such as collecting garbage from backyards, from up to three flights upstairs, and multiple times in a period. By this time, we had keys to probably 30,000 residents and businesses. As I said earlier, our customers trusted the scavengers more than the police department!

After some discussion, we leased IBM's 360 Operating System, the top of the line at the time.

One nightmare in billing conversion appeared because there was no standard fee for the multitude of services being provided. Even the people at IBM, as smart as they were, realized that converting collection services from Sunset Scavenger Company into a database or data processing system was going to be a challenge. We retained the services of a programmer, Thomas Dolan (my board wanted an Italian programmer but could not find one), who would work with IBM. The John F. Forbes Company also came in to assist in the transition.

I requested that the computer be able to print out a book similar to the one scavengers presently used. This way the scavengers could manage their routes with a form that looked familiar to them. The computer would generate this information and provide access to the account to determine who had paid and who was delinquent. The route supervisor and scavenger company would have a record showing which accounts were tardy, and then the scavenger would go out personally to collect overdue funds.

The concept sounded great but, in reality, it was not. The Forbes Company advised us that each account would have to have a customer code or account number. For example, A. Abbott would be 001, B. Abbott would be 002, and so on. However, A. Abbott and B. Abbott would end up in different parts of the city and *not* on the same route as the Boss Scavenger. It was clearly impossible to use that method of assigning account IDs. The concept had to be reformulated into a better method, one the scavenger could understand.

Simply put, we had to train the computer to think like a garbage man rather than having the garbage man think like a computer.

The program was ultimately modified, and we finally got the new system running, but it took approximately two years for the new billing method to be accomplished for the whole company. In a sense, we were leaping from the Stone Age to current-day technology in one big step. It finally worked, and we realized that we had better control of cash flows, projected cash flows, and things of that type.

We learned from IBM that we were one of the first garbage companies in the United States to incorporate that scale of database billing. In doing so, we set the groundwork for many other companies to emulate what we did.

As new computer programs were developed, of course, we upgraded and improved our billing system to meet modern-day standards. But we were pioneers in developing a computerized billing system, and it was certainly a first for Sunset Scavenger Company.

During the difficult transition, two board members favored an antiquated addressograph system and were vehemently opposed to the IBM data-processing system. When they lost the debate, they left Sunset Scavenger and sold their shares and equity, complaining that the company was going backward.

These two men did very well. They purchased shares in a company doing business in Santa Rosa as Empire Waste. Waste Management Company eventually bought Empire Waste, and one of the former employees retired with a lot of cash. He was able to purchase a working cattle ranch and put his son in the business in Eureka and Ukiah. Meanwhile, the other person is still active in the solid-waste business and has done extraordinarily well.

Perhaps I should have gone with them but, at the time, I was morally committed to the shareholders because of the confidence they had placed in me. That may sound silly, but I really believed that.

Over the years, the new management of Sunset Scavenger Company improved the corporate structure. Sunset Scavenger came into its own and was becoming a leader among the privately operated solid-waste collection and disposal companies. In my opinion, there may be some companies as good but none better.

Entering the Political Arena

As noted, the Sunset Scavenger Company and the Scavenger's Protective Association/Golden Gate Disposal had no direct contact with the public relations side of the business. The company attorneys and the public relations firm Whitaker and Baxter did this work by attending political functions and fundraisers on behalf of the two companies.

As I was to find out, this lack of company involvement originated in its basic historical philosophy: Our business was nobody's business, and the less anyone knew of the internal affairs of the company the better off we were. It was forbidden for employees to cash their payroll checks except at the Bank of America. If you cashed your check elsewhere, you could be fined $100 and be called in front of the board. As a result, the scavengers had no public face other than the Boss Scavenger ringing doorbells to collect for their services. The company's policy was to keep out of the public eye. It was like a secret society that, for no useful purpose, did not want its business known by the public.

This was rapidly going to change with Sierra Point, the pending waste-disposal site. With our philosophy of being invisible, we would have surely lost that battle, so we had to change our means of doing business. The battle over this landfill project began to take shape within four months after I became president. I knew that we had to take a proactive role if we were to become successful.

Prior to assuming this stance, I thought of the philosophical advice of an old Italian, Primo Repetto: "If you don't blow smoke up your own ass, no one will do it for you."

In other words, let people know what you are doing well because no one else will give you credit.

My longtime friend Jack Ertola followed in the footsteps of his father, City Supervisor Charles Ertola, who had passed away some years earlier. The mayor appointed Jack to complete his dad's term in office.

Later, he was elected by a vote of the people and became the president of the San Francisco Board of Supervisors. He was a popular and respected elected official and eventually became a prominent and respected leader in local and state politics. Because of my personal friendship with Jack Ertola, within several weeks he set up meetings with San Francisco mayor Jack Shelley and Chief Administrative Officer Thomas Mellon, the most powerful bureaucrat in San Francisco and, coincidently, chairman of the Scavenger Rate Control Board.

In similar but less formal environments, Jack introduced me to his colleagues on the board of supervisors, one of whom was Dianne Feinstein, who became mayor of San Francisco after George Moscone was assassinated and is now a US senator, and with whom I still maintain a personal friendship. I also met the director of public works, S. Myron Tatarian, the director of public health, the city attorney, and others in a whirlwind tour that proved to be an invaluable resource in the months to come, especially considering the battle over the proposed and controversial Sierra Point disposal site.

Jack Ertola's message to me was twofold. The primary reason for the meeting was to introduce these people to the new president of Sunset Scavenger Company. The other reason was for me to ask for the city's support in developing the Sierra Point landfill site. I learned at these impromptu meetings that the city was totally unaware of how important this site was, mostly because garbage service had never stopped, so everyone—the citizens and the city itself—took it for granted.

I got the attention of these city politicians by explaining that, if we could not use Sierra Point in 1966 as planned, in less than a year the city's garbage service would terminate. In these face-to-face meetings and those that followed, Sunset Scavenger Company gained credibility and respect with the City of San Francisco by blowing smoke you know where.

We established ourselves as professionals and not the traditional stereotype that many held, including my dean of boys at Polytechnic High School, who defined a scavenger as being "a strong back, weak mind, and as an added caveat, an Italian."

The introductions and mentoring that Jack Ertola provided me with proved to be an extraordinary resource, not only for me and the company but for the industry as a whole. The industry eventually benefited by the respect that was generated when garbage became "solid waste."

Although no one wanted to be associated with garbage, people began to realize that garbage was a multibillion-dollar industry, particularly as environmental concerns arose. One could not change the product, so the elite and the educated renamed garbage "solid waste." As a result, public opinion became overwhelmed by "experts" who, in reality, did not know their ass from a hole in the ground. The only real specialists in the field were the local scavengers.

Dealing with the so-called experts had its advantages. By working with municipal government instead of being in competition with it, the scavengers demonstrated that they knew the business best, paving the way for the City of San Francisco to eventually enjoy the most comprehensive, cost-effective, solid-waste system in the world.

But there was one added piece of advice from Jack Ertola: "When election time rolls around for the politician, he or she will come to you seeking funds to help pay for a reelection bid, and you'll need to respond accordingly." He added, "However, don't ever think that by giving the person money, you will have any influence directly or indirectly over the individual. But if you respond correctly, the individual's office door will always be open for you to present your case. The door will always be closed if you don't give them money. In other words, don't think you will influence the politicians if you give money, but they are sure to forget your name if you don't."

I found that advice to be true in the twenty years I was president of Sunset Scavenger and all the years to follow.

14

The Development of the Sierra Point Landfill

The practice of dumping in the bay and burning the garbage continued until 1952, when the current Bayshore Freeway blocked off the landfill. The residents of San Mateo County began to notice the pungent odor of garbage being dumped in saltwater and the smoke from burning fires. As a result of their legitimate complaints, we changed our methods of operation and pioneered what was to be known as a true sanitary landfill operation.

We eliminated the odors but also demonstrated the need for a higher standard of waste disposal. Although our new operations were state of the art at the time, they still resulted in some negative environmental effects, such as groundwater pollution and methane gas migration. Sanitary Fill Company eventually blocked off all the bay waters to the landfill and ordered cells receiving waste to be covered daily.

Engineering projections suggested that the bays currently diked offsite, as well as a lagoon just south of the sanitary landfill site, would continue to be used, giving San Francisco a disposal site until 2020.

That was a bad assumption, though, because Southern Pacific Railroad received a complaint from Van Waters & Rogers, Inc., a company that shipped about $80 million worth of goods on the railroad. Van Waters & Rogers protested that they didn't want a garbage dump in their front yard. To complicate matters, the lagoon was subject to tidal action and came under the jurisdiction of the Bay Conservation and Development Commission (BCDC). Filling it would require another costly and time-consuming effort.

As a result, Southern Pacific told Sanitary Fill Company in 1960 that once the site was full, we would have to seek another location. In response to the public outcry, Southern Pacific wouldn't allow the lagoon to be filled with garbage. Our engineers calculated that at the current rate of fill, this site's useful life would end sometime in 1968.

I wasn't involved with that matter at the time, but records show that Sanitary Fill Company notified San Francisco of the Southern Pacific Railroad's intention to terminate use of that site sometime in 1968. The City of San Francisco urged the scavengers to seek additional bay lands to expand existing operations. At that time, bay fill was a generally acceptable means of reclamation. It was not considered "ruination," as it would soon be called.

As the new freeway blocked off all access to the bay from the dump's current location, the only site available became Sierra Point. The Crocker Land Company, which owned San Bruno Mountain and the submerged tidelands associated with it, did not want to sell the property because the company anticipated a southern crossing for a new bay bridge. Sierra Point was the center point for the proposed bridge.

When the City of San Francisco put political pressure on Crocker Land Company, the company reluctantly agreed to sell us the submerged tidelands, some 260 acres, but retained an easement on the property to gain access if the projected bay crossing became a reality. This easement could reduce any potential value of the property once the bay was filled. We had to consider that possibility because it had the capacity to contain San Francisco's disposal for at least twenty-five years.

The price of the property was an outrageous $4,000 per acre—similarly submerged land was selling at the time for $50 per acre. But Crocker Land Company knew we had no other site available, and the city knew damned well that we—the city, scavengers, and ratepayers—were all being screwed.

The city had proposed that we borrow the money and provided us with a twenty-year disposal contract to pay for it through customer rates. That was when we found that, because the scavengers had always paid cash for everything, the company had no record of borrowing money. Because of that lack of credit history, even Bank of America (which the scavengers had done business with since it was the Bank of Italy) would not lend the projected $2.1 million needed to buy and develop the property.

As a result, we had to seek a secondary source of funding, which proved to be a very expensive process with Occidental Life Insurance Company. Bank of America agreed to lend us $600,000; Occidental lent us $1.5 million. This was all accomplished in 1962, prior to my becoming president.

The primary lender was the Occidental Life Insurance Company. The 6 percent interest on the money was outrageously high for the time, and the restrictions on the business were equally outrageous—

almost to the extent that we could not change our toilet paper brand without formal written approval from Occidental.

As time went by and I got my feet wet, I began a slow but positive process to circumvent these extreme restrictions. If I had not made these changes, we could never have accomplished improvements, grown the business, and achieved the goals that we set.

Once the funding was established in 1962, we applied to the necessary agencies responsible for the creation of an expanded landfill for San Francisco Bay. However, we concluded that the existing contract with the City of Brisbane allowed the current disposal operations to continue within the city limits and would permit us to continue to operate, but only on the east side of the Bay Shore Freeway. This should have been a simple process because the site in Brisbane had been used since 1906 for the disposal of San Francisco's waste, and the new facility was far removed and out of sight from the city's residents.

Unfortunately, our Sierra Point site became the focal point for stopping all filling of the bay, especially with garbage. An environmental organization known as Save the Bay raised vehement objections to our request while our application was being processed, and the bay-fill controversy raged on in earnest. Meanwhile, the Utah Construction Company applied for and got a permit to dredge mud and sand from San Francisco Bay and reclaim some 800 acres in Alameda County. Despite the adverse environmental impact of dredging upon the San Francisco Bay, environmentalists and the public remained silent. No one protested because that project was considered "reclamation," whereas our site designated for garbage was "ruination."

All of this took place right after I became president of Sunset Scavenger Company and vice president of the Sanitary Fill Company.

Don Sherwood, a local radio celebrity, began to talk about the project. Politicians from all over the area jumped on our project and zeroed in on the site. One state assembly member running for reelection came to our site wearing a gasmask, condemning the site, and got his picture on the front page of the morning paper.

The City of Brisbane, which had willingly accepted the garbage for more than sixty years with hardly a peep, now demanded a "host fee" for San Francisco to dump its garbage: $125,000 a year and an advance fee of $250,000. This from a city with a population of fewer than 4,000 people! We reluctantly agreed to pay the fees and entered into a binding contract to use the Sierra Point site for the disposal of San Francisco's waste; but instead of twenty years' capacity, disposal was drastically cut to only five years.

Then some of Brisbane's constituents commenced to raise hell about any garbage being dumped anywhere in their beautiful little hamlet, even after we had a signed contract with them to develop the Sierra Point site. As a result, voters passed an initiative ordinance that allowed the garbage to continue to be dumped in Brisbane (only on the west side of Highway 101) and prohibited garbage from being dumped on the east side of the freeway, the new site being developed for San Francisco's long-term disposal needs. This was clearly a blatant and discriminatory violation of the current contract.

It was an unbelievable turn of events since we had already spent close to $1.75 million to develop the site. Because of unanticipated expenses, a decision was made to dike 130 acres instead of the entire 290 acres and leave the balance for future development. Once we completed construction of the dikes, we placed the final load of dirt at low tide, sealing off the area and minimizing the quantity of bay waters within the 100 acres that were diked off.

At that point, we did not need any further delays. But as soon as we put that last load of dirt on the levee, the California Fish and Game Commission staff filed a complaint against us, claiming that we had one million pregnant striped bass within the confines of the diked area and demanding that we break the dike open and let the fish out. We argued that opening the dike would be physically and financially impossible, but to mitigate the alleged problem, we hired several commercial fishermen to put rowboats within the remaining low-water confines of the 130 acres just diked off.

The fishermen came in with nets and found only six small striped bass within the confines. Nonetheless, it cost thousands of dollars to acquire this information and prove that no fish were present—especially pregnant ones.

In the meantime, our attorneys had filed legal action against the City of Brisbane, arguing that the ordinance passed by the voters was discriminatory. This was a valid argument since the ordinance allowed garbage dumping on one side of the freeway but not on the other. Plus, both sites were M-2 zoning areas, which allowed companies with the correct permit to dump garbage. We had that permit.

Brisbane had very little money because of the lawsuits we filed against the city, so it retained the services of a prominent San Francisco attorney (Caspar Weinberger, who eventually became the US secretary of defense) with the $250,000 we paid them in advance. In the process of taking depositions and in an informal off-the-record comment to me, Weinberger said, "Lenny, if we win this case I hope you won't stop my garbage service."

I answered, "What, are you kidding?"

The sad thing was that even he didn't realize the magnitude of the problem we were facing. Virtually everyone in the general public and, more alarmingly, among the City of San Francisco's governing officials, did not realize that we were faced with the prospect of not having a place to dispose of San Francisco's ever-growing quantities of waste.

Even worse, Weinberger won the case on behalf of the City of Brisbane. We of course filed an appeal but, because it was such a legal hot potato, none of the local courts wanted anything to do with it.

As a result, the case was heard in some far-off rural community's superior court in Northern California. Time was running out—by now it was July 1966. The current waste site would fill to capacity in three short months.

In the interim, attorney Angelo Scampini, a sharp, TV-type attorney (and pure Italian), short in stature but as tough as they come, represented Sunset Scavenger with a plan to appeal the decision of the courts. But that appeal would not be heard before the pending deadline.

The new site was now completed. Access roads had been built and utilities were in place, all in preparation for San Francisco's waste to be deposited there, but the new site could not be used because it was technically illegal.

Angelo Scampini came to me with an unbelievable scheme that would bring the matter to a head. With my approval, along with the people of Sanitary Fill Company and the Easley & Brassy Corporation, Scavenger's Protective Association agreed to proceed.

The plan was confidential and would be implemented through tactics similar to a well-planned military action. On a Friday in late November of 1966, we would terminate the current operations on the west side of the freeway in the City of Brisbane and begin dumping garbage at Sierra Point.

We selected Friday because it was a comparatively light day and most of the garbage trucks would have dumped their loads and finished for the day. Only fifty or sixty trucks would still be on the way to dispose of waste at that time. The plot was kept secret to ensure a successful outcome; not even the drivers knew about it. The plan was for someone to go to the landfill at one o'clock, close the barricade on the existing dump road, and direct trucks to the new site at Sierra Point.

We knew that it was just a matter of time before someone noticed what was going on. Sure enough, the police department showed up and started issuing citations for illegal dumping of garbage. However, the garbage trucks kept coming, and they kept dumping since there weren't enough police officers to issue tickets before the other drivers dumped their loads and left.

Finally, the frustrated police department put a barricade across the entrance to the new site, leaving about thirty-seven trucks parked and waiting to dispose of their garbage. By this time, the newspapers and TV stations had heard what the scavengers were up to and what the City of Brisbane was doing to stop it.

As planned, about twenty minutes before the blockade was put up, Angelo Scampini, other executives, and I were present to watch the action. Then Angelo directed me to get in the driver's seat in the lead truck and drive the truck ahead. I drove forward and smashed through the first barrier.

There I was, in suit and tie, cigarette hanging out of my mouth, and Angelo hanging on the side of the garbage truck, yelling in Italian, "Avanti!" (Give it the gas!)

Bud Dyer, then chief of police (and a friend of mine), stood behind the barriers along with several of his officers. As I drove over one barrier and headed for the second, Chief Dyer shouted for me to stop.

Angelo again gave me the command: "Avanti!"

"Lenny, don't do this. I'm going to have to shoot you!" The chief drew his gun and pointed at me.

I looked at Angelo, and he said, "Hit it!"

The press cameras were flashing, and I didn't really know what the hell to do. Frankly, I was scared as hell that Chief Dyer might just pull the damned trigger.

Unbeknownst to me and to everyone present, Angelo Scampini had in his pocket a temporary restraining order to stop the City of Brisbane from enforcing the initiative ordinance approved by Brisbane voters.

Angelo jumped off the truck and finally brought out the restraining order. He reviewed it and gave it to the city attorney, who confirmed its validity. Then the police reluctantly took down the barriers and allowed us to continue operations. Needless to say, this was a dramatic, memorable day, looking down the barrel of a gun, heart pounding. The whole thing was scripted like a movie.

We eventually went to court with the case, but were denied the use of the 160 acres of land that were still under water. We were precluded from using the site beyond its full capacity, which was estimated to occur sometime in late 1970.

This, of course, created another crisis of sorts; we needed to develop yet another facility to meet garbage disposal needs if we were expected to continue with the uninterrupted service that San Francisco had enjoyed for more than seventy years.

Getting Exposure and Receiving the Public's Support

During the controversy of the Sierra Point site, the allegations were that our only goal was to fill the bay with garbage and create valuable bay-front properties for "profit and screw the environment." In reality, our goal was to blow smoke and get the public and politicians to realize that the companies were only seeking means of disposal other than landfill. But in the short term the Sierra Point site was absolutely necessary.

One of the rare humorous phases of this ongoing saga was a presentation I made before the Academy of Sciences in San Francisco as part of the unrelenting controversy. We were challenged by the Save the Bay Association to come before its members and other interested environmental parties and set forth the reasons why it was necessary to fill San Francisco Bay with garbage.

Our attorneys and public affairs people urged me to not attend the meeting because they were afraid that the company was about to be crucified by the public. My argument was simple: We were already being crucified, so why not take on the challenge and confront the skeptics once and for all?

John Moscone and I appeared before the San Francisco Bay Conservation and Development Commission District, Save the Bay

Association, the Academy of Sciences in Golden Gate Park, and about 300 environmentalists bent on stopping any filling of the bay under any circumstances.

After I was introduced, I gave a brief history on the garbage trucks, the scavengers, and the company of which I was now president. The key point I attempted to make was that the garbage we were disposing of was not *my* garbage; it was in fact *our* garbage. I said, "What you people do not seem to understand is that if I can't dump the garbage truck, I cannot collect the garbage. That is the simple logic here, ladies and gentlemen. I hope you will understand and support us in getting the use of this site and allow the time for us to seek an alternate disposal site."

At this point, I also emphasized that every disposal system in any city in the world must start with a landfill to get rid of today's waste *today*. I told the audience that we could reduce the dependency on landfill by recycling, composting, and converting waste to energy, but that there would be a residual component requiring landfill disposal.

A permanent landfill site would always be necessary in case the alternate disposal facility should fail. This would ensure that today's refuse would be promptly disposed of in a clean environment; a sanitary landfill was the only form of disposal that could guarantee that.

Then came questions and opinions from the audience. In the course of the conversation, a woman stood up and asked, "Well Mr. Stefanelli, why aren't you compressing garbage into concrete blocks and building houses like they do in Japan?"

That question exemplified some of the problems facing us at that time. Everyone seemed to think that there was a proverbial "black box" somewhere around the world offering a cure for all the solid-waste problems of the world.

The fact remains, though, that there will never be a cure-all for every community in the world. I knew this then, but I confirmed it in later years when I toured the world looking for that magical "black box." I have learned that composition of waste varies substantially throughout the world, and that you have to custom design your disposal needs by your particular waste composition and consideration of a multitude of environmental issues.

After hearing her question, I responded, "Garbage generates methane gas. If you compress garbage into a confined environment such as cement block, it could blow up. To compensate for that possibility, you could drill holes to vent the gas, thus preventing an explosion. However, because of the methane gas, it is flammable. You could blow up your house. A less significant hazard, but a hazard nonetheless, is that you might smell dead crabs in the bedroom."

I was looking into the audience, and I could see they basically agreed that my response was logical and reasonable.

But the woman was not satisfied, and she retorted in a distinctively critical tone. "From your own admission, you're only a scavenger. What do you know about the solid-waste disposal business?"

Looking down at her seriously, I said, "Madam, until you have had the joy of inhaling a fly, live maggots crawling down your neck, and warm watermelon juice drizzling down the crack of your ass, don't ever say I don't know anything about the product at hand. Whether you want to call it garbage, solid waste, or whatever, it's the same product—and ma'am, no one knows that product better than I do."

That response brought the house down with a laughing and cheering audience.

The next day, I was quoted on the front page of the *San Francisco Chronicle,* which stated in part: "The Great Debate . . . bay fill and garbage—the environmentalist versus the scavengers . . . the scavengers win hands down . . . that handsome young president of Sunset Scavenger Company told it like it really is."

From that first positive step in blowing smoke, the scavengers were finally being recognized and, yes, respected as experts in the solid-waste business. After a series of public presentations, court cases, and public forums, we were allowed to use the Sierra Point site.

15

Immediate Challenges: The Mountain View Project

The life expectancy of Sierra Point was cut to about four years, so we knew we had to develop a long-term master plan for San Francisco's waste. In the interim, many people and large firms came up with solutions to get rid of garbage: composting, waste-to-energy products, and mass-burning technology to mention only a few, with names like Westinghouse, Monsanto, and Combustion Engineering.

One of the most promising methods to come before us was from the Western Pacific Railroad, which had options on property in Lassen County, some 300 miles north of San Francisco. Western Pacific suggested that garbage be transferred from the scavenger trucks into large, custom-designed containers, loaded onto flatbed railcars, and transported by rail from San Francisco to a site just southeast of Susanville, California. Serious negotiations commenced immediately between the City of San Francisco, the scavengers, and the Western Pacific Railroad.

The city wanted to jump on that idea because the site offered 100-plus years of disposal capacity, and the railroad wanted revenues to enhance its economic stability. Negotiations started with S. Myron Tatarian, San Francisco's director of public works; David Copenhagen, vice president of the Western Pacific Railroad; and John Moscone and me, representatives of Sanitary Fill Company.

Initially, the estimated rate offered by Western Pacific began at $10 per ton, making it attractive to the city. There's a rule of thumb in the garbage business: If you have to haul garbage for more than twenty miles from the point of collection to the point of disposal, it becomes inefficient. Some form of transfer station would be needed so the smaller garbage trucks could dump the waste into larger, more efficient hauling vehicles.

If the proposed landfill were more than fifty-five miles away, the garbage could be put on a railcar. In this situation, the idea of rail hauling waste to Lassen County could work, but only if the proposed disposal rate did not exceed $15 per ton. (The current disposal rate for a nearby landfill was $3.50 per ton.)

The concept of rail made sense, but the matter of cost became questionable. Over the two-month negotiations, the $10-per-ton maximum rate originally being negotiated began to increase to $35–$40 a ton. I was concerned that the rail company was putting us into a corner; with each passing day, we were losing valuable time to seek an alternate system and being forced to accept the railroad's proposal, regardless of price. My suspicions became fact in time.

I guess what helped was my training in submarines, where you use every system you have on board and make sure that you have redundancy (backups). In other words, we needed a backup system for garbage disposal if we could not generate a reasonable contract with the Western Pacific Railroad.

During the course of the negotiations, I was informed by a colleague, Jessie Weigle, that Foothill Disposal Company, which served the City of Mountain View, had received a federal grant to build a regional park. It was planning to create this park, totaling over 700 acres of land, within the city limits of Mountain View, only thirty-two miles south of San Francisco.

It was a little known, negative environmental fact that approximately 25,000 acres in the south end of San Francisco Bay had subsided below sea level because of aggressive and excessive pumping of aquifers over the years. To compensate for this loss, state and local agencies had built an extensive levee system to keep the tidal water out. However, when it rains, freshwater flows into these areas as well as the area below sea level, or the high mean watermark. This may help restore the aquifers, but it is useless for any other purpose.

I was informed that the City of Mountain View owned some 700 acres of this land and was planning to create a regional park with lakes, a golf course, bike trails, and related recreational facilities; however, before the park could be built, the site had to be filled with earth to bring the acreage above sea level.

The engineers for the City of Mountain View concluded that six million yards of earthen fill would be required to raise the property above sea level; it was estimated that the cost for fill material would be $6.5 million. However, even if Mountain View had had the $6.5 million, it did not have access to six million yards of dirt. There were also many environmental restraints at this time that would surely restrict the city from tearing down a mountain-top to get the dirt.

Again, I guess my submarine history kicked in. Have a backup system for everything in life (for example, an extra garbage truck in case one quits or breaks down). I contacted the City of Mountain View and suggested that we could create the regional park, incorporating the use of San Francisco's garbage in place of earth fill. In the process, we would apply the highest degree of sanitary landfill technology to ensure that the City of Mountain View would have no environmental liability for the operation.

Of course, there was initial public skepticism, not to mention the negative psychological impact of the City of Mountain View becoming the garbage dump for San Francisco; but if presented properly as part of a proposal to create a regional park at no cost to the City of Mountain View, it made economic sense. The city agreed to consider our proposal if the City of San Francisco would approve it.

We made the proposal to the City of San Francisco, citing that we believed we could create this regional park in Mountain View and resolve San Francisco's immediate short-term disposal needs at the same time. Some city leaders, as well as some of the general public and the environmentalists, expressed skepticism. We responded to the negative questions, and over time we were able to demonstrate that we could in fact take the liability of one city (San Francisco) and create an asset in another city (Mountain View). We were prepared to prove that the plan could be engineered properly and operate efficiently, aesthetically, and in an environmentally friendly way to the highest degree.

In the interim, we continued to negotiate with the Western Pacific Railroad. The anticipated rate per ton to receive, transfer, transport, and dispose of garbage in Lassen County had increased to close to $50 per ton, with no end in sight. It was apparent the railroad believed that San Francisco had no other option available for its disposal needs.

Still another problem with railroad disposal was the design of a waste transfer station, commissioned by Kaiser Engineers. It was clearly designed by people who had little or no knowledge of the complex composition of solid waste. In our opinion, the Kaiser waste transfer station, if actually implemented, would be a disaster because of poor design.

In early 1969, Sanitary Fill Company drew up a contract with the City and County of San Francisco and the City of Mountain View to transport San Francisco's garbage to Mountain View and dispose of it in an engineered sanitary landfill in strict compliance with our then-current rules.

The plan included twenty-two holes of golf built around lakes and recreational facilities. The park would be created at no cost to the City of Mountain View. In fact, we paid the city a royalty, or "host fee," of thirty-two cents per ton and allowed the city to dispose of its waste as well.

The next step, of course, was how to get the garbage to Mountain View in the most efficient way possible. We decided to use a solid-waste transfer station that would be the largest ever built in the world at that time.

It was determined that such a facility would require the ability to receive and dispose of garbage, accommodate at least twelve trucks at the same time and more than sixty trucks per hour, be completely enclosed, and be able to store one day's waste production.

The facility would have to be available for use 24 hours a day, 7 days week, and 365 days a year. To be efficient and to have the proper storage capacity, it had to be able to transfer fifty-two tons of waste into waiting transfer trucks by way of a gravity feed every six minutes and operate only five days a week.

In the past, other scavengers and I had traveled to different cities looking for the proverbial black boxes to solve the world's garbage problem. The fact remained that the sanitary landfill offered the only total solution.

With that thought in mind, we began developing the transfer station using a design we had observed in Portland, Oregon years before. It used a direct means of dumping garbage into the collection vehicle, which any engineer would recommend as the most efficient means of transferring waste to a transportation vehicle.

Engineers agree that the less you handle refuse, the more efficient the system becomes. But from a garbage man's prospective, that is not necessarily the correct way to proceed. Direct dumping was the most efficient means of transferring systems but hardly the most logical. For example, if a transfer trailer had sixty-five yards of capacity and three twenty-five-yard trucks came to discharge their loads, the first two could dump their loads, but what happens with the third truck?

Obviously, in the matter of flow control, the last twenty-five-yard truck would have to wait until another transfer truck arrived; or, its driver could try to dump only ten yards of his truck. Neither of these options was realistic for many reasons.

The Portland Transfer Station originally dumped garbage directly from the collection truck, as described earlier, and experienced the delays that I cited.

However, what Portland did was unique: It utilized a large pit of sorts. Furniture demolition materials and a large bulldozer were stationed inside the pit and could roll over bulky material, compact it, and (when a transfer vehicle was available) receive a signal to push the compacted waste into a waiting transfer vehicle at a lower level.

After some consideration, we concluded that we should discharge all types of waste into a large pit and use two bulldozers to compact and level the waste. Then when the signal was sent that a transfer truck was available, the operator would direct the bulldozers to shove the material into the transfer truck, using scales to determine the weight.

It takes less than six minutes to transfer and load twenty-six tons of waste (the maximum legal load in California). With two loading bays, fifty-two tons of waste can be transferred and be on its way to the disposal facility every six minutes.

The long and short of this saga is that the transfer station was conceived by garbage men, not by the so-called professional engineers who were hell-bent on using the concept of direct transfer— that is, collection vehicle to transfer trailer. As time went by, these experts reluctantly agreed that the garbage man's concept was, in fact, the best, since no one else knew the complex composition of mixed solid waste and the problems related to handling it as well.

One of the most difficult problems was the scheduling of incoming trucks. Scheduling the trucks was virtually impossible, so the design of the facility had to consider this factor; the "pit" concept made this all possible. We were able to create a solid-waste transfer station that would do the following:

1. Have a 600-foot x 400-foot completely enclosed facility with no center support posts, anticipating the probability that sometime in the future a careless driver might hit and knock down the building. By eliminating the posts, this hazard was eliminated.
2. Receive up to fifty trucks per hour.
3. Operate 24 hours a day, 7 days a week.
4. Receive and transfer 2,500 tons of mixed solid waste a day.
5. Have the capability to transfer solid waste into transfer vehicles at the rate of 52 tons every 6 minutes.
6. Become operational by late 1970 to comply with the closure of the Brisbane Sierra Point landfill site.

We accomplished all of the above and more from concept to reality. I believe that, after I was elected president, we began to earn long-overdue respect from others who recognized that scavengers had experience and knowledge about garbage disposal. Merging the scavengers' expertise with the experience of engineers, politicians, bureaucrats, and environmentalists could help expedite the permitting process. This was demonstrated by the fact that it took less than eleven months to design, permit, fund (this time Bank of America was first in line to finance the $3.5 million needed), construct, and place into operation this magnificent world-class facility.

Predictably, the realization of a project of this magnitude involved major challenges as well as memorable experiences along the way. Some of the residents filed suit against us for the use of explosives to break up the rock, a practice we had used for many years with no complaints. According to the permits, we could only use specific amounts of explosives. However, a group of residents got together, hired a prominent hotshot attorney, and filed suit for an unspecified amount of money for damage to their homes. To boost their case, they claimed that the blasts were so severe that they were "knocked off their toilet seats."

During the course of the jury trial, our attorney, Angelo Scampini, made an unexpected suggestion: the jury should go to some of the plaintiffs' homes closest to the site, where they would be assigned to sit upon the toilet seats on a given schedule. We, on the other hand, would set a charge of explosives, double the normal amount. Not one jurist felt anything, let alone was blown off the toilet, and the case was dropped.

Once again, it was Jack Ertola's mentoring and introducing me to the political infrastructure of San Francisco, plus my following the advice of Primo Repetto about the need to "blow smoke up my own ass," that allowed the scavengers and the City of San Francisco to find this important solution to the needs of garbage disposal. Because of the then newfound working partnership with the city and the respect that we scavengers had justly earned, San Francisco's solid-waste transfer station is still in place after more than forty-seven years.

At the dedication ceremony of the transfer station on November 1, 1970, S. Myron Tatarian, the director of public works, stated:

> This magnificent facility, best described as the "Palazzo della Immondizia" (Palace of Garbage, coined by Leonard Stefanelli), would have never been possible if [it] were not for the joint effort and mutual respect between the City of San Francisco, recognizing the scavengers' experience and commitment to the city and the service they provide; and, in turn, the scavengers recognizing and respecting the administrative powers of the city. Together, we have created this magnificent project.

On November 2, 1970, we dumped our first loads into the transfer station. Our partners and subcontractors of the landfill operation, Easley & Brassy Corporation, prepared the Mountain View site to accept San Francisco's waste stream, estimated at 2,500 tons per day. The plan was to phase in the transfer station over two weeks. Full startup was completed in less than five days, though, clearly confirming that the design offered by the scavengers was an extraordinary example of knowledge and professionalism, spawned by actual experience cultivated and brought forward by the Boss Scavengers.

The disposal contract between Mountain View and Sanitary Fill Company was initially slated for only five years. The first year of operations went smoothly. Rain or shine, 2,500 tons of San Francisco's waste was received, transferred, delivered, and disposed of in the City of Mountain View with no problems or controversies.

It was not only the first contract of this magnitude, but the combination of San Francisco's garbage disposal and Mountain View's own needs created a perfect working relationship between the two entities. Not only did we pay Mountain View to receive our refuse, we also paid all the necessary fees and landfill operation expenses in a truly wonderful working relationship among the three entities: San Francisco, Mountain View, and the scavengers.

As noted, we paid a "host fee" of thirty-two cents per ton (about $175,000 a year). After three years, our engineering projections concluded that we had capacity for at least three additional years over and above the five-year contract. At the then-current rate of fill, we could conceivably work under the contract for eight additional years and possibly more.

The sessions discussing the extension contract began in 1972, two years after the commencement of the initial contract. One of the surprising requests by the City of Mountain View was a demand to increase the current host fee of thirty-two cents per ton to $2 per ton, or approximately $1.2 million a year. Initially, the City of San Francisco went berserk over such a proposal, suggesting, "Mountain View should be paying us, for building their beautiful park."

After the smoke cleared, we convinced the City of San Francisco that the sensitivity (politically speaking) of paying the increased host fee was a thorny issue; but when we calculated the actual cost, it was less than three cents per month for each residential ratepayer.

After some discussion, the city agreed that it was a fair cost to gain an additional eight years, for a total of thirteen years, of disposal capacity. We agreed at the time that $1.2 million a year was a significant amount of money. Yet compared to today's costs, that increase was only chump change; some counties now get $5 a ton to accept another county's garbage. At the time, though, we demonstrated that out of every dollar paid to collect the garbage, about sixteen cents was allocated to the actual disposal of waste, formulated on a per-ton basis. Using that formula and adding the $1.2 million host fee into the disposal rates and into the collection rates, the real impact on the average ratepayer was less than two cents—cheap, for the assurance of eight more years of disposal.

We entered into an extension of the original contract to carry us through the additional eight years, into 1983—providing more than adequate time to seek an alternate disposal site. Reluctantly, the City of San Francisco and we agreed to pay the $1.2 million fee to the City of Mountain View and to save millions of dollars in a trust account mandated by law to be set aside in perpetuity for what was known as Post Closure Funds. That fund would always be available for mitigation if an environmental problem should develop after the closure of the landfill.

While we were discussing this contract with the City of San Francisco, Dianne Feinstein, then president of the board of supervisors, urged us to seek innovative disposal methods. We tried to find alternatives but found none that we could pursue at that time. (One process we looked at was waste-to-energy, a process that I will address later in this book, because I believe it is the proverbial black box and a long-term disposal solution, one that is good for the world.)

The planned regional park began taking shape, featuring golf courses with green fairways constructed on top of refuse cells.[3] These cells were created to capture methane and leachate and make sure they were properly processed to eliminate any environmental hazards. The site and soil conditions were ideal; in essence, we were creating a cut-and-cover operation. Dig a hole, line it with clay, install a channel surrounding the cell, backfill the cell with gravel, and place the refuse in the cell. This would bring the ground up by forty feet or more, well above the watermark and high tides. Everybody was happy with the situation, and we were happy with the money it brought in.

Epilogue to the Mountain View Project

In addition to golf courses, recreation, and hike-and-bike paths, the new regional park was going to include an entertainment facility. Shoreline Amphitheater now hosts a vast spectrum of big-name entertainers, including heavy metal, rock and roll, and other musical styles on the landfill site.

When the City of Mountain View was building the Shoreline Amphitheater, it decided to put a grass berm seating area (the cheap seats) above the arena. We bid on the job, but another contractor submitted a lower bid and was hired. We were directed to

---

3. A cell is an excavation in the area, where clay and an artificial membrane (or liner) is laid on the bottom of the cell, to allow any leachate formed by the decomposing waste to be forced into "channels" filled with gravel; it is then pumped out and processed, thereby eliminating groundwater contamination between the liner and clay base. Once the cell is completed, another membrane is laid upon the waste and covered with clay soil, which creates a sort of "cap" upon the top of the cell. The purpose of this process is to allow the captivation of methane gas, which is a normal byproduct of decomposing waste. The process eliminates this gas from migrating or causing air pollution where it is flared or, in this case, used to generate energy.

place the refuse on the ground to create the berm. The other contractor was supposed to cover the waste with dirt and plant grass
on top. The plan was to add six inches of earth cover and plant
grass. Concert fans would sit on the grass berm.

However, the contractor forgot to line the berm area with an
artificial membrane before putting dirt on it. When the soil dried
out, it cracked open and the generated methane gas from decomposing waste slowly leached out because it wasn't properly sealed.
I know of at least ten incidents of people sitting on these berms,
smoking cigarettes or dope, and seeing a very light blue flame suddenly appear between their legs, burning their pants and shoes.

Fortunately, no one was seriously hurt, but these events were
hilarious. The City of Mountain View called us back to correct
the error, ultimately paying substantially more than was saved by
selecting a cheaper, amateur contractor.

Not only did we develop a technology for sanitary landfill that
collected leachate, but we also developed the new means of collecting methane gas by inserting perforated pipe into the landfill, and
using negative pressure or vacuum sucking to draw the landfill gas
from within the cells. We would then condense the gas and filter it.

Using the main natural gas line, owned by PG&E, feeding the
Bay Area, we were able to capture the flammable methane gas,
which has 50 percent of the energy value of natural gas. The two
are compatible and can be merged together; as a result, this recovered gas was fed into PG&E's main line to be used commercially,
rather than just being "flared" (ignited before being released to
the atmosphere).

The technology we pioneered in Mountain View set a standard for all landfills throughout the United States. Today, many
of the larger landfills generate electrical energy from methane
gas turbines rather than from flaring. (Flaring becomes necessary where small landfills generate small levels of methane.) Some
larger producers of gases at mega-landfills are taking the gas recovery programs to the next level and converting that gas to diesel
fuel supplements.

Looking back forty years, I can say with some pride that the
scavengers of San Francisco pioneered many innovations in San
Francisco's long-term solid-waste program, innovations that have
been emulated by others in the industry.

The *Palazzo della Immondizia* (Palace of Garbage) was and

still is a model for major solid-waste management transfer stations or material recovery facilities (MRFs) throughout the world. People who truly comprehended the complexities of the solid-waste business conceived strategies such as the Palace of Garbage.

I can say, "Not too bad for a bunch of scavengers!"

16

Beyond Mountain View

After we signed the contract for additional years with the City of Mountain View, we hoped to develop a landfill somewhere else within seventy-five miles of San Francisco or the transfer station. Opening a new landfill was an expensive and time-consuming effort because of NIMBY (not in my back yard) issues; people did not want their garbage—or anybody else's—within their city limits.

We zeroed in on an 800-acre site in Solano County. Lynch Canyon, actually on the border of Napa and Solano Counties, was ideally located; a freeway underpass provided ready access to the site, which could be developed for about $15 million. We took an option to purchase the property at $2.5 million and commenced the process of filing for an application to dispose waste in Solano County.

As soon as the application became public, there was rampant opposition, which we had anticipated when we began the environmental assessments work. We found that the soils included a substantial amount of clay, which was ideal for landfill operations. Artificial membranes lining the cells would be an added safety guard. All in all, Lynch Canyon was a perfect site for San Francisco's garbage.

Public rejection of landfill sites throughout the State of California was commonplace, and we anticipated resistance. However, we were not aware of the intricacies of the legislative process and that permits for a sanitary landfill site (or even just for parking a garbage truck) depended on a legislative act by the governing bodies, such as a county board of supervisors.

The simple fact was that you could site a sewage treatment facility, go through all the complicated environmental assessment work, and get a permit to build a sewage treatment plant through an administrative act of the board of supervisors under the auspices of the California Health and Safety Code without being subject to voter referendum.

In our case, siting a sanitary landfill, transfer station, material recovery facility, or even parking garbage trucks involved a legislative act that, after compliance with all the necessary environmental laws and getting all the necessary permits, could be overruled by the voters. Even if we went through all the rigmarole of getting the permit, the public could vote us out of business, as in Brisbane, where the voters overruled the city's approved permit to operate at Sierra Point.

We approached a major state legislator, requesting that solid-waste, garbage-disposal, and collection facilities—and the permitting of them—be designated as administrative acts under state law, so that voters couldn't overrule decisions based upon California's Health and Safety Code.

The legislator agreed that our logic was reasonable, and we proceeded to pay him and his law firm a substantial amount of money to work to modify the law that would put the permitting of these facilities under health and safety provisions, the same as a water treatment facility.

Despite all the payments we made, he never produced any legislation in that regard to benefit not just us but the entire solid-waste industry. (That's another story, yet to be addressed.)

Nonetheless, we commenced the development of Lynch Canyon because of its great potential to become a true regional landfill, something that the State of California surely needed, rather than continuing the traditional and archaic method of each city having its own dump.

On the other hand, Solano County already had two other major landfills, and that surely could become part of an argument about the county becoming a dumping ground for the entire region.

Serious opposition came from a small community called Green Valley, whose citizens were vehemently opposed to the site factor and expressed their opposition on chalkboards at a bar called Thompson's Corner. Their slogan was "Keep SF Garbage Out of Solano County."

As time went by, we learned that two garbage companies were funding this campaign: Richmond Sanitary Service and Concord Disposal Company, the developers of the Potrero Hills Landfill. Both saw us as the competition. I knew the presidents of both these companies on a personal basis, and when I challenged them to stop funding the anti-garbage campaign, they facetiously looked me in the eye and said, "Well, business is business." I had to bite the bullet, so to speak. They did stop, but the damage had been done.

We began to realize that getting a permit to use Lynch Canyon for garbage disposal would be an uphill battle. Unfortunately, we continued to try, although it became clear that we would not get it permitted for at least five to six years—too late for our needs. We needed a landfill site for San Francisco trash by 1983, and we were running out of time.

Oakland Scavenger Company had been working since 1970 to get a regional sanitary landfill in Alameda County. In late 1979, Oakland was finally getting the permit, clearly demonstrating the significant time and money it took to open a new landfill anywhere in the state.

For example, there is a large open pit—a former rock quarry—in southern California, with spur rails in place, very little rain, some groundwater, 2,000 feet deep, adequate cover material, and so forth. If God ever made a place on this earth ideal for a sanitary landfill or garbage dump, this was it. Starting in 1980, a company called Western Wastes in Los Angeles County realized the long-term potential of this site.

After many years of work to permit it for solid-waste disposal, Western Wastes sold its position to Browning-Ferris Industries, a New York Stock Exchange Company, which spent hundreds of thousands of dollars and many years of fruitless efforts. Two other major entities threw their hats into the ring with the same results. According to the records, after some $10 million spent and thirty years of work, not one pound of garbage has been disposed of at this Iron Mountain site in San Bernardino County. Permitting a new site and making it operational in California is a virtual impossibility, as any of my colleagues can surely confirm.

So, we needed a backup in case we couldn't get Lynch Canyon by the time we had to stop using Sierra Point. A backup often includes efforts to expand existing landfills (assuming the leachate and methane gases can be controlled) and in some cases to expand completed landfills (such as Mountain View and Sierra Point).

At one point, Oakland Scavenger Company was working to permit the Altamont Landfill. When I became president of Sunset Scavenger in 1965, I met and worked with former Oakland Scavenger executives Dewey Vittori and Tony Delcino.

Aside from Benny Anselmo, Dewey was one of the most influential people in my life. He was twenty years my senior and, for whatever reason, he took me under his wing when I was thirty-one years old.

He taught and shared with me the other side of the business, which I had been totally unaware of—determining the value of a franchised waste-collection company. Dewey proved to be an invaluable resource in the years to come.

Although Dewey Vittori maintained the title of vice president, it was clear that he was the real ramrod of Oakland Scavenger Company. He had too much respect for then-president Tony Delcino, but I was to find out it was Vittori who envisioned using and converting the Altamont site. Dewey, who smoked like a chimney, died of heart failure at age fifty-six, a great loss to the company and the industry.

Because of my longtime relationship with Oakland Scavenger Company, I knew company president Peter Borghero on a first-name basis. I contacted him in 1979 to talk about taking San Francisco's garbage to his yet-to-be-permitted Altamont Pass site. Of course, San Francisco's waste stream would be a lucrative account for him, but his first response was that he was not really interested. I knew that was not true.

When the Altamont site was conceived, it was to replace the existing landfill in San Francisco Bay just south of the Oakland International Airport. To commence operations at the Altamont site, Oakland Scavenger Company had to pay for the capital cost of land, development, engineering, financing, operational expenses, and so forth, which was projected at $7.50 a ton and was to be paid for by the company's own waste stream and customer base, as well as amortized over a twenty-year period.

An interesting side note was that Oakland Scavenger also operated a major landfill in the bay. When they planned the Altamont landfill some forty miles away, they realized they would require a solid-waste transfer station. As a result, I worked with Oakland Scavenger and one of its board members, Ron Proto, who was a Boss Scavenger at one time and then the project manager for the proposed new facility. Today's similar San Francisco projects use some improvements obtained from the experiences gained from our operations. My point is that, from the get-go, the San Francisco design was almost 100 percent accurate, conceptually designed by garbage men, not engineers.

I knew, therefore, that every ton delivered to the Altamont site over and above 700,000 tons a year was pure profit. After some serious discussions, Peter Borghero reluctantly offered $15 a ton for us to dump San Francisco's waste stream at the Altamont landfill. After some fierce negotiations, Peter knew that he had me by the balls because we had no other options. However, he finally agreed to $7.50 a ton, plus a host fee. That was a fair price because 90 percent of that $7.50 was pure profit to his company.

So, in 1983, the thirty-two-mile haul distance from the transfer station to Mountain View grew to sixty-five miles from the transfer station to the Altamont site. The change required that we purchase new transfer trucks and trailers to accommodate the longer haul distance. We also had to factor in heavier traffic conditions and bridge tolls.

Overall, the increased cost of doing business was minimal because the transfer station had already been paid for through the rates applied in San Francisco. The City of San Francisco was still getting the best deal possible, considering the fact that we had to transport the refuse some sixty-five miles for disposal. This contract has been in effect since 1983.

The move by Oakland Scavenger to acquire the Altamont Pass site proved to be a wise one. It was the last major site to be permitted anywhere in the State of California.

Oakland Scavenger Company and Waste Management Inc.

Some years after I left the company and went to work for Waste Management Inc., I orchestrated the purchase of the Oakland Scavenger Company. When efforts were made to extend the existing disposal contract between the two entities, the negotiations failed, much to my surprise and disappointment. I personally felt it was a loss to both parties.

Wedding day photo of Emilio Rattaro, original founder of the Sunset Scavenger Company, early 1900s.

Scavenger workers and wagons in Colma, California, 1916.

Gino Demartini (*left*), North Beach, San Francisco, 1916. Courtesy of Eugene Demartini.

Garbage pickup, via horse and wagon. Aldo Ballestrasse (<u>left</u>) and Paolo Belli (*right*), 1917. Photo courtesy of Leon Belli.

Allesandro Ballestrasse (*left*) and Augustino Mangini (*right*), Mission Scavenger Company, Mission District, San Francisco, 1918.

Three White Trucks, owned and operated by the Sunset Scavenger Company, in front of San Francisco City Hall, January, 1924.

One of Sunset Scavenger's "new" waste collection vehicles during the 1920s in the Mission District. These trucks replaced horsepower with gasoline and featured a 1921 White chassis and a custom-designed body with "stairs." According to the person who provided the picture, the man in front is Lenny's relative, Elmo Grazziani, the others are unknown. Note the portable "fence" made of cardboard and wood posts, which increased truck capacity and minimized the need for the time-consuming trips to the dump.

Lenny's three uncles: Pasquale (*left*), Dominic "Mingo" (*right*), and Alfredo "Freddy" (*standing*), 1934. At that time, the Sunset Scavenger Company was still using horse and wagons on routes closest to the disposal facilities.

Carlo "Charlie" Guaraglia (*left*) and his son Giovanni, aka "John", 1956. Charlie moved from Fontanarossa, Italy and started his company, One Horse, One Italian, one of many that merged with Emilio Rattaro's Sunset Scavenger Company in 1920.

Lenny, working on Truck 27, Fulton and Steiner Streets, 1954.

Very specialized and unique waste collection services provided by Scavenger. Garbage cans might be stored as many as three stories aboveground, but the worker still climbs to the top three levels with his barrel, fills it up, then hauls it back downstairs.

A scavenger providing so-called "back yard" services, revealing the extreme difficulties sometimes faced in gaining access to refuse storage areas.

Lenny with colleague and friend Donald Bonzi during
Lenny's fourth month as president of the Sunset Scavenger
Company, 1965.

Trash pickup enters the modern age: The new, state-of-the-art packer truck
sits aside the 1920 version in front of San Francisco City Hall, 1966.

Lenny (*right*) with the newly elected mayor of San Francisco, Joseph Alioto (*left*) and Lenny's mentor, Bennie Anselmo, Sr. (*kneeling*), 1968.

In flight: Lenny with another influential mentor, Dewey Vittori, Oakland Scavenger vice president, 1969.

Lenny and his pet pig, Cinderella, 1972.

Refuse-crammed barges readying to unload onto dump trucks for hauling to the Dream Island disposal site.

Tokyo Bay garbage being delivered to Dream Island, or more accurately Nightmare Island, which occurred regularly from sixty sites by tugboat. The refuse was then taken from barges and loaded by clamshell cranes onto trucks to be delivered to the disposal site. Note the significant amount of spillage, much of which ended up in Tokyo Bay.

Dream Island disposal site, ca. 1970, displaying 800 acres of uncovered garbage. Dream Island, reputedly, later evolved into a vast, open-space recreational area. *Left to right*: Leo Conte, Lenny, and Bennie Anselmo.

Compressed and baled garbage from the Tyszuka process.

The now-infamous Japanese proposal to "compress garbage, bale it, coat it, and build houses out of baled garbage," shows that they were instead used to fill in rice paddies. The Tyszuka Press claimed that the bales were environmentally secure, yet this photo from May, 1970, clearly shows the rice is dying from contaminants leeching into the field.

Sunset Transfer Station, first day of operation, November, 1970.

Left to right: Lenny, John Moscone (president of the Golden Gate Company), and S. Myron Tatarian, checking plans to add a ferrous metal recovery system to the Sunset Transfer Station, 1971.

An impromptu photo of a portion of Lenny (*top row, fourth from right*) with a group of waste management VIPs, waiting to access Lenin's Tomb in Red Square, Moscow, Russia, May, 1972. Photo by John Greenagle.

The Russian refuse delegation trips into San Francisco in 1973 were hosted by Lenny and Richard Campadonico, president of the Pepsi-Cola Bottling Company of California. The event was requested by the U.S. State Department, which did not have the necessary funds to pay for the tour.

Lenny greeting Senator Ted Kennedy at the San Francisco
Airport, 1975.

Left to right: Senator Dianne Feinstein, Governor Jerry Brown, and Lenny, February, 1975.

Lenny with George Moscone, November, 1978, shortly before Moscone's assassination.

Lenny, dressed as a rodeo clown and inhabiting the "barrel," Grand National Livestock Exposition, Cow Palace, San Francisco, 1982.

Lenny (*right*) with a framed blessing from Pope John Paul II, Italian Day, at a San Francisco Giants game, Candlestick Park, 1986.

Lenny and former San Francisco mayor Willie Brown, San Francisco
Historical Society luncheon, Mark Hopkins Hotel, San Francisco,
September, 2015.

Growing the Business

By 1970, the new board of directors and I had accomplished many things, including:

- establishing new, good, and positive working relationships with Golden Gate Disposal Company;
- incorporating a new fleet of trucks designed to improve working conditions for waste collection services;
- converting hand collecting 136,000 garbage bills to data processing;
- providing better service to customers;
- improving relationships with the City and County of San Francisco, as well as with the state and federal governments;
- getting the respect rightfully due to the men who provided this unglamorous but necessary service.

Other accomplishments, all of which added to the economic stability of the company and equity among the shareholders, included:

- developing and using the controversial Sierra Point site;
- developing a new alternate site in the City of Mountain View;
- creating a huge transfer station, the largest in the world at the time, which eventually developed a thirteen-year disposal program at that site; and
- signing a twenty-year contract with the Oakland Scavenger Company.

Rate increases were sought and approved by the City of San Francisco; there was little or no resistance from the public, as people began to appreciate and, more importantly, respect the services the companies were providing with new and modern equipment and improved means of collecting waste.

Wages in 1965 were $9,200 a year for shareholders; in 1975, wages were in the area of $28,000. We significantly enhanced the pension programs and medical and health benefits for the shareholders and all the employees of the company. Company shares at one time sold for $14,500; by 1975, shares were commanding prices in excess of $35,000 because of better wages, employment security, working conditions, and benefits.

The lingering fact that stood out in my mind, though, was that Sunset Scavenger Company had no growth potential because, for all practical purposes, every available square foot of the city had been covered with housing. Sunset Scavenger was actually losing revenues because of increased freeways and redevelopment programs that failed to preserve any additional land for housing or for our company. Hunters Point Naval Shipyard was closing and the city's population was decreasing. Because the cost of doing business was "fixed," so to speak, we had to seek rate increases to offset the loss of revenue.

The other company offering garbage-collecting services in San Francisco was Golden Gate Disposal Company, which serviced high-rise buildings and businesses. Golden Gate Disposal was experiencing a growth factor, not necessarily in square feet, but in "airspace." Downtown San Francisco was experiencing significant growth and many tall buildings were being built, while Sunset Scavenger was losing business. I tried to explain this new development to my shareholders during a "How Come...?" question-and-answer period.

Why did Golden Gate Disposal have better benefits? I sarcastically referred to the fact that we used the same 29-cent postage stamp to collect $10.50 for two months of service in the Richmond District, while the same 29-cent stamp brought in a $10,000 check from some high-rise building.

This was a difficult time for me, as we had 280 shareholders while Golden Gate Disposal had only 152. Therefore, a Sunset Scavenger dividend of $100,000, for example, had to be split into 320 parts with each shareholder getting $357.50.

If Golden Gate Disposal had the same $100,000 dividend, each shareholder would get $657. I tried but I could not demonstrate the logic and math to my shareholders. It was very hard for Sunset Scavenger's Boss Scavengers to comprehend why Golden Gate's Boss Scavengers got bigger dividends, even though it was a simple matter of mathematics.

At the same time that Golden Gate Disposal was experiencing substantial growth by selling "air rights," Sunset Scavenger was losing revenue.

The San Francisco Garbage Rate Control Board used Sunset

Scavenger Company income to establish the rate structure for the entire city. When this board was established in 1951, the city determined that it could regulate only residences, such as houses and apartments. The "commercial" component was served by Golden Gate Disposal and was unregulated, with commercial account rates designed essentially on an antiquated "time and motion" formula.

Back in those days, residential scavengers had to break cardboard boxes by hand, collect the garbage, carry it to the open truck, and more. The commercial account rates at that time were set by the time it took to service the account, multiplied by the number of men involved at the hourly rate for labor.

As time went by and modern refuse collection equipment became available, newer equipment made the commercial business highly profitable because of reduced labor expenses, whereas the residential service was still labor intensive—crews had to go to the backyard, climb the stairs, open the doors, and so forth to collect the garbage.

Because the city regulated only "residences, flats, and apartment houses," and Sunset Scavenger had the majority of those accounts, Sunset Scavenger was used as the model to set the rates for the entire city.

Because 40 percent of Golden Gate Disposal's revenues were from commercial accounts in downtown San Francisco, its income flow was greater.

The rate structure allowed Sunset Scavenger Company a 5 percent operating ratio in setting the rates in San Francisco. In other words, for every dollar in revenue Sunset received, it was allowed to keep five cents (after taxes), to be divided among shareholders and for capital improvements or whatever else the company needed.

The problem for Sunset Scavenger Company was that the cost of doing business not only increased due to regular inflationary trends, but it was further complicated by the loss of the Hunters Point Naval Shipyard commercial income. As a result of new freeway construction and redevelopment projects, many businesses moved out of the city limits.

Our revenues were static at best, whereas Golden Gate Disposal's continued to rise unabated. Part of Sunset's problem was an amendment to the 1932 San Francisco Refuse Ordinance, which created the San Francisco Refuse Rate Board. This board could regulate only "residents, flats and apartments" and had no rate-setting authority for commercial businesses. The provisions adopted by the city allowed the garbage companies to make a 10 percent pre-tax profit on gross revenue.

While this was great for Sunset in the 1950s when it was still experiencing growth, Golden Gate Disposal's service areas were losing substantial revenue sources because, at that time, downtown San Francisco was economically dormant.

Golden Gate Disposal was lucky to break even during this period, while Sunset was experiencing an income well within the allowable rates of return. Given its considerable losses, Golden Gate needed to increase service rates, but could not because Sunset's more than adequate revenues couldn't justify the application for a price hike.

In less than ten years, all that changed. In downtown San Francisco, countless one- and two-story buildings were torn down, replaced by twenty-, thirty-, forty-, and sixty-story buildings. Golden Gate's income began to soar with the rising commercial base.

At the same time that Sunset Scavenger's revenues became stagnant, expenses continued to rise, thus reducing the profit margin of Sunset's shareholders. Golden Gate was making big-time money, well in excess of the allowable rate of return, and the city could do nothing about it because of the inflexible rate model.

This situation created political problems for me as a president, and there was nothing I could do about it. That's just how the rates were set. Golden Gate "laughed all the way to the bank" every month and was able to split those excess profits among 152 shareholders.

Sunset Scavenger applied for and received a rate increase to achieve an approved 90 percent operating ratio. However, this meant that Golden Gate got the same increase as Sunset, despite far exceeding that 90 percent operating ratio, which only added insult to injury. The city could do nothing about it.

Seeking a Solution

We had taken Sunset Scavenger Company into the modern age. It was now a fierce, cost-effective, smooth-running machine collecting waste in San Francisco. I felt that in order to compensate for lost revenue, it was necessary for Sunset Scavenger to acquire businesses outside of the San Francisco city limits.

In the 1940s and 1960s, some Sunset Scavenger partners sold their shares and started smaller companies in the South Bay. For example, Los Altos Garbage Company was made up of nine former Sunset Scavenger partners who had sold their shares and went into these small, rural South Bay communities.

These men were getting older, and I approached them to see if they would like to sell their shares in the Los Altos company. I worked out arrangements to purchase five shares of the company, one the first year and the other four the following year.

The most difficult problem I had in putting a deal like this together was to convince our CPAs and board of directors that it was worth the money the partners were asking for their equity. I had to show them a formula to justify the cost of purchasing the business. Up to this point, no one had ever evaluated or placed a dollar value on the "franchise" the company held. In the Los Altos case, the company had a twenty-year franchise that was transferable and a tangible value in the acquisition of any given company.

The CPAs concluded that a franchise was an intangible value or asset—in other words, it was worthless. I argued the contrary. In my opinion, the franchise provided a guarantee that the company would be in business for twenty years, come hell or high water. Therefore, the franchise had a real dollar value that could be capitalized on the date of purchase and depreciated for income tax purposes. My argument, I'm proud to say, proved to be correct. Over time, I articulated the concept in writing, explaining that a franchise did in fact hold substantial tangible value in acquiring a company.

I hasten to add that I didn't develop the notion entirely on my own. I depended on the guidance of two old-timers who educated me well: my good friend, colleague, and mentor Dewey Vittori, vice president of Oakland Scavenger Company; and later, Benny Anselmo of Golden Gate Disposal Company. Dewey explained to me why a franchise was valuable and gave me a simple formula to determine the fair value of a garbage company holding one.

We used my method to determine the worth of Los Altos Garbage Company. In 1970 when we purchased that company, its gross revenue was some $5 million. In 2010, with growth and rate adjustments, the company was grossing in excess of $35 million, clearly confirming that my assessment of its value was accurate.

Using the same concept to purchase other garbage companies would serve us well in the coming years. For example, the service areas of the company being considered for acquisition might have two or three residential blocks between one customer and the next customer. In the years to follow, the same street would soon have more housing; therefore, it would cost the same to send a truck to collect 100 new accounts as it did to send a truck to those original few clients. In essence, the company would be making much more money at minimal additional cost. In this way, Sunset Scavenger Company did not have to rely only on rate increases to boost revenues.

In addition to Los Altos Garbage Company, over the years we acquired Foothill Disposal Company, South Valley Refuse Stockton Scavengers, City Sanitary Service (Medford, Oregon), and others.

When I became president in 1965, Sunset Scavenger Company's gross revenue was some $3 million a year. Seven years later, the company's reported annual income was in excess of $45 million a year.

18

The Creation of Envirocal, the Holding Company

A new problem arose. We were required by law to include all income from Sunset Scavenger Company in a certified public audit that was used to develop the rates in San Francisco. On the other income statements, revenues from outside of the city were reported as "other income" and added to the net profits of Sunset Scavenger Company. We believed that these income sources had no relationship to the cost of collecting and disposing of waste in San Francisco. Although we could legitimately argue that fact, I concluded that it would be better for each regulated subsidiary to operate on its own.

The point was that even though San Francisco had nothing to do with these other entities, it was conceivable that someone could integrate the revenues from these acquisitions within the rate structure. Our rates might be adjusted downward if that happened, a prospect that was not in our best interest.

After due consideration, I concluded that we should create a new holding company with Sunset Scavenger Company. The directors were a little nervous when I first proposed this concept, because they did not understand the need to exchange the traditional Sunset Scavenger stock certificate of thirty-two shares for a certificate in a new corporation.

Despite this, I was convinced that if we gave shareholders the proper notice and explanation, they would vote to adopt the plan. According to our attorneys, 100 percent of the shareholders had to agree to turn in their stock certificates for the new company's certificates.

At first, I picked the name Consolidated Environmental Industries Incorporated (CEI Inc.), but I was saddened to learn that someone already had that corporate name on file, so we couldn't use it. After some discussion with the attorneys and PR people, we considered combining two words, *Environment* and *California*, to create a simple word. Envirocal Inc. was not necessarily as glamorous as I wanted the name to be, but it was better than nothing, and it made sense to have a name like that.

With the help of attorneys and certified public accountants, we filed for permission to start a new corporation in the State of Delaware (because of favorable tax incentives) and to transfer equity from all subsidiaries. As a result, Sunset Scavenger, Los Altos South Valley, Stockton Scavenger, Sanitary Fill Company, Joseph Petigera Company (our independent salvage/recycling entity), and others became subsidiaries of Envirocal Inc. in June 1972.

To my pleasure and surprise, all of the shareholders did exchange their Sunset Scavenge Company shares for the new certificates in Envirocal Inc. Each Sunset Scavenger share certificate was canceled and given back to the original shareholder.

For the record, the bylaws of Sunset Scavenger Company were incorporated into the new Envirocal Corporations, so all working shareholders' compensation, benefits, and voting rights continued to be "treated absolutely equal and alike, regardless of office position or responsibility." The only change was a general omission of the term *Boss Scavenger*.

Public Companies Entering the Northern California Markets

Garbage companies in Northern California operated on their own for many years; no physical connection of any kind existed among the people who managed them. However, Benny Anselmo, Dewey Vittori, Rudy Vacarezza, and other men who ran small one- or two-truck companies (similar to Oakland Scavenger and Golden Gate Disposal) formed an organization called the California Refuse Removal Council. It had its first meeting in June 1962 in Reno, Nevada, headed by Benny Caramela, then president of Reno Disposal Company.

As an aside, Rudy Vacarezza, who left Sunset Scavenger to develop a business in Lodi, California and was an up-and-coming leader, suggested to the newly formed association that we use the term *refuse collector* instead of *scavenger* as well as change the word *garbage* to *trash*. He emphasized that he was not ashamed of the work he did, but wanted to put a better image on the industry as a whole. I, for one, agreed with him.

Initially, the concept was solely to set up communication among the refuse companies and have them meet one another to work out common problems. But after several meetings and some research, it was concluded that private industry provided 95 percent of the waste collection services in Northern California, from the Oregon border to Fresno, with the balance provided by municipalities, including Berkeley, Palo Alto, and Fresno. From 1962 to 1965, we urged all these private companies to join the California Refuse Removal Council. After I became president in 1965, Sunset Scavenger joined the ranks of the California Refuse Removal Council at the urging of Benny Anselmo.

Between 1965 and 1968, two publicly traded companies entered the field of solid-waste management. One was Waste Management Incorporated, founded by Dean Buntrock, president of a company called Ace Scavenger Company in Chicago. Waste Management merged with several others in Florida and took the company public, raising not only working capital but also shares of stock to acquire a number of operating companies around the nation. The other company was Browning-Ferris Industries (BFI), a small, publicly held equipment rental company purchased by two Dallas entrepreneurs: Tom Fatjo (a CPA) and Norman Myers (an insurance agent). They issued a secondary offering with public money and started buying garbage companies throughout the United States. Many privately held companies in California watched these actions closely, but most were reluctant to consider selling their companies by taking "paper" (stock) in lieu of cash, especially those in Northern California.

These companies contacted me, of course, as well as Oakland Scavenger, Golden Gate Disposal, and others in the Bay Area, offering to purchase each one of them and add it to their growing list of acquisitions. Sunset Scavenger, Golden Gate Disposal, and Oakland Scavenger were ideal candidates for acquisition, but the offers did not make selling attractive enough to shareholders.

I knew the presidents of Oakland Scavenger and Golden Gate Disposal on a first-name basis, and we had serious concerns about these large Texas companies entering the Northern California market. We knew that sooner or later one of them would creep onto our turf whether we liked it or not. The first actual companies to come up for sale were San Jose Scavenger Company and Garden City Disposal; they were offered as a single package.

In 1959, Paul Madsen Sr. had formed Garden City Disposal Company with no prior experience in the garbage disposal business. He bid on the City of San Jose's contract to collect garbage and won against the San Jose Scavenger Company, which had held the contract since 1926.

As time went by, Paul Madsen lost money and was on the

verge of bankruptcy due to his lack of knowledge about the solid-waste industry. Madsen demonstrated some business sense when he proposed to subcontract half of the city's waste collection back to San Jose Scavenger Company using Highway 101 as the dividing boundary.

This arrangement initially benefited everyone. Garden City Disposal held the primary contract and collected half of the city's garbage; San Jose Scavengers collected the other half. Both companies dumped the refuse at Newby Island Landfill, a site developed and is still owned by the San Jose Scavenger Company.

But by the late 1960s, the operators of these companies were getting older and mutually agreed to put the entire package on the market for sale.

They contacted me, thinking that Sunset Scavenger Company might be interested in the deal; but I knew that Sunset Scavenger didn't have the resources to purchase a landfill and a company grossing close to $40 million a year. Most garbage disposal companies in Northern California were worried about the intrusion of publicly held companies into their markets. To fend off the competition, I contacted Oakland Scavenger, Golden Gate Disposal, and the San Mateo Scavenger Company and proposed forming a joint venture to purchase Garden City Disposal, San Jose Scavenger, and Newby Island Landfill.

I was a personal friend of Norman Myers, the vice president of Browning-Ferris Industries, and he knew of our intentions to purchase the three San Jose entities. He made no secret of BFI's efforts to purchase the San Jose operations as well. In 1972, after I'd held several meetings with Oakland Scavenger, Golden Gate Disposal, and the San Mateo Scavengers, we agreed on a final proposal. Meanwhile, Browning-Ferris was also preparing an offer. The San Jose companies informed us that they would announce their decision sometime before Christmas Eve.

In the interim, I had a cocktail at Bertolucci's restaurant in South San Francisco with Norman Myers. We toasted to whoever won the offer and got the prize. Several days later, we heard that the San Jose companies had accepted Browning-Ferris's offer. We felt that we had made a sincere effort to succeed but failed and left it at that. This was our first introduction to the big leagues. The big public companies were now in our backyard, and we had to deal with them, for better or worse. A whole new chapter in our company's life was about to begin.

Never Trust Anyone But Yourself

The intrusion of major publicly held companies into the Northern California market caused us some concern, even though we had friendly one-on-one relationships with the principals of the companies. The newcomers posed a threat to the companies that had been doing business in the Bay Area and Northern California for more than fifty years. We were afraid that if they could not buy us, they would actively become our competitors.

The president of San Mateo Scavenger Company was Valentino "Val" Arata, an old-time respected gentleman. His son-in-law, Louis Devencenzi, was vice president and secretary. San Mateo Scavenger Company was similar to Sunset Scavengers in that both had equal partners who were all paid the same. San Mateo had only fifty-two partners but had the garbage collection franchises of virtually all of San Mateo County, except San Bruno, South San Francisco, and Daly City, which were still held in private hands. It wasn't until I joined the California Refuse Removal Council and began to meet people and create personal relationships there that I found out Sunset Scavenger Company's former management had always thought they were superior to the other garbage companies, especially those in San Mateo County.

In my early years as president, Val Arata, John Spino, and other old scavengers often told me, "Tu parli troppo"—you talk too much—when I was on television, in newspapers, and on the radio over the Sierra Point landfill controversy. They practiced the old ways of doing business: Keep everything quiet; don't talk about your business in public. Contrary to tradition, I was blowing smoke.

Regardless of these disagreements, we were great golfing buddies and friends. We drank, played golf at the Peninsula Golf Club (where Val did not hesitate to brag that his membership ID was #1), and attended functions together. We were good friends. So we included San Mateo Scavenger Company when we bid on the San Jose contract in the hope of purchasing it and keeping Browning-Ferris out of the area.

In 1971, while we were waiting to tee off and reminiscing about Browning-Ferris Industries entering the market, I asked those who had moved to the Northern California area how they would react to a BFI proposal to purchase their company. They replied with no hesitation. No way would they sell their company under any circumstances. They added that BFI couldn't afford it.

Later the next year, San Mateo Scavenger Company joined our team largely to increase our chances of acquiring the San Jose companies. About three months after we had submitted the proposal, the San Jose entities rejected it. My board member, John Armanini (whose brother was a partner at San Mateo Scavenger), came into my office and told me that his brother had heard rumors—San Mateo Scavenger was in the process of being sold to Browning-Ferris Industries.

I couldn't believe what I was hearing, so I called Louis Devencenzi.

After some pressing, he admitted, "Yes, the company is in the process of being sold to Browning-Ferris Industries."

I couldn't contain myself. "How in the f--k could you sit in confidential meetings, preparing a multimillion-dollar deal against Browning-Ferris Industries' bid to purchase the San Jose operations, with the knowledge that you were in the process of selling your company to them?"

Devencenzi vehemently denied any knowledge of the sale of the company prior to submitting that bid in December of the previous year. He insisted that the deal was cut in thirty days, starting on March 1, sixty days after we had submitted the proposal to San Jose. He also said he never traded any secrets or confidential information to Browning-Ferris prior to the bid opening.

I didn't hesitate to tell him that he was spewing absolute bullshit.

There was no way that he could have put that deal together within thirty days, especially with fifty-two Italians. Clearly, he was lying through his teeth, and he knew that I knew it, but it was too late to change anything. The deal was done. All that remained was a lesson for me: You can somewhat trust a person you're doing business with, but keep everything to yourself because you're the only one you can really trust in this life.

As time went by, I learned that Browning-Ferris Industries was still attempting to stay on my good side. They even flew me to Houston in their corporate jet to meet their president, Harry Phillips. Then they offered me the title of vice president of market development, Western Region, with a starting wage of $125,000 plus incentives. That was three times what I was making as president of Sunset Scavenger Company. Definitely a tempting offer but, as stupid as it may sound to the reader, I had a moral commitment to my shareholders. I rejected the offer.

While I was there, though, I asked Phillips how they justified paying $17 million for San Mateo Scavenger Company, which grossed only $20 million a year. Turns out it was a real bargain because, in addition to the operating company and the real estate, BFI purchased Ox Mountain Landfill, which is a permitted, high-capacity, regional landfill tucked away in the San Mateo County mountains. They paid for the San Mateo Scavenger Company with BFI common stock; no cash was involved.

Browning-Ferris issued some 520,000 BFI shares, valued at $32 per share. Each of the fifty-two shareholders of the San Mateo Scavenger Company received approximately 10,000 shares. At the time the deal was consummated, each of the fifty-two participants and San Mateo Scavengers shareholders received roughly $320,000. On the surface, this appeared to be a wonderful opportunity for the fifty-two shareholders because, prior to the deal, their shares in San Mateo Scavenger Company were valued in the area of $50,000.

They should have known there would be strings attached.

The first condition on the deal allowed each man to keep the job that he was doing before, but his salary would be reduced by $10,000 a year. Even though the company's profits at the time fell by about 5 percent (about $750,000 a year), the company actually increased its earnings by cutting the salaries of the shareholders by $10,000 each. The company's earnings rose to $1.3 million a year.

BFI not only received the properties, a fully permitted high-capacity landfill, and a company with a long-term franchise, but it also increased earnings to a projected $1.3 million a year by slashing the wages of the fifty-five shareholders.

Compared to the overall earnings of Browning-Ferris Industries at the time, the San Mateo Scavenger Company generated per-share earnings that were more than twice those of the parent company. Between the properties, equipment, landfill, and the per-share earnings, I was forced to agree that BFI had made an excellent deal.

The fifty-two selling shareholders also appeared to have made a good deal since the investment they had in San Mateo Scavenger Company at $50,000 was now valued at $320,000, an increase of almost 500 percent, assuming the selling shareholder could convert those 10,000 shares into hard cash by selling them to his stockbroker.

As is typical in transactions of this magnitude, the purchasing entity usually restricts number of shares allowed to be put up for sale. One reason for these restrictions is that placing 520,000 shares on the market all at the same time could dump the traded stock price. Therefore, the senior management was required to maintain its shares for a period of one year, whereas the working shareholders were restricted to liquidating only up to 10 percent of their equity the first year.

In the two years prior to that transaction, the BFI stock rose an average of 5 percent a year. It was suggested that the selling partners could expect the same growth. Translated into dollars, the $320,000 in BFI stock could increase by $15,000 in a year's time. But a year later, BFI stock had dropped from $31 a share at the time of the sale to a low of $12 a share. This meant that the $320,000 that each shareholder received dropped to less than $112,000 in a year. As a result, BFI had a black eye of sorts, and most companies showed little interest (if any) in a stock purchase of any solid-waste company in Northern California.

On the other hand, those who held onto the original shares of Browning-Ferris stock for twenty years would be much richer. BFI no longer exists and now operates under the umbrella of Republic Services Incorporated, but the original 10,000 shares of stock from that 1972 sale would be worth more than $1.5 million today.

This situation clearly exemplifies the unpredictability and uncertainty of the public market's new fast bucks and suggests that people should hold out for the long haul. However, sometimes things really work out well for people who take a chance and have the guts, patience, and deep pockets to sustain a down market.

19

Addressing the 1968 Civil Rights Act

Among the many significant problems the company faced after I became president (in what seemed to be a never-ending series of controversies) was the requirement of completing and filing the federal reporting of each employee based on gender and ethnicity.

In 1969, I personally completed the initial filing of the form of the 1968 Civil Rights Act, realizing that our workforce was nowhere near the so-called "quota" when it came to racial balance according to federal guidelines for minorities, especially African American employees. I concluded that we might be in deep trouble with the federal government, especially since we held many contracts with federal, state, and local governmental agencies.

Nonetheless, I filled out various categories in the following manner, based upon the standard form submitted for completion. In the questionnaire, we were asked for our total number of employees. Then the survey asked that our employees be broken down into the following categories: Female, Hispanic, African American, Asian, American Indian, Others. As I recall, I responded in the following manner:

Female	17
Hispanic	72
African American	8
Asian	0
American Indian	2
Others	324
TOTAL EMPLOYEES	423

I signed the document early in 1969 and mailed it to the appropriate governmental office. In September, I received a call from Jonathan Anderson, representing the federal government's Office of Equal Employment Opportunity (EEO), to schedule a meeting with him to review the document that I had signed and verify the information provided.

Mr. Anderson showed up promptly at my office at ten in the

morning as scheduled. He was obviously a well-educated and elo-quent black gentleman, about forty-five years of age. After the for-malities and introduction, he brought up my signed document and proceeded to ask questions to clarify what I had recorded.

He went through each category that I had listed. I explained that all female employees worked in administration because of the physical demands of collecting garbage. To my surprise, Anderson did not ask about the fact that we only had eight African Ameri-cans. He was more interested in what the "others" were.

I didn't blink an eye. "Italians."

He seemed somewhat uncomfortable—maybe even embar-rassed. I actually saw him blush somewhat when he responded, "Well, Mr. Stefanelli, according to the 1968 EEO guidelines defining minorities, Italians are not considered minorities as compared to Mexican Americans, African Americans, Asians, et cetera."

I responded, "When this company was created, it was the result of gross discrimination against Italians. They could not get jobs at the turn of the century because Irish and other English-speaking immigrants were given all labor-orientated jobs within the city. The Italians had no place to go to earn a living but to pick up garbage." I added, "For that matter, just the other day some irate customer called me a dirty wop—and if that's not discrimi-nation, then I don't know what being a minority is."

Try as I may, my argument did not go far. But as a result, I de-veloped a respectful working relationship with the inspector over the years. He knew that the company was nowhere near the stan-dards set forth by the EEO, but he also recognized and respected the long Italian history of the company and, at the same time, ac-knowledged that we were making sincere efforts to mitigate that problem of having limited minorities employed by the company.

As hard as it was for me to believe, Mr. Anderson gave Sunset Scavenger Company a clean bill of health, indicating that we were conforming to the federal EEO guidelines, even though we clearly weren't at the time.

I guess my honest and straightforward response made sense, but he also solicited an unofficial commitment from me to do better at hiring more black employees without discriminating against cur-rent employees—a promise that I would keep.

I shared with Anderson conversations that I'd had with the black leaders in the community over this specific issue of hiring blacks to work in the garbage industry. The fact was that good workers from the black community did not want "to haul trash." I showed Mr. Anderson where we tried on many occasions to hire kids from Hunters Point to work with the regular scavengers. They refused the offer. I later realized, though, that the company did discriminate, and this became one of the issues I worked to change.

I had worked on a truck for eight years with Booker T. Day, one of the eight black workers we had. Like the other seven, he had been with us for a great number of years, and I could personally attest to the fact that he was an excellent employee. Booker proved to be an invaluable resource for me, teaching and sharing the black community side of life, including culture, philosophies, concerns, and more. As he was schooling me in this manner on a daily basis (unknown to me at the time), it was an experience that very few so-called white people had access to. Booker Day turned out to be another great mentor in my young life. When Day passed away at sixty years of age, I was the only white man present at his funeral.

I also shared with Mr. Anderson the fact that third-generation Italians no longer wanted to be in the garbage business because of the job's heavy labor demand. Add to this the fact that they were educated and could find work other than garbage collection. As a result—just like the Italians that came to the United States at the turn of the century—another ethnic workforce was clearly coming from south of the border, people who worked with their hands and were not afraid of hard physical labor. In my opinion, this was the future of the solid-waste business, at least in California.

For the next six years, Mr. Anderson came every November, and he was more than pleased with our hiring practices, which increased the ranks of blacks and other minorities, getting ever closer to the standard set forth by the federal government. I am pleased that I was able to build up a strong relationship with him for the ultimate benefit of the company.

Of all the problems facing the company, I believe we had slowly addressed and resolved the minorities issue. Sunset Scavenger had embarked on a program to purchase, at fair market value, shares that became available from retiring shareholders. But people were not retiring, so we had no shares available to sell to anyone, regardless of ethnic background. Given the circumstances, there were no grounds for a potential discrimination lawsuit.

However, at Golden Gate Disposal, black employees were concerned that they were not offered shares or the ability to become Boss Scavengers and shareholders in the company. Golden Gate Disposal *did* have shares for sale and *did* in fact discriminate against blacks by selling shares to Mexican Americans who had less seniority in the company than black employees. As a result, black employees filed a racial discrimination suit against Golden Gate Disposal in 1970, alleging racial discrimination in the sale, purchase, and transfer of shares within the company.

About six months after the initial lawsuit was filed against Golden Gate, we were convinced that no one from our company would file a similar suit. But the plaintiffs of the Golden Gate Disposal case convinced one black employee in our company to join them in a class-action suit. Sunset Scavenger, Golden Gate Disposal, and the Teamsters Union Local 350 Sanitary Truck Drivers and Helpers became the defendants.

Golden Gate clearly had a problem, because the suit included close to seventeen employees, whereas the suit against our company included only one individual for a total class of eighteen. It was impossible to settle with our employee and not the others because a class action had been approved against all three entities and—whether we liked it or not—Sunset was involved.

Keep in mind that this was a $7.5 million lawsuit. Clearly, we, especially Golden Gate, were guilty of racial discrimination, pure and simple. There was no way to get around it. Not only was this a lot of money for the companies, but a guilty judgment would have terminated all our governmental contracts. In comparison to that, a $7.5 million settlement would look like a bargain.

We decided to take an aggressive and proactive approach because of the potential of negative publicity and the possible loss of business. We settled out of court for $650,000. This may sound like a lot of money, but it really wasn't considering what it could have cost us if we had gone to court. We had no defense against the huge racial imbalance of whites versus blacks within the corporate structures, even though we were in the process of correcting that disparity.

The settlement was paid as follows: the union picked up $50,000; Golden Gate and Sunset Scavenger each paid $300,000 divided into three annual payments, into special trust funds for the plaintiffs.

Sunset filed a claim with its insurance carrier (this was suggested by our agent) and collected $200,000 from the insurance company. We wrote off the balance of $100,000 as deferred wages. Aside from attorney's fees, we paid only $100,000 and had no on-going liability for racial discrimination. I worked with our attorneys on the settlement, and I now see this as one of my greatest achievements during my tenure with Sunset Scavenger Company.

Some years later, the same group that sued us filed a racial discrimination suit against the Oakland Scavenger Company on the same grounds: The company was accused of both not selling shares to minorities and having discriminating hiring practices. I have mentioned Peter Borghero, president of the Oakland Scavenger Company, throughout this book. He was a friend and colleague, but he also had the reputation of being a *testa dura* (hard head). The lawsuit against the Oakland Scavenger Company for racial discrimination in 1970 asked for $15 million—double what they had sued us for before, and the whole burden was to fall upon 140 shareholders of the Oakland Scavenger Company.

When I heard on TV that Pete Borghero and his company were being sued, I contacted him and advised him to settle the lawsuit before it got out of hand.

His response surprised even me: "No f---ing n----r is going to tell me what I can or cannot do!"

"How can you talk like that?" I said. "Peter, you have no ground to stand on. Your own records show that your company has discriminated against blacks, Hispanics, et cetera. Whatever your policy has been in recent years, at one time you or your company discriminated even against other Italians with the policy of selling shares *only* to Genoveses. Only in recent years did you allow one or two Toscanos, and five years ago, a Sicilian. So how can you claim that you don't discriminate against anyone?"

In 1988, the lawsuit was still pending. By that time, I had left Sunset Scavenger Company and been hired by Waste Management Inc. and was responsible for working out a deal to acquire Oakland Scavenger Company. A part of the purchase agreement included Waste Management's participation in any settlement in this $10 million lawsuit. As an incentive for Oakland Scavenger to sell, Waste Management agreed to pick up the first $2 million of any settlement or award in this discrimination suit.

The end result was that the court awarded the plaintiffs $10 million for discrimination. Waste Management did pick up the first $2 million, but the 142 Oakland Scavenger Company shareholders had to pay the balance of $8 million.

20

Seeking the Proverbial Black Box for Waste Disposal

Houston and New Orleans

My infamous speech at the California Academy of Sciences in 1966, with the now especially infamous commentary—"Madam, until you have had the joy of inhaling a fly, live maggots crawling down your neck, and warm watermelon juice drizzling down the crack of your ass. . ."—gave me the confidence to speak in public, especially because I certainly knew my subject. In time, I became known as a leader in the newfound and complicated field that began to be called *solid waste*.

My colleagues and I decided that it would be to our advantage to take time to look at facilities in other places, evaluate them, and possibly learn from them as we did when we built the transfer station for San Francisco. That transfer station worked perfectly from day one because we inspected other facilities before building it. By observing what other people did—both errors and successes—we learned.

Through the auspices of the California Refuse Removal Council (CRRC), which I joined in 1966, we started to meet others in our industry. Because of the informal relationship between companies, we created a special bond among the garbage men, scavengers, and other waste haulers—the only real experts in the solid-waste management industry in Northern California. I started to learn more about the multitude of the alleged, proverbial black boxes, the answers to garbage disposal. I planned trips to Houston and New Orleans for a group of garbage men and politicians.

In Houston, there was a "God's Way" operation (composting garbage and putting it back into the earth) that was somewhat primitive although ecologically sound. Browning-Ferris Industries had purchased a composting operation that allegedly took municipal solid waste and converted it into usable compost and fertilizer. Our inspection of this system, especially by those who knew the industry well, found that the operation's end product, as fertilizer, was negligible at best—and clearly no solution to a large city's disposal needs.

Then Westinghouse Corporation, a big name in the corporate world, spent several million dollars developing a system to convert municipal solid waste (MSW) into compost. Westinghouse's touted process consisted of a huge six-story digester with an engineered moisture and temperature-enclosed environment.[4] From the digester, the MSW was thrown into a grinder to open all the bags and run the ground waste through a magnetic field to extract ferrous metals. Westinghouse planned to use St. Petersburg, Florida as an example.

What is common knowledge today—but only a few knew then—is that to make a viable compost byproduct, you need high percentages of two components: food waste (bugs) and biodegradable material such as paper and green waste (and no plastics, glass, etc.).

The waste stream in St. Petersburg was less than 6 percent food waste and had an equally low percentage of biodegradable materials. The system also lacked an efficient front-end separation to recover materials not compatible with the compost process. While the system was a rather innovative concept, practically speaking it was seriously flawed. The methods used were too primitive for anything other than introducing the waste stream to a grinder, breaking up the bags of waste, extracting ferrous metals, and homogenizing the material.

Far from producing the envisioned fertilizer, the new system created nothing more than a land "enhancer," of which the primary and only value was to allow sandy soils to retain moisture.

Westinghouse was undaunted and promoted their byproduct as a "soil enhancer," which they used in cattle grazing areas. The livestock consumed the lush grasses, which grew as a result of the soil conditioner's ability to retain water in the normally sandy soil. However, as the cows pulled at the grass they ingested the root system as well.

As time went by, the cattle became ill. We learned later that the livestock were suffering internal bleeding. The grass's root system was infused with glass particles generated from the initial grinding process when residential solid waste was introduced to the composting process.

---

4. A digester is a means to accelerate the normal decomposition of biodegradable materials, such as paper, leaves, and grass. This decomposition is a normal process in the forest, but in placing this material into a "digester" with putrescible waste, constantly moving it, and interjecting air in a confined environment, it is possible to accelerate the process, and that is what Westinghouse attempted to do.

The cows died—not exactly a glowing endorsement for this new method of converting garbage into compost.

The plant was closed down permanently. Westinghouse, the great American name in industry, got out of the garbage/solid-waste business as quickly as it came into it. Like so many big-name companies, they had charged into the unknown and complex field of "garbage," assuming that it was a simple problem to solve.

From Houston, we went to New Orleans to look at a waste-to-energy plant in Jefferson Parish. Refuse right out of the truck was dumped into a mass-burning furnace. There was no energy recovery and surely no air quality control equipment, as evidenced by the dark smoke plume, which was illuminated at night by sparks shooting up into the muddied sky. This was clearly not a solution to San Francisco's long-term solid-waste disposal needs.

The problem was further compounded by the fact that the New Orleans system burned only residential waste, making it unfeasible for San Francisco, where only 60 percent of waste was classified as residential. The remainder was commercial and industrial waste—hardly compatible with the New Orleans system. Industrial waste could hold hazardous and possibly flammable or, worse yet, explosive materials. To effectively deal with San Francisco's waste, it was obvious that we needed to create a highly sophisticated front-end processing system before adopting any alternative to the landfill.

From New Orleans we flew to White Plains, New York to inspect another mass-burning facility which, like the one in New Orleans, had little if any air quality control equipment on site. The black, noxious fumes that resulted would never have been acceptable in California from aesthetic and environmental points of view.

The trip proved to be an extraordinarily good experience because we learned that the technology purported to be advanced was not necessarily a solution for San Francisco. Another trip to Germany followed in 1968 to inspect waste-to-energy plants in East and West Berlin, Düsseldorf, and Munich. I was elected again to lead our group to Germany to study what was, at the time, the most advanced waste-to-energy system in the world.

Our group included the president of the board of supervisors, the chief administrative officer and director of public works for the City of San Francisco, the president of Pacific Gas & Electric Company, the president of the San Francisco Chamber of

Commerce, and representatives from the solid-waste industry in northern California.

Germany

Our first stop was West Berlin, where the city operated a large, mass-burning waste incinerator that processed waste from East Berlin as well. We Americans were really interested in the relationship between the two cities since, at the time, their respective ideologies—communism and capitalism—clashed.

Yet despite the Wall that separated them, the West Berlin Waste Incinerator was shared with East Berlin. The ash residue from the combustion process was disposed of in East Berlin. Even though the two governments were miles apart politically, they agreed that they had a common problem, and they worked together to resolve it. This was an interesting relationship, and few people in the world were aware of it.

From there we went to Düsseldorf.

Düsseldorf had a huge waste-to-energy plant that had in place all the equipment necessary for maintaining good air quality. While there was nothing new in the preprocessing, they also accepted only a residential (predictable) waste stream, like the New Orleans plant.

As a bit of interesting trivia, Düsseldorf's topography is flat, but off to the side, there is a large landscaped hill of sorts. It was brought to our attention that Düsseldorf was where all the ball bearings were made for the military during World War II. It had been a major target for US bombers and was almost blasted out of existence. When the war ended and Düsseldorf was being rebuilt, the debris caused by the bombing was collected and piled, resulting in the huge section of high ground next to the city. This may be one of the biggest landfills in Germany.

Also interesting was that, by our 1968 visit, the major German cities had state-of-the-art waste-to-energy systems, but the smaller communities still had open burning dumps in operation. Germany exemplified both extremes of waste treatment, but open incineration was clearly unacceptable in California.

The highlight of the trip was a 2,000-ton-per-day waste-to-energy plant built right next to a major residential area in the City of Munich. The plant managers explained how the facility operated using an advanced, German-designed Von Roll internal fire grate system, resulting in a 90 percent volume reduction while generating substantial amounts of steam for energy development. The system also incorporated state-of-the-art electrostatic precipitators that recovered fly ash and microscopic matter—in laymen's terms, "smoke"—resulting in virtually no visible pollution.

The facility also incorporated an advanced method to maintain a constant internal temperature of 1,600 degrees Fahrenheit during the entire combustion process. Such an extreme temperature neutralized the toxic dioxins and maximized air quality.

However, as we inspected the system, we discovered that this facility could only process residential waste, the same as previous sites we'd toured. If we were to adopt this particular model, we would need a front-end processing system to eliminate potentially dangerous materials from entering the combustion system.

During our visit to this facility, we were very impressed with its cleanliness and efficiency. On top of that, the residents living near the facility had no objections to the manner in which waste was processed at the site, clearly demonstrating that the plant was accepted by the community as a good neighbor.

One of our colleagues, Richard Granzella, president of Richmond Sanitary Services, commented to the general manager, "You have one hell of a garbage-disposal facility here."

The man dryly responded, "Sir, this is not a garbage-disposal facility. It's a power station that uses two sources of energy to create electrical power, namely refuse and coal. Because we look upon refuse as a secondary source of energy, we solve a secondary problem, which is refuse disposal."

That was an accurate reflection of how Germany relates to solid waste in general. This was a valuable learning experience for all of us, and their system promised to be a viable option for the scavengers/City of San Francisco to consider as a long-term waste disposal solution.

Japan

The Tyszuka firm in Japan had claimed since 1966 that it possessed the means of solving the world's waste disposal problems by baling refuse, coating it with cement, and building houses out of the resulting blocks. Here was another black box idea that many environmentalists believed in.

In 1970, the Japanese were still proposing this flimflam system.

Sometime in 1969, Mr. Tyszuka, the promoter of this system, took a picture of himself on the working face of our garbage landfill at Sierra Point. He used the photo in his brochure, which stated that garbage, unlike Adam and Eve, "needed to be clothed."

In 1970, the world's fair was set in Suita, Osaka, and we rode the bullet train to the fair. Prior to that trip, we passed through the factory, where this magic garbage press was in operation, so we scheduled a visit to "Dream Island."

When we arrived at the facility, we watched a 16mm film showing how the system was designed and how it worked. The impressive video featured London Philharmonic music, and I'm sure every environmentalist in the world who saw the video was convinced that the Tyszuka method was a cure-all.

After the presentation, we went out to the facility and observed the actual operation. The results were unbelievably ugly to say the least. To begin with, the composition of Japanese waste is 90 percent putrescible (wet garbage); no matter how much you compact it, this type of waste will not "weld" and hold together unless it has some form of membrane.

Japan's waste stream in 1968 lacked solidity because, before the collection truck arrived, someone scavenged every can of garbage, taking out bottles, metals, wood, and whatever might have value. What was left was smelly and wet material to be processed by the Tyszuka Press.

The garbage truck picked up the remaining garbage and dumped its load on a cement floor inside a building. A small tractor shoved the smelly load into a slanted pit, where a conveyor carried the raw material into a trench and fed it into a form lined with chicken wire. Then the material flowed into a three-foot-square shaft, about six feet deep, which was essentially a kind of caisson (a watertight structure).

When the three-foot-square shaft was topped off, a vertical hydraulic ram compressed the garbage under high pressure into a chicken-wired lining. Afterwards, the hydraulic ram and the three-foot-square steel caisson were withdrawn. Sitting there was the ugliest block of garbage anyone would ever see.

Then, what appeared to be an enlarged set of ice hooks was attached to a cable and picked up the waste baled in chicken wire. The bale was taken to an open, hot vat of tar and submerged for about thirty seconds; once tarred, it was taken outside to cool and stored on site. The bales were not encased in concrete.

Eventually I asked the logical question, "What do you do with the tarred bales?" They showed us that they filled rice paddies with the bales, covered them over with dirt, and reclaimed "valuable land" adjacent to the facility.

I asked, "If the goal is to reclaim rice paddies, why don't you just fill them with garbage and not go through the added expense of baling the waste?"

The answer was that by baling the garbage first, the company would be protecting the environment by not releasing contaminants into the water.

An inspection and the photos I took of the baled refuse confirmed that the bales were *not* sealed completely—anyone could see raw garbage peeking through the chicken wire.

The bales that were placed in the rice paddies showed leachate pouring out into the water, and the rice grown in the paddy near and around the bales showed severe stress.

When the refuse went through the compression process, it extruded a liquid so dirty and pungent that one of the garbage men facetiously referred to it as "V8 Juice." When I asked what they did with that liquid, they said it went through a comprehensive process to neutralize any contaminants. They showed me an aquarium with carp in it; the fish were used to determine the purity of the water on a continuing basis. Two of the pond's carp were floating belly up.

Remember the woman at the Academy of Sciences in 1966 who asked, why are we not baling our garbage in cement and building houses out of it? Clearly, I knew what I was talking about when I answered her.

During our trip to Japan we learned that, advanced as the Japanese were (cars, electronics, engineering, and so forth), they seemed to pay little attention to safe solid-waste collection or disposal.

While we were in Japan, we enjoyed the famous bullet train, truly an engineering marvel. Trains would rush along at 180 mph and run through stations at 120 mph while another train was stopped and loading passengers. The bullet train was so fast that the vacuum created in its wake made you feel like you could be sucked off the platform.

When Osaka was nominated as the city for the 1970 World's Fair (aka Expo '70), the public relations experts realized that millions of people visiting Japan would see and experience every phase of its civilized society—including its less than ideal waste-collection system.

Before the World's Fair, the people of Japan, especially in the big cities, had regularly scheduled waste-collection days. Residents and businesses would place their garbage (which, as noted, was 60 to 70 percent putrescible—wet food waste) in the gutter. When the garbage man (*gomi son*) came by, he used a shovel to pick up the garbage and threw it into an open truck. A water truck would follow, washing down the street. When the garbage truck was full, the garbage man would take it to the dump, which in Tokyo's case was "Dream Island."

The public relations people, whoever they were, evidently convinced the powers that be that Japan needed to clean up (pardon the pun) its waste-collection system. To do that, the government mandated that the population use a garbage can, a standard twenty-gallon yellow plastic container with a lid. This "advanced" form of waste collection and storage equipment was not used until 1969, prior to the opening of the World's Fair. The use of garbage cans eliminated the need to wash the streets on a weekly basis, thus preventing substantial water contamination and debris from going down the storm drains in the major cities.

Dream Island—clearly a misnomer—was an environmental nightmare. A series of pilings allowed water to move in and out of the so-called "island" of some 800 acres. The only protection to prevent floating debris from going into Tokyo Bay was a crude series of cyclone fences woven between the pilings. As the picture shows, the garbage was unceremoniously dumped into the salt-water and seldom covered with earth.

The stench was overwhelming because the saltwater and refuse were mixed together, which created hydrogen chloride gas. The water pollution was unbelievably bad, with leachate flowing freely into Tokyo Bay, especially at outgoing tides.

I thought about the mystique of the so-called black box and pondered what the environmentalists in San Francisco would say if they could see this environmental disaster. Other countries had better means of disposing of their wastes. There was nothing to learn, let alone adopt, here.

I wished the environmentalists could see this and realize what an excellent job the scavengers in San Francisco were doing at Sierra Point, a true sanitary landfill with no air, water, or land pollution. The only real environmental issue at Sierra Point was that we were filling San Francisco Bay. We had developed the transfer station, the landfill contract with Mountain View, and were starting to make long-range plans for the city's waste.

Ironically, people from around the world were now coming to San Francisco to learn from us, the "scavengers," how to handle their garbage.

Scandinavia and the Soviet Union

In spring 1972, a third trip was planned to visit Scandinavia. Stockholm, Sweden had developed an exotic waste-collection system using pneumatic means of transferring waste in a series of pipes brought to a centralized stationary compactor. In Copenhagen, Denmark, they had just created a 3,000-ton-per-day waste-to-energy project that was in full operation. In Oslo, Norway, a full-scale composting operation and a waste-to-energy system were under construction and could be in operation by mid-May, when we were scheduled to visit.

Just about that time, President Richard Nixon and Leonid Brezhnev signed an international treaty providing for technological exchanges between the United States and the Soviet Union, a step forward for international peace. I hadn't paid much attention to this development because it didn't involve our industry or me. That all very quickly changed when, sometime in February, I received a call from a man who introduced himself as the consulate general for the People's Republic of the Soviet Union.

The call made me somewhat skeptical. Why he would be calling me of all people?

He explained that he knew I was taking a group of politicians and solid-waste experts to the Scandinavian countries. Would I be interested in extending our tour and visiting the Soviet Union for further exchange of technologies?

I was convinced that someone was playing a joke. "Okay, knock off the bullshit. Who is this?"

"Mr. Stefanelli, I assure you that this invitation is legitimate and not 'bullshit,' to use your American term. I respectfully understand your apprehension; but if you are interested in coming, please provide me with the names, and I will work directly to provide the necessary travel information and hotels in the Soviet Union."

For the first time in my life I was embarrassed, but in my defense it *was* an extraordinary situation because the Soviet Union was off-limits to Americans unless they were in the diplomatic corps. No one had direct contact with Russians, and here I was speaking with the Russian consulate general in New York.

I sent notices to the members of our group, informing them of this change in plan. We were still going to Stockholm and Copenhagen, but Norway would be eliminated so that we could spend ten days in the Soviet Union, meeting with their experts and exchanging technologies.

The response by our group was overwhelming—the group of twenty grew to forty because of the "Russian connection." (I was limited as to how large a group I could bring and had to reduce the total.) By the time we left, April 26, I had a group of thirty-six, which included not only garbage men but also a few elected officials, including several high-end corporate executives that I believed could help the industry and a representative from ABC Radio/TV. I realized that this trip was a lifetime opportunity that could provide a public relations advantage for the looked-down-upon garbage/solid-waste industry.

Our group met at the San Francisco International Airport, flew to New York, and then on to Copenhagen. We had scheduled a four-day trip to inspect collection systems in the 2,000-ton-per-day waste-to-energy project. We also planned to take in a few days of rest and see some sights. I observed that Denmark at that time had quite liberal attitudes toward sex; this was clearly apparent from newspaper ads and books.

Next up was to inspect Copenhagen's uniform 2,500-ton-per-day waste-to-energy plant using German technology—the Von Roll Grate system. It was a clean, well-designed facility using traditional means of mass-burning technologies. As with some of the other waste-disposal processes, if San Francisco adopted a similar approach, it would have required a front-end processing method to prepare waste prior to the application of a Von Roll Grate system.

The primary reference source was from residential waste and did not include industrial commercial operations, which in most practices always had to include front-end preparation. The waste had to be processed before being introduced to the combustion chamber to eliminate or minimize the possibility of hazardous waste contamination.

By adopting this concept, we would maximize the recovery of materials that could be recycled and create a uniform and predictable fuel source, making it substantially easier to control or eliminate air pollution. While considering adoption of this process, I was reminded of the comment made by the Munich engineer who considered "refuse" to be a secondary source of energy. By incorporating a front-end process, we would use the entire waste stream and create what the industry refers to as RDF or refuse derived fuel.

Next up was Stockholm, where we toured and inspected a 1,500-ton-a-day waste-to-energy project that basically used the same mass-burning technology that we had inspected in Copenhagen: boilers with waste used as a fuel for steam-generated electric power. The same air quality standards were applied but to a lesser degree than we observed in Copenhagen.

We also noticed a new pneumatic waste collection system that was unique in many ways. Unfortunately, it was applicable only to new construction such as large condominium developments.

There were two requirements for making such a system function efficiently. One was the use of a single, uniform paper bag. All tenants in these large complexes were issued a supply of standard-form, round garbage bags with sealed tops. Each tenant filled a garbage bag, sealed it, and took it to a station inside the building. The station had a specially designed receptacle with a two-phased system to accept the bag. The primary charging hopper had a button that opened on contact. The tenant would place the bag on the hopper and push the button to close and seal the bag. When the door closed, another internal sliding door opened, and the bag was exposed to a constant negative pressure (vacuum). The bag of waste was transported by air to a stationary compactor. When the compactor was full, it was picked up.

This was an exciting next-generation waste-collection system, but it could be utilized only for new construction; the cost was prohibitive to try to make it work for older apartment complexes.

Then there was the inevitable "human" factor, where someone might not use the custom bag, instead dumping the refuse in a different bag—or no bag at all. Or perhaps a person would create a major problem by dropping a broom handle down the chute (a fact of life that the experienced scavenger is acutely aware of).

The night before our departure from Stockholm for the Soviet Union, our passports, visas, and so forth were checked and verified by a representative of the Soviet Union, and we were provided an instruction booklet of "do's and don'ts" concerning what we could take with us into the country. The list of do's and don'ts didn't exactly inspire confidence.

No sexually explicit materials could be brought into the Soviet Union. Cameras were to be kept in suitcases—with no exception. No photography was permitted while flying above or within Soviet territory. You couldn't even take a picture as you approached the airplane.

That night I called my wife in the United States to talk with her about our upcoming trip. At the time, placing a call to the United States took approximately three hours on the international telephone system. While we all felt apprehensive about our next destination, we were also excited about being allowed behind the "Iron Curtain."

According to the pre-established itinerary, we were to fly from Stockholm to Leningrad via Swiss Air, and then we would be taken to our hotel. The following day we would meet with Soviet experts in solid waste.

Prior to our departure from Stockholm, we were instructed to be in the lobby of the hotel at 6 AM to receive our boarding passes and visas. At the last minute, we learned that the Russians had forbidden the ABC reporter from entering the Soviet Union. Naturally, the reporter was stunned and outraged, but his pleas were ignored.

The barring of the reporter had a chilling effect on us all, and everybody became concerned about the restrictions and the unknowns that we were facing. Two security guards separated us from the ABC representative, and we boarded the bus, leaving him on the curb still ranting and raving. I learned later that he got home safely. We met him again when we returned home and gave him some press coverage about the trip he'd missed.

As we boarded the Swiss Air jet, the airline crew reminded us again of the rules and regulations, especially the one about no cameras being allowed outside of our luggage.

Four hours later we landed at the Leningrad airport. It was freezing outside. We did not get off the plane at a terminal, although there was one in sight. The plane parked on the tarmac. All other passengers were allowed to leave en masse, while our group was instructed to "stand by." Once the other passengers had deplaned, a small bus arrived, and we were permitted to leave the plane six at a time. They transferred us to the terminal, where we finally passed through customs.

As the leader of the group, I was among the first six to be interviewed and sent through customs. If there were any problems in the terminal, I wanted to be there to try to correct them.

Leo Conte, president of Golden Gate Disposal Company, was in the second group of six. The inspectors were going through his luggage, and the next thing I saw was a very nervous Leo Conte being escorted into a private room. Leo was a nervous person to begin with, and you should have seen the look on his face when the armed officer carted him away. I asked where he was going. The inspectors said they had to look into his suitcase and ask him some specific questions. About ten minutes later, Leo came out with his suitcase, waving his hands up and down.

"What happened?" I asked.

He said that he'd forgotten that he had a copy of *Playboy* magazine inside his suitcase, and the inspector had raised his eyebrows and said, "Come with me!"

They took Leo, his suitcase, and the *Playboy* magazine into a back room, where the inspector opened up the magazine and stared at Leo.

Leo said he was convinced that he was going to Siberia. Then the inspector mentioned that he had heard of this magazine but had never seen one. Leo immediately gave him the *Playboy*, and the agent walked him back to the group, to Leo's great relief.

We wondered what would have happened if we had brought in any of the magazines from Copenhagen, where free-sex magazines abounded. Thank God nobody did. Of course, a *Playboy* magazine in those days was mild compared to what is available today.

Even though we were warned against bringing pornography into the Soviet Union, it was quite apparent that Russian men had the same interest in the subject as American men. (You think?) It was obvious to me that the inspector had not seen *Playboy* because of the Iron Curtain. As we were to find, many of the things that we took for granted in America—toothpaste, soft drinks, fast elevators—did not exist in the Soviet Union in 1972.

Once we all cleared customs, our group of thirty-five (minus the ABC person) assumed we were on our way to the Leningrad hotel, as noted on our itinerary. Instead, they took us to a waste disposal site in Leningrad to meet with their experts. We were tired—and some of us had a bit of a hangover—and the last thing I personally wanted at that moment was a tour of garbage trucks.

Our bus drove into a large corporate yard. It was a Sunday and a fleet of various types of garbage trucks was on display, including snow-removal equipment. We had assumed that, even in Russia, Sunday was a day of rest, but to our surprise the entire labor force that manned this equipment was present to greet us. They were not dressed in their work clothes but in Sunday clothes, and some even wore ties. I was not just looking at dressed-up administrators but at the men and women who actually worked the trucks.

It was clear they wanted to be there, to show with pride their workplace and equipment. They had even gone so far as to paint the sidewall of the truck tires white. Unbelievable.

Their refuse collection equipment was astonishingly primitive. There was no standardization, and the machinery was obviously inefficient, but the workers and especially the management had what they assumed to be the best that the world's technology could offer.

Because of the Iron Curtain, they had nothing to compare their equipment with, so they no doubt concluded that they had the best equipment and working conditions—a conclusion that was to be challenged in the coming days.

It was a great and memorable experience for all of us. Through our interpreters, we were able to meet and communicate with colleagues in our business. Russian scavengers were excited and pleased to meet Americans.

After the impromptu and unscheduled visit to Leningrad's Public Works Facility, we were finally taken to our hotel, which was just as well. We were all very tired.

Our accommodations were at Leningrad's finest hotel, an eight-story structure overlooking a major waterway. Docked in front of our hotel was an old battleship, called the *Aurora*, from which, according to history, the officers and crew fired the first shot that was the beginning of the famous 1917 revolution, which brought communism into power in the Soviet Union.

The next day, we were scheduled to meet at a government building known as the International Friendship House, where our solid-waste experts, corporate executives, and politicians were to meet their Russian counterparts: non-elected bureaucrats, businessmen, and so forth.

As President Nixon's staff had directed me, I brought a series of slides showing our waste-collection equipment, transfer station, landfill operations, and resource recovery (recycling) operations. With some effort, I carted along a state-of-the-art Kodak 880 Carousel Projector with wide-angle lenses, automatic focus, and the capability of carrying 140 individual slides at one seating.

Since the Soviet Union was a major military power, everyone assumed that it would have an advanced waste collection and disposal system. Visiting and discussing advanced technologies with representatives of a country as big and powerful as the Soviet Union was supposed to be an outstanding learning opportunity, and we had been eagerly looking forward to observing their methods.

However, our unscheduled visit to the facilities in Leningrad rapidly tempered that vision of finding solutions for San Francisco in Russia. The antiquated method of waste collection that was put on display for us shattered our optimistic expectations. Russia's lack of modern technology was clearly evidenced, all the way down to its outdated projector, which required the slides to be hand-fed one at a time.

Unlike their American counterparts, Russians were accustomed to late cabs, busses, elevators, and the like. The men in charge of the projection booth took the better part of an hour examining our Kodak Carousel. They were awed by its advanced engineering in comparison to their primitive "one in and one out," hand-operated projector.

Once the review of our Kodak Carousel was completed, the slide presentation commenced with a group of about 100 people from all walks of business and political life in the Soviet Union. I started the show with a display of specialized waste-collection units, our modern waste-collection packer trucks, and the delivery of the waste to the world's largest, 2,500-ton-per-day, fully enclosed, San Francisco solid-waste transfer station. From there, the slides themselves and my personal commentary demonstrated the system's capability of transferring fifty-two tons of solid waste every six minutes into the huge, clean, solid-waste highway transfer vehicles, which hauled twenty-six-ton loads to the landfill, where the truck and trailer were raised on a portable lift mechanism.

The pictures of the portable lifting equipment were especially impressive because they showed how the entire truck and trailer were raised hydraulically and how—with gravity's help—the refuse fell to the ground. Slides depicting huge bulldozers pushing and compacting the waste followed. We showed the Russians how the garbage, or solid waste, which was originally a liability for San Francisco, was now being used to recover substandard land by the "cut and cover" method. The end result was a 900-acre regional park with a golf course, freshwater lakes, hiking trails, and recreational land—all built with garbage.

Observing their expressions and reactions, I was convinced more than ever that our Russian counterparts had never seen, let alone envisioned, waste equipment and disposal means of this magnitude. The audience was visibly overwhelmed by the advanced technology used in the United States—and specifically by the scavengers of Northern California—for collecting and disposing of waste.

As a result of my presentation, the Russian government abruptly canceled the scheduled tours of Leningrad's landfills and composting facilities. The images we showed at the International Friendship House clearly demonstrated that the waste-management collection and disposal methods practiced in California were far superior to anything available in the Soviet Union, especially in the major metropolitan areas.

A Russian official said that garbage delivered to landfills was fed to hogs, a practice that the United States ceased in the early 1940s. I dared not ask if the food was boiled prior to giving it to hogs. The United States had stopped feeding hogs raw refuse for fear of trichinosis and other diseases. Adding water or boiling the wet waste prior to feeding usually eliminated the possibility of trichinosis, but it also substantially reduced the nutritional value of the wet garbage being fed to the pigs.

The situation in the Soviet Union was horrendous. It was clear that the country offered nothing to the world about advanced collection waste-disposal systems. In fact, unless they learned from us, they would continue to be substandard in this field.

Another interesting observation was the actual composition

of Russia's waste stream and details about what ended up in the landfill. Russia's garbage could be estimated at 70 percent putrescible (wet garbage), compared to less than 7 percent in the United States, primarily due to our huge volume of packaging wastes and garbage disposal.

Because of Russia's high percentage of putrescible wastes, the country would have been great for a compost program, but there were no efforts by the governing bodies to require residents to separate their wastes for collection. Waste segregation would be necessary to integrate that portion of the waste stream with green waste or other biodegradable materials to create an ideal compost byproduct. In San Francisco, we had already commenced composting on a major scale.

To complicate the matter with the Soviet Union, most waste that ended up in the garbage can was biodegradable or recyclable. Soft drinks were not served in disposable cans and bottles. In Russia, people filled a container, drank from it, washed it by hand, and then used it again. In businesses, a worker simply rinsed a container in clear water, and filled it with the soft drink or beer requested by a customer. The customer would drink the contents and hand it back to the purveyor, who would rinse it and await the next customer.

At that time in Russia, milk, bread, vegetables, coffee, and other staples were sold fresh and in bulk; most consumers had their own containers. As a result, "packaging waste," as we call it in the United States, was practically nonexistent in Russia. The volume of garbage per capita in Russia was less than 50 percent of what the United States produced in 1972. According to a national study, the average American created an average of six pounds of waste per day while the average Russian produced less than three pounds per day. This difference demonstrated that US residents used substantially more "packaging and convenience" products. In other words, America had a higher standard of living, which my personal observations seemed to confirm as the days passed in the Soviet Union.

Our originally scheduled trips in Leningrad and Moscow were changed to tourist destinations. We never saw a packer garbage truck in Russia, other than one primitive and very small "advanced/experimental" truck, which one good scavenger in San Francisco could fill to capacity in less than fifteen minutes.

While no new waste solutions were learned from the Soviet Union, a year later a contingent of Russians came to the United States under a similar exchange program and with the same types of arrangements. What was really special was that the Russians specifically asked to see me at Sunset Scavenger Company, having remembered our presentation a year earlier in Leningrad.

Visiting Russia in 1972 was an extraordinary and memorable experience for our entire group, especially me personally. Being there and speaking with the people—especially at that time—was a rare and wonderful experience. Seeing Russia and meeting Russian citizens gave me a significantly higher respect for the country in which I lived and for the standard of living that we Americans take for granted.

The Soviet Union may have had advanced military, aircraft, submarines, space travel, electronics, and ever so much more, but it sure didn't know how to collect the garbage.

South America

In 1974, our group visited Rio de Janeiro and Sao Paulo in Brazil and Caracas in Venezuela. Each of these cities had purportedly implemented large-scale composting systems that took large volumes of solid waste and converted them to compost for land enhancement and higher agricultural productivity.

Composting is deemed by many environmentalists to be "God's Way" to handle solid waste. Other professionals and I know that this process can be feasible only if it has substantial bacteria to commence the process and is enhanced with prepared green wastes and other biodegradable materials, such as paper.

At that time, these countries used the Dano Composting Process, which was of Austrian origin and licensed to an American firm, to convert waste to compost. The process had limited success in the United States because of the advent of garbage disposals, which reduced the amount of putrescible (wet) waste that ended up in the garbage can. Wet garbage is a necessary component for successful composting. Consequently, the less putrescible waste found in residential garbage, the less the chances are of making a meaningful compost product. How ironic that, in an attempt to create a more convenient and cleaner environment in our homes by the installation of kitchen garbage disposals, we removed the material from the waste stream that was necessary to create a useable compost byproduct. As a result, the solids being disposed of in our already overloaded sewage treatment plants increased.

The Dano Process is a series of large metal cylinders that are approximately eleven feet in diameter and 125 feet long. Each cylinder is mounted on bearings on a five-degree slope. The prepared refuse (after glass, metals, and other non-biodegradable materials are removed) is run through a grinder of sorts in an attempt to merge it with the bacteria within the biodegradable mass and deposit it into the cylinders, which turn at fewer than four revolutions per hour. The interior of the cylinder is a closed environment, where constant moisture and temperature are maintained as a necessary condition for expediting the composting process, which typically takes ten days.

Inspections of these three South American facilities proved that the system functioned well but, in all three cases, the major composting facilities processed only a small fraction of the total waste generated in major cities. In addition, none of the facilities accepted commercial or industrial wastes. The balance of the residential waste not being composted was disposed of in the local waterways, with little to no concern for water pollution. What was not dumped into the water was lit on fire, compounding an environmental disaster.

The Dano Process used a raw product of garbage with a high percentage of putrescible waste (fruit, meats, and so forth), along with a front-end process that removed non-biodegradable materials prior to the composting process. All this made for a fine end product, but it was not economically feasible. In any composting operation in the world, and especially in California, two sources of revenue support the process: disposal charges and the sale of the product. If there is no product to sell—composting, for example—then there is no incentive to compost garbage.

Landfill operations in South America were so cheap and ugly that there was no economic incentive for anyone to bring garbage to the composting plants for disposal. At best, only 15 percent of the waste generated in cities was handled by these facilities, and the municipalities that owned them paid whatever it cost to operate them. There was no income from the sale of material recovered from the raw incoming refuse.

The South American cities we inspected had historically high yielding, rich soils, so there was no market for compost. Because there was no market for the byproduct and therefore no related infrastructure, it ended up in the dump, adding to the cost of disposal. At one time, the government in Sao Paulo mandated that all farmers who wanted to sell their goods had to go to the compost facility, pick up a load, and take it back to use at their farms. The result was that the farmers picked up the compost but dumped it on some road on the way back to their farms.

Last time I checked, all these facilities had been closed, and the cities are now trying to replace them with environmentally sound landfills instead of dumping their wastes in the waterways or lighting it on fire to the detriment of the natural world.

Australia and New Zealand

While composting solid waste makes theoretical sense, the process is—at best—only a partial solution to the world's waste-disposal needs.

The inspection trip Down Under provided no new means of solid-waste disposal. In both Australia and New Zealand, the primary means of disposal was sanitary landfill. One composting operation in Canberra used a variation on the Dano Process, but it was unable to keep the processed waste in a closed environment. As a result, the plant and equipment were infested with huge quantities of large maggots—clearly not conducive to aesthetics or health.

One unique landfill that we observed in Melbourne was the reuse of a huge rock quarry, some 300 feet deep. The city was using it for long-term landfill purposes and expected it to meet the city's needs for the next 200 years. The solid-rock interior prevented any leachate from contaminating groundwater. With an active methane gas recovery system, the landfill could meet the city's long-term disposal needs at an attractive cost and with no negative impact on the environment. As an added dividend, the system would restore the earth to its original topography.

Neatly summed up, there was nothing in these two countries that offered us a new or enhanced means of waste disposal, aside from a demonstration of the feasibility of back-filling large rock quarries with solid waste; but in our service areas, we did not have access to such sites without significant water pollution issues. It was clear that in most cities of the world the primary means of waste disposal was sanitary landfills. As we observed these varied operations, it clearly reaffirmed our belief that our industry, especially in San Francisco, was well ahead of the curve.

So, What about the Black Box?

What most people do not or refuse to understand and most die-hard environmentalists refuse to acknowledge is that garbage, or solid waste, is matter. Anyone with a PhD in physics will tell you that *matter cannot be destroyed*; it can only be converted, to wit:

A solid into a liquid
A liquid into a gas
A gas into a solid

And so on.

You will always have something that needs disposal, regardless of what process you may adopt—waste-to-energy, composting, pyrolysis, or even nuclear destruction—but currently, and in the foreseeable future, sanitary landfills are the *only* means of *total disposal*.

You can reduce your dependency on landfill by composting, recycling, or changing waste to energy, but you will still need a landfill to dispose of *something*.

For people to live in a healthful environment, waste has to be collected regularly. To maintain the collection schedule, you also need to empty the collection vehicle regularly. The only real guarantee of successful disposal is through sanitary landfills. Alternate methods of disposal will reduce the dependency on landfill, but you need to *get rid of today's garbage today*—contrary to the environmentalist philosophy. Sanitary landfills are the only real guarantee.

We traveled the world and inspected the best and worst waste disposal practices conceived by mankind. The proverbial black box does not exist. Because of the multifaceted composition of waste generated throughout the world, each community must customize its disposal solutions to meet its specific needs. One can learn from successes—and yes, from errors made by others—and make good decisions about how to formulate and implement a system of waste disposal.

21

A Good Proposal—Not Implemented in San Francisco

I am totally familiar with San Francisco's waste composition. I learned about it through in-depth personal contact with it during my fourteen years on the truck, by studying it in our yards, and by sending crews to hand-separate solid waste into nine categories so we could accurately determine the components through measuring and recording weights and percentages. I did this work not by computer analysis but by physically breaking down components from residential apartment houses, commercial construction debris, and the like.

In 1972, the City of Mountain View increased the royalty fee from thirty-two cents to two dollars a ton, attracting the attention of then San Francisco supervisor Dianne Feinstein, with whom I had worked personally in the development of the transfer station and other waste processes in San Francisco. Feinstein came to me claiming that it was outrageous that we had to pay all this money to the City of Mountain View, even though that city would provide us with a disposal program for at least ten years. While objecting to Mountain View's move, Feinstein urged us to find ways to generate energy from the waste stream.

The timing was perfect because the nation was in the throes of an energy crisis, so there was no better time to develop an alternate method of disposal, reduce dependency on landfill, recycle a portion of the waste stream, and generate electrical power. We could do this by developing a new predictable fuel source called refuse derived fuel (RDF).

Based on my personal experience and on the knowledge gained on trips to Western Europe, I knew that, with some front-end preparation, San Francisco's waste stream had the potential to generate electric power. Since this change would move us into a higher level of waste processing—far beyond the scope of our experience or knowledge—it was clear we needed to find someone who had the credentials necessary to create such a program.

After some research, we found Richard Cottrell, a graduate of MIT and former president of Aerojet General, Rocketdyne, in

Sacramento. Cottrell had experience converting biomass waste to energy projects and knew how to develop an RDF system. He clearly had the credentials necessary to develop this system for San Francisco, and he would complement our team in making the proposal.

We worked in conjunction with Pacific Gas & Electric Company, which agreed to purchase the power generated at six cents per kilowatt-hour for any waste generated from this potential project at forty-two megawatts, which would provide about 8 percent of San Francisco's electrical needs. Coupled with that commitment and the city's willingness to give us a twenty-year disposal contract based upon our already demonstrated experience, we were able to get more than $100 million to finance the project.

We already had control of the waste stream and a disposal rate in existence that was high enough to offset the funding and operational expenses to create this project.

So we made a proposal to the City of San Francisco, formally referred to as The San Francisco Resource Conversion Center. We proposed using the existing solid-waste transfer station as a starting point to receive waste. But instead of transferring the waste to the long-haul transportation trailers, we would use a front-end system of separation and recovery to process the waste into two categories: "heavy" (non-combustible) and "light" (combustible).

The heavy/non-combustible sections would be run through ferrous and nonferrous magnetic fields to extract metals, glass, dirt, concrete, and any materials that could not be recycled. This heavy material would be taken to a landfill for disposal. The light/combustible waste, representing about 70 percent of the total waste stream, would be sent to "rough grind" and through an "air cyclone," transforming the waste into a homogeneous mix, uniform in size and moisture balance.

By this point, the mixed light component would become a predictable source of energy, what the industry refers to as refuse derived fuel, similar to natural gas or coal.

By developing a uniform, consistent, and predictable fuel source, it would be comparatively easy for us to apply the appropriate technology to maintain air quality control and minimize air pollution.

With the proposed system, the City of San Francisco could produce 8 percent of its electrical needs from its own garbage while reducing the dependency on landfill by 90 percent and recycling as much waste as possible.

Everything was perfect. We had a site available in the City of Brisbane, existing truck traffic control in place, funding, and proven technologies formulated and designed to meet our specific needs and known waste compositions. Even the archenemies of our previous deal with Brisbane were in favor of the project. It promised annual revenue in excess of $3 million to a small-town community of 5,000 people in a city with a budget of only $4 million.

As noted, an added incentive at that particular time was the 1972 energy crisis, which was leading to higher fuel prices. Our project made economic and environmental sense at a time when the United States was seeking new sources of energy. (Some environmentalists were even talking about capturing elephant farts in the zoo to see if they could be converted to energy.) We were ready to proceed. It seemed as if all the windows of opportunity were in perfect alignment.

However, it was not to be. In a series of unpredictable and unfortunate events taking place in rapid succession in San Francisco, the city's political structure changed, and the project was eventually terminated.

The first change was that the mayor of San Francisco, George Moscone, a good friend who supported our project, was assassinated along with City Supervisor Harvey Milk.

Just prior to that tragedy, Thomas Mellon, the city's chief administrative officer, retired. Mellon's post at the time was more powerful than the mayor's. He was an extraordinarily intelligent individual who was not afraid to make a decision. He supported our project, but his retirement resulted in the appointment of a new chief administrative officer, former city supervisor Roger Boas.

In my personal opinion, all the great talent and experience that Tom Mellon brought to the office, Roger Boas completely lacked. He had a great penchant for hiring consultants to help him make decisions for the city. When the results of the consultants' work proved positive, he would take all the credit; when they were bad, he would blame the consultants. Using all these consultants cost the city millions of dollars and, in our case, valuable time that we did not have.

To compound an already bad political picture, the voters of San Francisco approved district elections to replace large elections for the eleven members of the board of supervisors. The supervisor who was elected to the area where the proposed waste-to-energy project was planned was vehemently against the project.

As a result, the project was delayed almost two years. By then, a lot had changed:

- The capital cost of $90 million for the project had soared to $200 million.
- Because the value of energy had decreased, PG&E's guaranteed payment of six cents per kilowatt-hour was reduced to less than four cents per kilowatt-hour.
- The California Pollution Bond Authority's interest rate on financing had soared from 5 percent to 8.5 percent.
- The City of Brisbane, which at one time had supported the project, no longer wanted it. Roger Boas opted for a site at the Port of Redwood City, which would require San Francisco's waste stream to be transported to Redwood City, adding substantially to disposal costs.
- As the energy crisis waned so did the public's acceptance of burning garbage, and the term refuse derived fuel lost meaning.

The California Air Resources Board (CARB) also exacerbated the problems when it publicly spoke out against any form of combustion, especially garbage. The Redwood City project created another firestorm of politics, and the whole project was lost. This was an unfortunate set of circumstances. I believed then and still believe now that refuse-to-energy projects (like those being used in Western Europe) provide the only solution to garbage disposal.

22

A Conceptual Solution for the State of California

As I write this book, after so many years of experience in this complex and sometimes misunderstood field, I am reminded again how my high school dean of boys suggested that, if I did not get my shit in order, I would grow up to be a garbage collector. For better or worse I did become a garbage man, and now I feel the need to at least try to give something back to the great State of California. That said, I ask myself: What is a long-range solution for the state of California?

As someone who has been in the business for sixty years, in my waning years and at no charge to the state, I respectfully offer a conceptual—but logical and feasible—long-term solution for a comprehensive regional and state solid-waste-management disposal system.

A solution must commence with an environmentally sound, regional, large, and long-term series of sanitary landfills. We need the appropriate number of regional landfills to serve the entire state, with haul distances of no more than 150 miles. In most cases, only material that cannot be recycled or otherwise used goes into those landfills.

Once we can agree to this, we must design and implement a regional plan for a specific series of material recovery facilities (MRFs) or transfer stations, where a program of flow control can be implemented. All waste generated within an area would be collected and disposed of in that area's designated facility, where all waste would be received, processed, and recovered—and all recyclable materials would be recovered, processed, and sold.

During the process of recovery, the secondary byproduct would be the refuse derived fuel (RDF). This raw material would be transferred into trailers and delivered to one of several strategically located biomass power stations. Once the RDF is delivered to the power station, it would be further processed to convert the material into a uniform size, moisture-balanced, and predictable combustible fraction and be introduced into a combustion chamber to create steam energy for electricity generation. The materials that cannot be recycled or used for fuel would be disposed of at the designated regional landfill.

Many independent waste-collection entities may be operating within a designated region, so those entities, using the MRF/transfer station, will be charged a uniform standard per-ton disposal fee.

If there should be a physical problem or a maintenance issue of any kind at an MRF or power facility, the landfill is always available, assuring a continuation of regularly scheduled waste-collection services.

As an added incentive for creating *dependable* electrical power along with these proposed regional power stations, they could be designed to use not only RDF for a power source, but also to include natural gas as a backup supplementary source of energy. This system would not only assure a continuing source of electrical power in the case of a breakdown of RDF delivery or an unpredictable increase in moisture content in the natural gas, but it would also provide a backup energy boost to increase internal combustion temperatures to assure maximum air quality efficiencies.

I recall the dramatic and extremely appropriate response from the German engineer in Munich. He said:

> Sir, this a power station first, one that generates a substantial amount of needed electrical power, that uses two sources of fuel to develop that power, namely coal and refuse. . .and because we look upon our refuse as a fuel, we solve a secondary problem, namely the need of refuse disposal.

A profound and accurate assessment? You bet!

Some may argue that this type of proposal would be difficult or impossible to implement on a grand scale. However, we could start with a study to determine how many tons per day would be necessary to justify the investment necessary to build a series of MRF/transfer stations and a single RDF/natural gas electrical generation facility. For example, let's assume that the per-ton-of-waste generation needed to justify the investment is 3,000 tons per day. We would then look at a region in California where 3,000 tons of waste is generated each day. Then we would determine the number and capacity of the MRF/transfer stations required to process that waste stream to create the initial development of RDF.

The next step would be to determine the best location for the RDF/natural gas electrical power generation within the region, taking into consideration haul distances and adequate highway access to the facility.

I have no idea how many regions would be necessary in the State of California (only studies can determine that), but I do know that the population in California will continue to rise, as will the generation of waste.

I hasten to add that some of my colleagues will disagree with this thought, because the term *zero waste* is the call of the future. I respectfully disagree, because although zero waste sounds appealing and desirable, it will never happen, especially if we want to maintain the high standards of health we enjoy today. I offer this observation because the United States of America has the highest health standards in the world, and much of that lofty goal has been achieved because of our packaging, which generates a substantial amount of non-biodegradable materials to create and maintain those standards.

As an added caveat: In lieu of burning agricultural wastes in the fields, as practiced throughout California, a program could be developed to recover, process, and convert waste to generate power rather than let it burn in the fields.

An energy consultant friend of mine has estimated that, if this conceptual program were commenced by developing an initial "region" and eventually the entire state, it is possible that the State of California could produce 12 to 15 percent of its electrical power needs from its own waste streams. This alone makes the idea worthy of consideration. Furthermore, the environmental and economic benefits derived from such a system would result in substantial savings to California's taxpayers. It currently takes three trucks in each area to provide waste-collection services throughout the state, to collect waste, collect green wastes, and separate recycling. In the past, one truck did it all; returning to this more efficient system would result in taking at least 1,000 diesel trucks off the streets.

This simple but logical solution from a simple scavenger is workable, and the technology and the need are here today. The first hurdle is the California Air Resources Board (CARB).

The Hurdles of the California Air Resources Board

In my personal opinion, CARB is a clear and present danger for the economic health of the State of California. I base this statement on a multitude of bad regulations, many of which I was personally involved with in the past and have observed over the years—and especially those that affect the solid-waste industry.

Years ago, CARB made efforts to clean up the trucking industry. The first segment CARB looked at was refuse trucks using diesel engines. I assume that CARB applied the logic that we were in a dirty business, and therefore our diesel trucks were dirtier than other diesel trucks, so CARB began to look at us, and the solid-waste industry, in order to establish minimum standards for the entire diesel trucking industry.

CARB had no data or baseline to determine what "minimum standards of diesel emissions" should be. CARB tested a multitude of concepts and systems then being developed by new companies to sell their diesel-pollution-control products in California. After some time and testing, one company was approved to sell its emission-control equipment in the state. CARB set new standards to force the industry to clean up its act. As for our company, we had the option to purchase new equipment with the approved emission system or add the system to our existing fleet.

To comply with the new regulations, companies had to pay an average of $50,000 more for each new or existing truck. A three-truck company added $150,000 to its capital cost; a fifty-truck company added $2.5 million. The sad part about this is that in most cases, a solid-waste collection company can recover this type of expense because it is a legitimate cost of providing waste-collection and disposal service; however, the small independent trucker has no means of recovery. An added $50,000 expense can spell financial disaster for the firm. CARB did not seem to consider the impact of such decisions on the independent trucker.

But it gets worse. One of the new companies whose air pollution equipment CARB approved to sell in California failed and went out business. The few truckers who had purchased and installed the equipment were left holding the proverbial bag. Nothing was ever publicly announced regarding this CARB fiasco.

Over the years, I have had many dealings with CARB, and its tunnel-vision staff, especially when dealing with the dirty word *combustion* and while considering alternate forms of waste incineration. For example, a system of waste disposal known as *pyrolysis* is a combustion process without oxygen. In laymen's terms, because there is no oxygen in the combustion chamber, there is no flame. But to achieve the temperature necessary to create combustion of the material inside the enclosed oxygen-free chamber, electrical or other means of indirect heat is required to force the structural breakdown of material to another form—from a solid to a gas.

You can never destroy matter, only convert it.

With that thought in mind, consider such a system designed especially for auto and truck tires, where the tires are heated to sufficient temperatures for the rubber base to melt and be converted into a combustible oil and gas, which can then be used for a multitude of purposes with further refinement. Once the system cools, the tires are then solid chunks of valuable carbon black. Through exposure to a vibrating table, the carbon black is released from the steel belt on the tire, and the steel is recovered and recycled.

In my professional opinion, this is a logical and environmentally sound means of disposal or recycling regarding the never-ending problem of used tires. I know of at least four efforts to permit one of these facilities in California, but there are no such facilities operating because CARB has concluded that the pyrolysis method of thermal reduction is a "combustion process," and therefore it has prohibited its use anywhere within the State of California.

Still another example of CARB's ineptness and lack of foresight was demonstrated some years ago when I was retained by a company known as WangTech as a consultant to evaluate another pyrolysis method of disposal—not tires, but liquid hazardous waste. At first I was skeptical but, after observing a demonstration project, I eventually saw hundreds of potential applications.

As this method developed and operated in Chicago, I emphasized to the promoters that the process would have to pass the "acid test" (CARB regulations). I stressed that if WangTech could pass CARB's requirements, the company could be permitted to operate anywhere in the world.

Realizing the legitimate need for an independent evaluation of the air emissions from the process, the company gave me permission to enlist an engineering firm in California. The results confirmed that the air emissions from the process were cleaner than the air in its natural (untreated) state.

The method involved heating the liquid hazardous waste to the boiling point, passing the resulting vapors through a patented filter (the "heart" of the WangTech process), and continually monitoring the waste until all contaminates were recovered from the vapors. At this point, the vapor being released was virtually pure water, which could be reduced and released harmlessly into the atmosphere.

Realizing that CARB would not take my word for the claims of clean air emissions, I applied to the agency for a permit to demonstrate the process in California. In order to file for the permit, I used two sources of evaluating the emissions: WangTech's measurements and my independent study and evaluation. The application to allow a demonstration of the process at WangTech's expense was summarily denied on the grounds that, in CARB's opinion, it was an "incineration process" and therefore ineligible for consideration. Need I say more?

Because of CARB's rejection, the State of California lost the opportunity to develop an economical and environmentally sound solution for small hazardous waste disposal generators in California. This system would surely have been a great step forward in resolving the state's hazardous waste-disposal needs.

23

The Winds of Change

After I became president of Sunset Scavenger Company in 1965, the company made substantial gains in all areas. We upgraded equipment and made it more efficient, enhanced working conditions, gave workers substantial increases in health and pension benefits, increased stock values, increased personal income, and—most important—implemented the transfer station, which virtually assured we would be in business in perpetuity.

After we acquired companies outside San Francisco, revenues increased substantially. The formation of a real estate holding company and an equipment leasing company—all under the umbrella of Envirocal Inc.—was another achievement. Each of our rate-regulated subsidiaries operated on its own, but had the advantage of purchasing equipment, fuel, and the like at large-scale discounts.

The most personally rewarding part of all this to me was to feel and see what we had accomplished for the partners. Their investment in the company was increasing, and they and their families received enhanced benefits.

But there was a problem: the "share," which created the Boss Scavenger in the company. When a shareholder chose to retire or leave the company, he could sell his share to another employee on the truck or have the company purchase it back. Starting in 1972, the company opted to purchase the shares from retiring partners; by 1982, we had reduced the number of shareholders from 320 in 1965 to about 280. We did allow a few young, eligible, desirable employees to buy shares. The value of a share in Sunset Scavenger Company in 1965 was $15,000. In 1972, the board of directors established that share value at $25,000.

The concept of purchasing the shares made economic sense on paper because the historical means of collecting payments for refuse collection services was provided by the Boss Scavengers, who physically collected each of the more than 146,000 accounts by hand. Once the IBM data-processing program began billing the 146,000 accounts, a Boss Scavenger's responsibilities were narrowed to monitoring his customer base and running down delinquent accounts. In other words, the need for Boss Scavengers to work as route managers declined significantly.

Without the need to monitor the customer base, a three-man crew was reduced to two. At the same time, the pay differential of a Boss Scavenger and a regular scavenger was some $10,000. We reasoned that, by eliminating a high-priced employee for one costing $10,000 less per year, the company could use those savings to purchase shares from selling partners. This arrangement would also benefit the selling partner because he would be paid off in five years instead of ten if the share were sold to another employee.

The downside to implementing such a program was the debt incurred. The purchase of another solid-waste collection company increased revenue to Sunset Scavengers, but purchasing shares did not result in income-producing debt. I considered the decision to buy shares an interim measure, while looking forward to creating a plan B in the future.

When we commenced the program, the value of each share was $25,000. If we purchased ten shares, it would mean a potential balance sheet debt of $250,000, which would be recorded as an intangible asset. I knew that such a program was nothing more than a Band-Aid solution; the company couldn't afford to buy all the shares back without unpleasant consequences.

As the company grew, I became rather frustrated doing business with executives who were making, in some cases, more than ten times my salary as president of a multimillion-dollar corporation. On the other hand, I also recognized that one of the reasons I became president of Sunset Scavenger was to ensure the preservation of salary equity between truck scavenger and corporate management, which effectively ran the company up to 1965.

I realized I had dug myself into a hole, and I couldn't get out of it. Some long-haul drivers working overtime at Sunset were receiving W-2 forms at the end of the year showing that they made $20,000 more than I did as president.

In theory, the "Equal Pay. . . regardless of office position or responsibility" covenant was still in effect, but I was not entitled to overtime, even though I endured many sixteen-hour days. Nevertheless, I did have some unique benefits. I drove a black Cadillac and belonged to the Olympic Club and other social clubs paid for by the company. I also had a limited expense account. I did my job and I loved it.

At about this time, Tom Peters, author of *In Search of Excellence*, interviewed me. Peters was giving presentations to inspire young executives to be the best they could be. I was honored when Peters interviewed me. He praised me in his presentations and ranked me as one of the six top corporate leaders in the United States, along with the presidents of IBM, Wal-Mart, and American Express. In his presentation–which had my picture in it—he said:

> See this man? His name is Leonard Stefanelli, and he is in an industry that you so-called white-collar workers would never consider being associated with...he goes to work every day, never looks at the clock nor how much money he makes...he puts his entire life and commitment into his job. Why? Because he loves what he does...and if you do not love what you do...you will never really be successful, so make every attempt to find a profession, job, or employment where you LOVE what you do.

Tom Peters would pause, point to my picture, and look at the audience. "What none of you would love, but Leonard Stefanelli loves..." (emphasizing his point by pounding his fist on the desk) "...is *garbage*. If you try to emulate Leonard Stefanelli's relationship to his job and work ethic, I will assure each of you success."

And I did love my work. It was frustrating at times, especially when I had to deal with the shareholders, but the job was extremely rewarding. It gave me the personal satisfaction of conceiving, implementing, and seeing new ideas come to life. I would not have traded it for anything else.

Tom Peters argued that my love for the job was its own reward, but I was caught in the no-win situation of being vastly undercompensated for my achievements. That was the hole I had dug, and I had to live in it.

During the 1970s and throughout my tenure in office, I was offered, several times, positions with Waste Management, Browning-Ferris, and other smaller companies. There was a shortage of professional executives in the rapidly growing solid-waste industry, and truly experienced personnel were in high demand.

I was flown out in private jets to corporate headquarters and given offers with very attractive compensation packages. I kept the written offers for five of these positions. One included a ten-year guaranteed employment agreement, with the title of vice president and a starting annual salary of $200,000, plus stock options. I carefully considered accepting that proposal, but (as cornball as it sounds) I turned it down because of my strong commitment to my company. I had deep roots in Sunset Scavenger, appreciated its rich history, and felt passionate loyalty to its shareholders. I believed that the company was going in the right direction, and that the time would come when someone would recognize and respect what it takes to effectively manage a company with such a unique corporate structure. I feared that a new president might amend the bylaws, allowing different compensation schedules, or change the entire corporate structure by tearing down the old ways upon which the company had been founded in the early part of the twentieth century.

My dogged commitment to the company eventually came back to haunt me. I was president for too many years, as was typical of many corporations at that time—being someplace too long sometimes can be a bad thing.

I was elected president when I was thirty-one. Some fourteen years later, I was starting to become frustrated with the job. The old ways of doing business were becoming less effective; we needed change or else we'd die on the vine. Despite the substantial improvements we'd made, some traditional Italian philosophies and practices within the garbage companies still prevailed. My personal feeling was that unless things changed—and soon—the company could slip into an economic rut. The prospect that I couldn't make the changes needed for the company to survive began to weaken my motivation and interest in my work.

Some years earlier, I happened to be in an airplane with Barton Shackelford, president of Pacific Gas & Electric Company. It was nighttime and we were flying back from Seattle when the pilot announced, "For those of you who are interested, we are flying over the Oregon-California border."

Bart looked out the window into the darkness below. "Look, Lenny. Every one of those lights below is a PG&E customer."

An extraordinary statement—until then, I had not comprehended, let alone respected, the magnitude and the awesome responsibility of Pacific Gas & Electric Company.

Then I thought, "For every light, there is a can of garbage."

Bart and I eventually became personal friends when we were brought together to consider a waste-to-energy plant for San Francisco. He assured me that the production of energy would remain in private hands and not allow any municipality to compete. Indeed, PG&E made every effort to support a private entity to achieve that goal, and our company would be the beneficiary of their commitment.

At that time (early 1970s), public companies were entering the California market, but there were still some forty private waste-collection companies in existence, ranging from small two-truck operations to as many as thirty trucks, in addition to Sunset, Golden Gate, and Oakland Scavenger Companies.

After the trip to Oregon, I had this vision of creating a super company, built on the foundation of our Italian heritage—the rich heritage that Sunset, Golden Gate, and Oakland Scavenger Companies had begun a half-century before as an organized industry.

La Cosa Nostra—"Our Thing"—is a traditional term used to refer to the so-called Sicilian Mafia, and it aptly described the program that I was beginning to envision, if it became a reality.

In 1982, I was really excited about this prospect, creating a public entity that would eventually include the majority of the private companies operating in Northern California. The first step in creating such an enterprise was a merger between Sunset/Envirocal, Golden Gate Disposal/Norcal, and Oakland Scavenger Company.

My board members and I developed a plan. While some old-school members had some reservations, the majority approved the plan. With the able assistance of Michael Sangiacomo, my new chief financial officer, I drafted a proposal to be presented at a future date to Golden Gate Disposal and Oakland Scavenger Company. The pending proposal included the following points:

1. After economic evaluations, each of the three entities would agree to the terms of the merger of resources.
2. The new organization, in theory, would generate a revenue flow of about $750 million annually.
3. The name of the new entity would be Consolidated Environmental Industries Inc. (CEI).
4. Each company participating in the merger, including the subsidiaries, would continue to provide services under its original corporate structure.

5. Creating a Public Offering: The funds created or common shares could be used for retirement of debt, development of new business (such as transfer stations or new landfills), and acquisition of other companies available in Northern California that were interested in participating in "Our Thing."

6. If more acquisitions occurred over the next five years, CEI could become a two-billion-dollar company doing business only in Northern California.

7. The shareholders/Boss Scavengers (or "high-priced garbage men") of the purchased companies would exchange their existing shares into CEI shares but would remain in their current employment positions until they elected to retire.

8. Upon retirement, workers would have the option to: (1) sell all their shares on the open market for cash, (2) sell a portion and retain some of their shares, or (3) retain all of their shares.

With the valuable aid of my CAO, Gal Campi, my staff, and representatives of Merrill Lynch (to support the financial logistics and feasibility of the proposal), I called a meeting with the presidents and staffs of the respective companies and submitted the plan for their consideration. I explained that if we adopted "Our Thing," we surely would give the so-called giants in the solid-waste industry a run for their money.

The presentation took about an hour. I went into great detail talking about this once-in-a-lifetime opportunity and the high probability of reaping greater dividends for our shareholders. Everyone listened with great interest. Once the detailed presentation was completed, I yielded the floor to the audience.

The first question was from Peter Gardella, vice president of Golden Gate Disposal Company. "Who would be president?"

Since sixteen Italians were present at the meeting, this question was inevitable. It didn't really matter who the president would be, though, considering the magnitude of what was being proposed.

I pointed out the irrelevance of the question. The answer would be worked out based upon the needs of the new corporation, and that the new president would be chosen by the new board of directors.

"As far as I'm concerned," I said, "I've been president at my company for seventeen years; and if that's a problem for anyone present, forget about it."

So the issue seemed resolved.

Then Peter Borghero, president of Oakland Scavenger Company, raised his hand. I anticipated a legitimate or important question from him because he ran a tight show at Oakland.

Borghero asked, "Okay, if we merged together, what color would the garbage trucks be?"

I damned near fell out of my chair. Here we were talking about a billion-dollar merger, and Peter Borghero's priority was what color the garbage trucks would be! I could not believe what I heard from both of these high-end executives. This merger offered awesome opportunities for all concerned in the company, yet those were the only two questions asked. When no significant questions came forth, I suddenly realized that I was five years before my time. The proposal went nowhere.

To say I was disappointed by their lackluster response is an understatement. The concept was far beyond these fine gentlemen's comprehension of what the companies needed to do in a competitive market. Although the majority of my company had endorsed the plan, some board members did not. Content with the old ways of doing business, they joined ranks with the narrow-minded leaders of these other companies.

Losing this great opportunity was like hitting a brick wall. Without that merger, Envirocal's growth opportunities were severely hampered, if not terminated. This disappointing lack of action rattled what I had always considered an unshakable commitment in myself to the future of the company.

Just another rock in the bowl, with more to follow.

After leaders of the two largest solid waste companies in the Bay Area turned down this project, my interest in the business started to wane. I thought they should have at least considered the proposal, if for no other reason than to meet their fiduciary responsibility to their shareholders. But they failed to do so.

Changing Politics within the Company

When I was elected president, I believed in free speech, the democratic process, and the shareholders. I pledged to the partners that, unlike in the past, people could speak about anything at the stockholders meetings. Seldom, if ever, had any Boss Scavenger ever asked about how the directors, let alone the president, managed the company—especially about any subject that might be considered critical or controversial. (If you remember, Uncle Freddy once asked why the company was sending money to Italy during World War II and, shortly after he asked that question, he was on his way to the army.)

When I was elected president, I wanted the shareholders to be able to express their thoughts in an open and unrestricted environment. I made it clear that free speech and the democratic way was the call of the day. Initially that idea was productive, but as time went by the meetings sometimes got stupid and ugly.

In the past, stockholder meetings had been necessary for one primary reason: to impress upon members the importance of providing the highest degree of service to our customers. Workers who did not do this were brought before the board of directors and penalized by a fine, suspension from work, or a combination of both. The board's decisions were read at the shareholders meetings, so the psychological impact and personal embarrassment of the board's actions, read aloud in front of peers, was an added incentive to provide good service and follow the rules. Members rarely asked any questions, and seldom was any corporate business discussed at these meetings.

That all changed under my leadership. At the stockholders meetings, we read the minutes of the board and went into some detail as to why and how decisions were made. I would elaborate on the decisions as necessary to share with stockholders the magnitude, complexity, and the political and economic implications these decisions would have on the company. As was done in the past, I always emphasized the need for good service, but now we had reached the point we were talking about multimillion-dollar decisions and sharing the information.

Typically, shareholders asked only a few questions, and I would respond accordingly. I believed that, in many cases, the information was over their heads—or they trusted in our judgment. I would like to believe that it was the latter, but sometimes I wonder.

At one shareholders meeting, after reviewing a recent acquisition, Guido S. Guido, a Boss Scavenger who was about forty-five years old, a Calabrese born in the Old Country, had a question. His actions and personal appearance often brought to mind the image of Benito Mussolini. Guido put his foot upon the bench and began to pontificate in a heavy Italian accent, addressing the shareholders directly.

"Patrone, are we all not equal in the company?" (The members present seemed to agree.) Guido continued, "The president has a Cadillaca car, so I'd ask the question, if he has a Cadillaca car, how comma we all do not have Cadillaca cars?"

The response from the shareholders was mixed. Some applauded, while others laughed at him. I stated that such a question hardly warranted a response and left it at that.

Unfortunately, it was an example of things to come. Although I had tried to bring up board decisions and share them openly with the shareholders, these men were slowly becoming complacent. Their income and benefits were now excellent and that was all they cared about. Instead of planning for the future, they began to worry about who might be getting something they were not getting.

The "Cadillaca car" comment showed that free speech was creating some problems. When the annual elections for the board of directors were being held, more people were signing up to run for office than ever before—including some who didn't have enough qualifications to be a dogcatcher.

The sad part was that the dogcatcher candidates were winning seats on the board. I recalled how fortunate it was that I had been successful in getting the bylaws amended to provide for three-year staggered terms. Otherwise, all eleven members would be up for reelection every year, creating much confusion and instability. These new members did not believe in some of the policies I was attempting to change and other important corporate decisions I was trying to implement. The board was becoming a body built on popularity rather than ability and commitment. Some even lacked the most basic commonsense knowledge of business.

I recalled that day during my brief college education at the University of San Francisco when my business administration instructor introduced himself and said:

I want to congratulate all of you for attending this class. I say this because you have established yourselves in a separate category of the workforce, as you are trying to get ahead in your lives. The other segment of the workforce is content to work 8 to 5, five days a week, stay home with a beer, watch TV, and bounce their kids on their knees. I hasten to add, I am in no way criticizing this way of life, but your decision to attend this class demonstrates that you desire to get ahead and contribute to making the world a better place to be in.

I never forgot that statement from more than fifty years earlier, but it was clear that I was losing control over the board of directors as more "beer drinkers" joined. Independent thought by reasonably qualified people is a sacred trust in the democratic process. But some of the people being elected to the board were hardly reasonable.

24

A Radical Change and a New CFO

Historically and especially prior to 1965, administrative and truck maintenance personnel were typically drawn from the ranks of the partners working on the trucks. This was especially true of those who had developed physical limitations and could not continue with the labor-intensive job of collecting garbage on an open truck.

When an administrative position opened up, a working partner who needed such a position because of a physical impairment would fill it, even if he had no knowledge or experience in the new assignment. The shareholders who still worked on the trucks would call the assignment a "gravy job," adding, "the guy is a bum . . . , must be kissing some director's ass . . . , there is nothing wrong with him," and suchlike.

Whether the guy was a bum was not the issue. It was the company's policy that when any position became available, it would first be offered to a shareholder. The reason for this policy was to maintain the tradition of taking care of the shareholders. This was one of the primary incentives to become a shareholder. Recalling the words of the former president: "Keep your nose clean and you will have a job the rest of your life." The problem was that 90 percent of the time the shareholder was assigned to a position about which he had no knowledge or experience. He needed to be trained, often by someone who *was* qualified.

This created a double-edged sword scenario. Most people with managerial skills who came from outside the company had no basic knowledge of the complexities of the waste-collection business; they would have to be educated about "garbage" as well. Regardless of who filled any position, retraining was always necessary.

As we acquired other companies, we adopted this employment policy by placing the "men on the truck" (shareholders) in new positions that became available. We had some success with this policy, but only after some proper mentoring and support. However, the degree of sophistication needed to meet the demands of the future surely did not come off the garbage trucks, so another challenge that had to be dealt with was the need to offer these new executives an attractive compensation package, more than what we gave the man on the truck. I had to explain and justify to my board—and to the shareholders—that not all positions can be filled by a man on the truck. To attract qualified people to fill certain positions, we had to compensate them more than the current wages earned by the Boss Scavengers.

They claimed that this was a bitter pill for them to swallow.

This protest was crazy because the company would pay whomever we hired more money than I was making as president. I realized, though, that I had to live with that situation because payment levels were an issue back in 1965 when I became president. Now I had to take my own bitter pill, whether I liked it or not.

Late in 1979, we hired a young CPA as our corporate comptroller. In the past, he had audited our books to prepare certified financial statements as required by law. His skills and knowledge of the company's affairs seemed to make him a perfect fit, and his compensation package was within acceptable range of the Boss Scavengers. Nevertheless, I had to do some hard selling to the board because he had "never carried garbage. . .and he was not Italian"—yet another "old way" to deal with. The board eventually agreed to hire him.

The new comptroller and I had some personality conflicts from the very beginning. I felt he had a superiority issue with me, suggesting that he was smarter than I was. That feeling came to reality in 1982 at a company Christmas party at Bimbo's, when he, like many of us, had indulged in some alcoholic beverages. He asked to dance with my wife, and she agreed.

When my wife came back, she said, "Where did you find this guy?"

I asked why she'd said that, and she responded, "I'll tell you on the way home." Once in the car, she told me that as soon as they got on the dance floor, my corporate comptroller proceeded to tell her how intelligent and educated he was, how he was more qualified than I was to be president, and that if he wanted he could have my job anytime.

Her response was, "Can you take over tomorrow?" and she left him on the dance floor alone.

Needless to say, his career with the company and me would be short-lived; but prior to making any moves, I needed to find someone to replace him. Thomas Kunz, the managing partner of our

CPA firm, said he knew of a person who may be interested in the position: Michael Sangiacomo, who was employed as chief financial officer of Pacific International Rice Mills Inc. and the previous assistant comptroller at a local coffee company. His being an Italian *and* Genovese was a real plus when considering the historical attitude of the board. I was also advised that his father was once a shareholder/Boss Scavenger of the Scavenger's Protective Association/Golden Gate Disposal. I liked what I heard and asked Tom Kunz to contact Sangiacomo to see if he would consider a position with Envirocal/Sunset Scavenger Company.

We met at Bertolucci's in San Francisco for an initial introduction. I found Michael to be knowledgeable of the business, as well as good-looking, with a great personality to go with it. During the course of the conversation, I asked him why, with these credentials, he did not work for Golden Gate Disposal. He explained that his Dad (although retired at the time) had in fact taken him there to introduce him. The company offered him a man-on-the-truck position as his qualifying apprenticeship until a position that needed his experience became available. Michael said that he was not adverse to hard work, but felt his education and experience could be put to better use than carrying garbage.

At our next meeting, after a review of his prospective duties, he said that he would consider working for us. I was convinced, then more than ever, that this was the individual I wanted and that the company needed to fulfill both its current and long-term goals.

The next step was the potentially controversial issue of compensation. After some serious negotiation, I explained the age-old tradition of not paying anyone more than a man on the truck. I suggested that he might take this matter into consideration. Michael responded that he was fully aware of that policy, but that it was outdated and none of his concern. If I wanted him to leave his current position, he would require a compensation package that was at least $40,000 a year more than I was making as president. I had to set aside my personal feelings and do what was right for the company, because the company surely was in need of the talents that Michael Sangiacomo had to offer.

I accepted his terms and conditions—subject, of course, to approval by my board of directors—by no means a slam dunk.

His three primary credentials—he was an experienced CPA, an

Italian, and the son of a Boss Scavenger—made the proposal easier to sell to the board. I will not bore you with the ugly exchanges at the board over the issue of compensation ("How dare you bring in a proposal to pay an employee more than a Boss Scavenger, the man on the truck, the real income producer?"). In any case, in mid-1983, by a seven-to-four vote, Michael Sangiacomo became Envirocal/Sunset Scavenger's first chief financial officer. Eventually he became my confidant—a personal and trusted adviser. Hiring him was a difficult effort for me personally, but surely a correct one for the future of the company.

A New Era and a New Chief Financial Officer

Michael Sangiacomo came on board and oriented himself to the Sunset Scavenger Company. He appeared with me to provide the financial status of the company and other information at the stockholders meeting.

Michael's financial reporting was comprehensive and professional. He also provided details that I knew were far too sophisticated for most of the shareholders to understand. This was confirmed by their questions, which were mostly about his salary and why he was worth more than the man on the truck. The shareholders believed they were the only *real* money earners in the company and that anyone who did not carry the can was a freeloader. In their minds, the money we were paying Michael was an example of violating the company's traditional philosophy of operation. In other words, no one should be compensated more than a Boss Scavenger, and unless there was a radical reform in the corporate structure, that would never change.

These arguments eventually waned but, at that time, I could see Michael was irritated by the repeated questions, always giving the same answers but never seeming to satisfy anyone. I shared his frustration because I had experienced the same exasperating treatment for seventeen years.

Michael handled the criticisms well and settled into managing the affairs of the company in a professional manner. He provided financial data that was in the best interest of the company, but there was always the nagging issue of the shareholders' attitude toward him because he was making more money than anyone else.

Another Negative Event: The Solano Garbage Company Acquisition

In December 1982, when I was working on acquiring Solano Garbage Company, another new member was elected to the board of directors, replacing one who had supported my basic business philosophy.

We had commenced the acquisition process in 1970. Since then, Golden Gate Disposal had followed our lead by beginning an aggressive program of acquisitions, including the formation of a parent company, then called Norcal Waste Systems. From our first acquisition of Los Altos Garbage and through the others that followed, combined with those that Norcal had acquired, few companies remained that considered selling.

If you want to purchase a company, experience dictates that you don't just walk in with a bag full of cash, even if you are personally acquainted with the acquisition candidate. Instead, you eat lunch, play golf, have a drink, hunt, or do whatever else is needed to become part of the "family," alluding to the *possibility* that someday they (the principals) might consider a sale. If you do all that 95 percent of the time, the principals will eventually come to you first. You then make a preliminary estimate of what you would offer as a financial incentive. Then, if you conclude there is some mutual ground, the first order of business is to sign a letter of confidentiality. This letter is necessary for several reasons, primarily to assure that any information exchanged between the parties remains private and that the sellers will not let it be known they are considering a sale of their company.

The next step is to ask for and evaluate the company's financial status. Once you have reviewed this information, you draw up a one-page summary of your proposal, meet the principals for lunch, and present the proposal to them informally.

Every one of the many acquisitions that I initiated began in this manner, followed by a simple handshake. Then I would take the proposal back for approval, have the attorneys draw up the formal sales agreement, and finally close the deal.

The Solano Garbage Company's general service area was in Solano County, which incorporated the cities of Fairfield, Suisun City, and Green Valley, as well as Travis Air Force Base and a huge undeveloped service area that was prime real estate for sizable population growth. Aside from the waste-collection service and related equipment and property, Solano Garbage Company had its own landfill operation, with an option to purchase several hundred acres of additional property adjacent to the current permitted landfill. This was important because increasing the capacity of this site would be a relatively easy and economic means to create a truly regional sanitary landfill, as opposed to opening a whole new site, which was and continues to be very difficult and expensive anywhere in the State of California.

If any entity (private or municipal) attempted to create a new sanitary landfill, my experience shows that one could spend in excess of $50 million and ten years of work, yet never turn one spade of dirt to develop the site, let alone open it up to receive waste. (Waste Management endured such a venture in Contra Costa County in the early 1990s, investing millions of dollars on a site before finally giving up.)

Solano Garbage Company's site offered substantial growth potential, came with a landfill site, had potential to become a truly regional disposal facility, and could be a significant income producer. I was extremely excited about this possible acquisition. The two partners, Nick Zunino and Frank Ottolini, agreed to my offer of $1.2 million. I knew that this offer was a steal because of the landfill, and that it was no doubt the best opportunity our company ever had to expand its revenue base and enhance pay equity.

I brought the proposal to the board of directors, which voted six to five to reject my recommendation. This turn of events was a complete shock to me because of the bargain it truly was and the extraordinary opportunity its acquisition would be for the company's prosperity over the short term (five years).

Aside from my disappointment was the embarrassment I experienced when I had to go back to my friends and colleagues to tell them that my board had rejected the proposal. The board's refusal to approve the deal made me look a bit stupid, and it demonstrated to both them and me that I was in fact losing power at the board level.

For the record, the Richmond Sanitary Service (led by my friend Richard Granzella) purchased Solano Garbage Company for $1.5 million—$300,000 more than I was ready to pay. As time went by, Richmond Sanitary Service did exactly what I had envisioned. It expanded the landfill site and maintained a regional disposal facility, now doing business as the Potrero Hills Landfill, which now receives waste from not only Solano Garbage, but from Contra Costa County (Concord Disposal), West Contra Costa County (Richmond Sanitary Service), Sonoma County, and NCR Waste Services Collections. The disposal amounts to more than 3,000 tons per day and significantly enhances the bottom line.

What is important to note is that Richmond Sanitary Service purchased this company for $1.5 million and then invested another $12 million in land acquisition, permitting, and equipment, most of which was paid for from increased disposal revenues from Concord Disposal and others. This successful venture substantially enhanced the value of Richmond Sanitary Services' investment, and when the company was sold to Republic Services, the value on the Solano Garbage Company component of the deal was in excess of $50 million. Need I say more?

The Solano Garbage Company fiasco and some other failed projects demonstrated my board's lack of foresight. I began to realize that any future opportunities I may want to pursue, although never as attractive as the acquisition of Solano Garbage Company, would still be turned down, so why would I even try?

Regrettably, the majority of the board's business philosophy and opinions on how the company should be operated—such as dealing with internal politics among shareholders and making policy—was based more on popularity than on sound business logic and was contrary to my way of thinking.

In December 1985, another new board member was elected. As I feared, this new board member was elected based on popularity, not talent. He could hardly speak English and had no business sense at all. To make the situation even worse, the person he replaced was not only an ally of mine, but also my vice president.

Prior to the election, one board member bluntly told me that I should stay out of the campaign process to fill the position of vice president. The director even went on to state: "If you do, you will be next."

My term for reelection was coming up in December 1986.

Even with my support, my vice president lost his position. Nothing much was said, but clearly my future as president of the company was in jeopardy, and I knew it. The board's continuing rejection of my programs convinced me that I had lost control of the board of directors. In truth, I was getting bored and, more importantly, frustrated with my position.

Aware of the board's adamant opposition to my ideas of how

the company should operate and where I believed it had to go to survive in the future, I concluded that I would be wasting my time even to try to save my position. I also admitted to myself that I had been president for too many years (twenty) and that, even though the shareholders knew that I had accomplished great things for them and the company, it was rare for anyone to stay in that position for such a long period.

I had no incentive to stay and made the difficult decision to seek other opportunities. I say difficult because of my long-term relationship with the company and its rich history, which I so deeply respected, as well as my moral and fiduciary obligation to the shareholders. I also felt a strong debt of gratitude to the company because of the wonderful opportunities it had given me, especially the personal satisfaction of seeing my visions become a reality.

I was considering moving to greener pastures, but where? I had no idea, but I assured myself that I would not give my board the opportunity to vote me out as president.

Unlike the past, when the shareholders voted the entire board of directors out of office, I was reasonably confident that I would be elected to the board. But I knew that the presidency was no longer within my reach, so I was making plans to see what might be available in the coming year of 1986.

25

A Significant Event that Changed My Plans

Finally, a matter arose that involved a working shareholder being charged with a major conflict of interest.

When the transfer station went into operation in 1970, it opened up new opportunities for the Boss Scavengers to get out of collecting garbage and be retrained as drivers, truck maintenance workers, and managers. Under this unique arrangement, Boss Scavengers remained on Sunset Scavenger Company's payroll, even though they were actually performing services for another entity. The transfer station would contract with Sunset Scavenger Company to provide the personnel for these necessary positions and reimburse Sunset at an hourly rate that would not only include the then prevailing hourly rate for direct labor, but also other related costs, such as pension, health, welfare, and so forth. The primary reason for this arrangement was to simplify payroll. Although physically working for another entity, the Boss Scavenger was still controlled by the rules, regulations, and bylaws of Sunset Scavenger or the revised bylaws of Envirocal Inc., the holding company. All employees of the other entities were still dues-paying members of the Sanitary Truck Drivers and Helpers, Local 350. The only exception to this arrangement was senior management.

In this controversial situation, a Boss Scavenger had been assigned to the transfer station, initially as a driving instructor training and certifying some thirty-five drivers to drive the 80,000-pound eighteen-wheeler waste-transfer vehicles. In time, as the need for drivers waned, the transfer station needed continual maintenance, periodic improvements, and upgrades—sometimes costing as much as $100,000. The protocol was, of course, to put these needs out to competitive bidding, review the bid based on the specifications, consider the contractors' qualifications, and award the contract.

Over the years, and especially between 1982 and 1986, the contract became awarded to the same entity. I personally thought this was strange, and other members of the board noted it as well. The shareholder involved was a longtime friend of mine, so I contacted him personally about the matter, wondering about a possible conflict of interest and noting that some of the board members had concluded that he was getting kickbacks.

He vehemently denied such a claim and facetiously said, "If I was getting kickbacks, the company was still getting the lowest bid." After further discussions with him, I concluded that he was somehow connected with the company financially. I cautioned him that, if he were connected with the company, he did have a conflict of interest and should clean up his act and find another contractor. Once again, he denied any wrongdoing and argued that the company always got the lowest bid. I told him that was not how I saw it and the board was on the hunt. I suggested that, in his own best interests, he should terminate his relationship with the contracting company. If the board were to make a move on him for a purported "breach," there would be nothing I could do to help him.

The next day, I received a call from the contractor asking to see me. When he arrived, he brought with him his bank ledger, corporate agreements, and other company documentation to prove, once and for all, that this shareholder had no financial interest, direct or indirect, in the contractor's business. He had me review his company and personal checkbooks, insisting that the shareholder's name never showed up anywhere. I thanked him for sharing this information with me. I was satisfied that there was no credible evidence to tie the shareholder to the contractor. My gut feeling, however, was still to the contrary.

Unbeknownst to me (until I was provided a copy of the board agenda the day prior to the next meeting), several members of the board had called for the shareholder to appear before the board to respond to charges of a conflict of interest. At the board meeting, the suspect shareholder denied the charges and showed us the documentation to demonstrate his innocence. After the presentation and a very short discussion, the board of directors voted eight to three to fine him $5,000 and give him a month's suspension, for a total penalty of $10,000. It was evident that this decision had been made in advance and outside the boardroom walls.

I and the other two board members who voted against the fine were harshly criticized for not voting with the majority of the board. I argued that each board member had the obligation to vote what he believed. I believed that the shareholder was not guilty because there was no tangible proof that he was. I added that, because he was a member of the Teamsters Union, he would most likely file a grievance, which would end up in front of a four-member commission, two members from management and two from labor. No doubt it would end up in the typical deadlock situations like this produce, with a formal arbitration hearing before independent parties. I also stated that I would be one of the members on the grievance committee, and that I had the obligation to support the board decision and would do so even though I disagreed with it. I predicted that the shareholder would be returned to work and would be reimbursed fully for the fine and time lost.

"In my opinion—aside from the loss of time and money—he will be reinstated, and the board of directors and the company will look like a bunch of immature idiots." That is exactly what I said, and I meant it.

As I predicted, the shareholder went directly to the union, which filed a grievance against the company. The grievance hearing was scheduled during the week that my longtime friend and mentor (and the president of the board of supervisors) Jack Ertola was scheduled to leave with me on a long-planned horseback ride in a remote area in Northern California. I asked Leo Conte, president of Golden Gate Disposal, to fill in for me.

My directions were as follows: "Listen to the arguments set forth and vote with management's and my board's decision to the fine and suspension. It will then be sent to arbitration, and it will be out of everyone's hands."

Leo's response: "No problem. I'll do as you say."

The following weekend, I left with Jack Ertola as planned. On the following Wednesday, I rode several miles to the nearest telephone and called my wife to check in.

When I got through, I could hear by the excited tone in her voice that something was amiss. She blurted out that I had been "excommunicated as president of the company" by the board of directors and that the information had come directly from one of the board members, Joseph Pesce, who was a longtime friend and supporter of mine.

I called Joe Pesce, and he told me that, at the grievance hearing, with a three-to-one vote—and Leo Conte casting the deciding vote—the committee decided to overrule the board's decision to fine and suspend the shareholder for conflict of interest. The committee also mandated that the shareholder be reinstated with full pay, reimbursed for the fine, and compensated retroactively to the day the suspension was initiated.

The board had convened a special meeting to discuss a presumed conspiracy between Leo Conte and me. The board adopted a resolution to demand my immediate resignation as president of the company because, in their view, I had conspired with the president of Golden Gate Disposal Company to overrule a board decision.

If I had not gone on the horseback ride, this surely would not have occurred. I had no way to present my side of the matter, and I could not get ahold of Leo Conte to ask why he did what he did.

The term *nightmare* certainly understated my situation. Once back in the city, I attempted to better comprehend the sequence of events that had, in a matter of four days, led to my dismantling as president of the company.

The Worst Was Yet to Come

Once I returned to San Francisco, I was called for an appearance before the board of directors to explain my side of the drama. The meeting was set for 10 AM the next morning. I also called Leo Conte and asked for a meeting with him at 9 AM

When I arrived at Leo's office, I could see that he was unsettled, although he appeared to be unaware (which, I was to find out later, was a charade) of the huge negative impact on my twenty-year career as president. I told him that his decision to vote resulted in a demand for my resignation as president. His face seemed to say, "You have to be kidding," as if to say he knew nothing of the board's decision to excommunicate me.

I went on to say, "Why in the hell would you do the exact opposite of what I instructed you to do?"

"I concluded that he wasn't guilty," Leo responded.

"I agree that he might not have been guilty," I said, "but that was not your decision to make. Look at the significant problems you have caused for me! Why in the hell would you do something contrary to what I specifically told you to do?"

Once more, he said that in his opinion the person was not guilty. I repeated that he did not have the authority to make that decision and, more important, because of what he did, I was about to lose my job. He made no excuses or apologies. I did not realize why until much later.

I asked Leo to come with me to the board and tell them that his decision to declare the shareholder in question innocent was his decision alone. Leo Conte said he could not come because of a previous commitment, so I left his office and went back to meet with my board.

I went into great detail, reiterating my meeting with Leo prior to meeting with the board. I explained that I had asked Leo to take my place at the grievance committee hearing, that I'd given him specific instructions to take the board's decision to maintain the shareholder's fine and suspension, and that Leo had agreed to do so.

Despite my explanation, the board renewed its demand for my resignation. Clearly, its intent was to terminate my position as president now for cause rather than wait until the December vote. I asked for additional time, but I was instructed to return to the board within twenty-four hours with my decision.

I left the boardroom, went to my office, and made some calls. I called my personal advisers, who said I should hire a lawyer. I made an appointment with Steven Breyer (now a member of the US Supreme Court), one of San Francisco's premier attorneys. Because he commanded a high degree of respect, he also commanded a $10,000 upfront retainer. It was a big hit financially for me but proved to be a good investment as the saga played out.

It was clear that the board was hell-bent on terminating me as president, but they couldn't terminate my employment since I was a shareholder. But where would they assign me? I had already been told by one of my anti-Stefanelli board members, Steve Barbagelata, that I would be assigned to a garbage collection route. (I was told that the men on the truck wanted me there because of the embarrassment I had caused the company.)

The fact was I could easily go back on the trucks because of the enhanced working conditions I had spearheaded and implemented, but that was not wise since that was exactly what the board wanted to do to me: belittle, embarrass, and step on me in another effort to discredit me.

As hard as it is to believe, matters got worse.

I worried about my reputation with the community after losing my position with the company, a position that I had held for more than twenty years. What about the respect I had earned during those long twenty years? What would happen when my unjustified dismissal became public?

As I thought about this, I came up with a possible solution to save some face. I called Leo Conte and set up another meeting. My proposal to Leo was simple. Aside from being president of Sunset Scavenger Company, I was also president of Sanitary Fill Company, the disposal arm of the two collection companies. Sanitary Fill had an eight-member board of directors, four from Sunset and four from Golden Gate. My plan included Leo's control of four votes on the Golden Gate board and my one vote as a member of the Sunset board. With the five members voting, I would tender my resignation as president of Sunset Scavenger/Envirocal to satisfy my board's demands but remain president of Sanitary Fill Company. I would work out of that office until December 31, 1985, when I would submit a letter of resignation as president of Sanitary Fill, to be effective December 31, 1985.

Leo readily agreed to my plan, admitting that he owed me. He assured me that his members would vote in favor of the plan, so I arranged to meet again before the board of directors. But much to my surprise and disappointment, before I could even submit the plan to the board, the pending president of Sunset, Livio Cristinelli, blurted out, "If you think you are going to Sanitary Fill Company until the end of the year, forget about it. That dog does not hunt."

It was readily apparent that immediately after Leo Conte and I had finished speaking about the matter in his office, Leo got on the phone and told Livio Cristinelli about my proposal. At the time, I was unaware of why he did that. I later learned that Peter Gardella (Sanitary Fill Company's vice president) had convinced Leo that he needed to renege on the deal he made with me "for the future of Golden Gate." Leo, not having any balls, caved in and told Sunset that I was coming with a proposal that Golden Gate Disposal would not support. I was to learn that this scheme was plotted out well in advance.

Leo did me in at the grievance hearing and now this. Talk about a stab in the back, something I never expected from him. Once was a tragedy; twice was inexcusable. Clearly, I had not followed my own advice: Never trust anyone but yourself.

After being crucified by my board and again by Leo Conte, I went back to his office where he was sitting with Peter Gardella and asked Leo, "What in hell are you trying to do to me?"

Abruptly, he started screaming at me (his usual modus ope-
randi when he was nervous or not in control), insisting that he was
justified—"Because I need to work with Sunset Scavenger's new
board, and I have responsibilities to my own shareholders. . ."

I was beside myself. "I don't need you screaming at me, and I
don't accept your lousy excuses, especially twice. Because of your
actions alone, I've lost my job at Sunset after twenty years." Then
I turned my back on him and left his office.

He followed me, put his arm around me, and had the gall to
say, "Hey Len, I know you are upset, but I hope you're not going
to do anything to hurt the companies."

I could not believe he would say that. If that was his concern,
I wondered why he hadn't supported me. I was intimately familiar with the most confidential of matters surrounding both companies, and *now* he was worried about what I might do?

"Leo, let me put this into perspective. I am going to do everything possible to f--k you. If the companies get in the way, they'll
become part of that effort. What do I owe you?"

The Hidden Agenda and Conspiracy

After that unexpected series of ugly experiences and months of in-
depth investigation, I found out how and why this all occurred.

It was now abundantly clear that it was not a spontaneous re-
action or error by Leo Conte over the grievance hearing, but an
extraordinarily well-planned and orchestrated plot to get me out
as president, combined with an equally well-orchestrated plan to
destroy my reputation. With my public image ruined, any efforts I
might have attempted to get back at the people who hurt me were
effectively neutralized. They might also have worried about how
I might get back at the company or its future operations. In a pre-
emptive strike to discredit any negative public responses I might
make against the company or the people who ran it, the company
tried to destroy my credibility.

Simply put, all bases were covered in the conspiracy, and this
is how it all began. As noted earlier, I was becoming disenchanted
with my position in the company. I had been president too long. I
had a board that did not appreciate or respect my proposals. Worse
yet, this board rejected whatever I proposed to advance the company's interests. I also believed that the traditional means of doing
business had to change. Unless things changed, the shareholders

would never realize the real dollar value of their investment because there were only two markets available to sell their equity: the company or another employee. Neither option could represent the real value of what shareholder equity truly was, in my opinion.

In 1985 a share had a value of $60,000, a substantial increase of 300 percent in value under my leadership, although still nowhere near the real value based upon what public entities would pay.

Under the conventional means of selling and buying a share, the seller (an employee shareholder) would offer a share for $50,000. The buyer would make a deposit of 10 percent ($5,000) and assume a note of $45,000, making payments of $300 per month on the principal of $45,000 plus 4 percent interest on the unpaid balance.

When an employee became a shareholder, his wages would be increased by $600 per month, and the added income would pay off his debt without changing his current standard of living.

Under this system, a shareholder would pay off the debt in just over twelve years. This exact same arrangement was in place when I bought my share in 1955, but the investment in Envirocal/Sunset Scavenger Company was more than just a job. It was an investment.

I believed that the company had to either go public or be acquired by a public company for the shareholders to receive true market value for their equity. My belief was confirmed when Waste Management offered each Boss Scavenger $335,000 in cash for his equity in 1989. However, the offer was rejected because of misleading information provided by the Envirocal/Sunset Scavenger Company's own attorney to the shareholders.

Some believed that an employee stock ownership program (ESOP) was the solution at Norcal Waste. I believed then and I believe now that an ESOP was not a viable option for Envirocal/Sunset Scavenger Company. My comprehensive research confirmed that an ESOP program was, in most cases, a great opportunity and provided great tax incentives for the owner of any company to turn over ownership to its employees. But this situation was unique since the selling owners were a majority of the buyers because of the company's unusual corporate makeup.

The significant profits that Golden Gate Disposal was enjoying and the ever-growing commercial customer base were not regulated by the city. However, these profits were far above the allowable rate of return permitted by the city's rate control board for the two entities, and that was a politically sensitive issue for Golden Gate.

However, the company had the cash flow to finance the ESOP while making principal and interest payments on ESOP. Making those payments and expensing them reduced Golden Gate's net income within the guidelines of the Rate Control Board. Therefore, when the company submitted its annual audited statement to the city, it appeared to be in compliance.

Sunset Scavenger Company's operating expenses dictate what the rates are in the city, based on the actual costs of providing waste collection: e.g., labor, insurance, fuel, disposal, etc. The payment of debt service and interest on ESOP is *not* a "cost of collecting garbage" and (ethically, and more importantly, legally) could never be considered by the city as a legitimate expense in running the business, and I knew that.

The point is that the Norcal ESOP was being funded by the extraordinarily high profits and cash flow that Golden Gate Disposal generated from its ever-growing commercial customer base. Because the city regulated only residences, flats, and apartments and the city used only Sunset Scavenger as its rate model, Norcal was able to fund its ESOP. In theory, it was possible that Envirocal/Sunset might be able to create an ESOP; but in practice, an ESOP would not materialize once a potential lender found out that the city did not allow that expense to be included in the rates. I know because I tried.

I went into great detail with my board on many occasions when the issue came up, and I assumed that they understood the matter. The majority of the board seemed to agree with me because the matter never went any further.

Oh, was I wrong in that conclusion! As I was to learn after I was unceremoniously excommunicated, a committee of my board had been formed (unbeknownst to me) and met on several occasions with representatives from Norcal, consisting primarily of Leo Conte and Peter Gardella, to explore the feasibility of Envirocal/Sunset Scavenger merging into the Norcal ESOP. Initially, they concluded that I, Leonard Stefanelli, was the reason the company was not going ESOP, and believed that the merger would not happen unless I was out of the picture. A plan was then conceived to get rid of me by preventing me from being elected to the board of directors that coming December. That meeting was eleven months in the future. While there were no assurances that I would not win the board position, they were confident that they would have enough votes to elect a new president (Livio Cristinelli). The problem was that such an event was a year away.

The committee began seeking pretexts to expedite the process of getting me out of the picture. This was the point in time when I requested Leo Conte to represent me at the now infamous grievance hearing. That was the opportunity the committee was looking for.

When I called, Leo agreed to represent me, and I told him how to vote. I did not know, though, that a plan was in the making at the committee's level. Leo voted not as I told him, but instead to put the employee back to work, providing cause for my board to demand my resignation.

Their well-engineered scheme not only terminated my position early but also destroyed my personal and business reputation, something I surely did not deserve under any circumstance.

Sometime after the official merger took place, I received a phone call from the El Dorado County Assessor's Office about a small Lake Tahoe shopping center that the company had purchased as an investment some five years earlier. I asked why the Assessor's Office was calling me, and the man said my name was listed as the contact person. They were questioning why, after buying the property for more than $1.1 million, the company had sold it for 50 percent or less of the appraised value.

I replied that I was no longer with the company and had no knowledge of the transaction.

I asked, "Do you know the name of the person who purchased the property?"

"Yes," he answered. "The party is Livio Cristinelli."

A payoff? Livio had been paid for helping to get rid of me!

As bad as it was for me, I did get some payback, because Leo Conte and Pete Gardella (and others) got what they deserved. From those many years of working with Leo, I realized that Norcal was his home, wife, kids, and dog. In essence, Norcal was Leo's family, and he loved and respected it in that manner since he never had a real family.

After the FBI raided the company, Leo was forced to resign. He lost his job, his reputation, and so much more. As far as I was concerned, he brought it on himself. I knew how badly this affected him because I'd experienced it myself. What happened to me was an embarrassing personal experience. But I had a family and a multitude of loyal friends to fall back on, and I survived and prospered in the industry after those dark hours.

Getting Even

I was successful in doing just that. Being president of Norcal Waste System/Golden Gate Disposal became the only thing in Leo Conte's life, and it was taken away from him in the same manner he caused my job to be taken away from me, only worse. I shed no tears when it happened.

People at Golden Gate Disposal informed me about the plan Leo and members of his board worked out. This was truly strange, especially after all the great things the two companies had achieved together, the great things we had achieved with the construction of the transfer station, and the new level of respect the companies now commanded from the city and the customers we served.

In time, I realized that this difference of opinion occurred because of the historical and philosophical rivalry between the two companies, each thinking it was better than the other. I must admit that from time to time I thought that way as well, believing that Sunset Scavenger Company was superior to Golden Gate Disposal and thinking about how great it would be for Sunset to buy Golden Gate Disposal someday.

But that fantasy was just that. Because of Golden Gate's huge (and growing) commercial base, Sunset Scavenger could never acquire Golden Gate; and even with Golden Gate's substantial, ever-growing cash flow from its commercial base, it could probably never acquire Sunset Scavenger. The logical solution would be to merge the companies, a plan that was considered in 1983 and failed to happen.

As I was to find out later, members of the Golden Gate Disposal board still clung to the traditional and meaningless rivalry between the companies. The thinking was, "Get rid of Stefanelli, and we will take over Sunset Scavengers." The reason was my opposition to the ESOP program, since the city would never agree to increase the rates to pay the ESOP debt necessary to fund the program. In time, I found out that was the exact plan.

The Next Phase of Destroying Me

After the board denied me the opportunity to phase out my career with any degree of dignity, I agreed to tender a formal letter of resignation, effective on the first of the next month, about ten days later.

During the course of this conversation, I asked about my company car, a nine-year-old (1976) black Cadillac sedan with a personalized license plate that read "RUMENTA" (a northern Italian term for garbage). I asked if I could purchase it.

The interim president, Livio Cristinelli, responded tersely, "You can keep that Mafia staff car; it's a bad image for the company."

About a week later, one of the directors came in while I was cleaning out my office. (I always referred to him as Shake and Bake, because he had a nervous habit of shaking his hands, which was really noticeable when he had a cigarette in his hand.) Shake and Bake walked into my office and blurted out, "After some additional discussion by the board, we have concluded that you need to pay for the car. . .and we want $2,500 for it!"

The next day, I brought in the check and gave it to Shake and Bake.

The following week, I was feeling a lot better and had sort of acclimated myself to all that had happened to me. I was in my office on Friday, around 11 AM, preparing for the Calamari Club Luncheon at Scoma's, when Shake and Bake, cigarette in hand, walked into my office.

"What are you going to hang on me now?" I asked.

He sat down at my desk, and I noticed that he had my check for the car in his hand. He shoved the check across the desk to me and announced, "When you leave the office today, leave the car keys on the desk. The board has decided that we need it in the family."

I took the check and said, "First, you give me the car, and then you say I have to pay for it, and I agree. Now you're telling me that I can't have it at all, under any circumstance. How can you or the board justify that position?"

His response was incomprehensible: "It's not the board's decision but the men on the trucks. They don't want you to have the car."

That clearly confirmed how badly this situation had deteriorated. Their outrageous demand pushed me to anger and frustration. It made no sense that I had to deal with an individual who did not have both oars in the water and yet was a director of a multimillion-dollar corporation.

My response was direct: "For the record, I am still president of this company until 12:01 Sunday. I am now taking the car to lunch. I will return it tomorrow, and I'll remove all my personal files and property on Sunday. Between now and 12:01 Sunday night, that 1976 Cadillac car will be stolen."

"You can't do that!" he said.

"Watch me!" I responded and walked out the door.

That night I put the car in my mother's garage and, on Saturday morning, I filed a stolen car report with one of my many friends on the San Francisco Police Department. No one knew where the car was, and there was nothing Shake and Bake or the board could do about it.

For a brief moment of personal satisfaction and joy—it was worth it.

Keeping the Car

Sometime later, a question came up about "first in and first out" funds in the company's pension plan. Management needed my testimony in court, and I asked, "What's in it for me?"

"What do you want?"

"I want the pink slip to the Cadillac," I answered.

And they reluctantly gave it to me. I still have that car, completely restored and with the same personalized license plate, "RUMENTA."

26

The Final Stab in the Back

When I thought that nothing could get worse and was contemplating the next step in my life, I was informed that the board of directors had retained the services of Pillsbury, Madison & Sutro law firm.

The purpose of retaining the firm at a cost of $50,000 was to have the attorneys review all my financial, political, and business dealings for any illegal activities. If that were not enough, a rumor somehow leaked out to the industry that part of the investigation was to confirm alleged theft of corporate funds. I had no income, no job, and I was in fact seeking work while being investigated for allegedly embezzling money from the corporation.

Three months later, the attorneys responsible for the investigation appeared before the board with their report and with information provided by Joseph Pesce, who was still on the board at the time. He reported to me a summary of the investigation:

Gentlemen, as per your request, we have completed a comprehensive review of all of Mr. Stefanelli's corporate and personal activities for the previous five years that he served in the capacity as director and president of the several corporations he has served in.

As result, we cannot find any evidence of inappropriate, unethical, or illegal activities, and we would respectfully suggest you not pursue this matter any further, for if you do, you may open the company to unnecessary litigation that could result in significant financial expense if Mr. Stefanelli opted to pursue action against the company for a defamation of character or some similar action. . .and as you are aware, he has retained a reputable and prominent attorney to represent his interests.

All this occurred within a period of three weeks. I had no idea how this investigation was to turn out, even though I *knew* that I did not do anything illegal. Regardless of the results, I already had a top-line attorney (Steven Breyer), and I was sure that Pillsbury, Madison, & Sutro knew this.

It should be obvious why I became angry and vindictive against the people who created this nightmare. I would like you to understand why I did what I felt I needed to do.

While all this was going on, Michael Sangiacomo, my chief financial officer—the man who made substantially more money than the "men on the truck" (and more than I did as president, though he deserved it)—contacted me at home. He expressed concern that I had been forced to resign and was convinced that he was next. He offered a couple of projects that he thought we could invest in together and seek work outside of the company.

The problem for me was that I did not have any excessive funds to invest. I appreciated that Michael thought enough of me to want to partner with me in some venture, but I couldn't participate. Fortunately, the people who had taken charge of the company realized that running it was not as easy as they had assumed. The termination of Michael Sangiacomo was put on hold.

Why do I say *fortunately*? Because Michael was the only person there who had the experience, knowledge, commonsense, and business logic (or in simpler terms, brains) to help the company. The new management could not handle it. Instead of being terminated, Michael Sangiacomo eventually became the chief adviser to the new president, Livio Cristinelli.

27

My World without Sunset Scavenger

One of the most difficult things for me was to explain to my political contacts, business connections, and personal friends why I was not president any longer. It was also hard to tell my daughter Gina. My wife, Virginia, stood by me during these difficult three weeks.

After I started my first day unemployed, Virginia said, "Wear a suit and tie every day. As you contact people to explain what happened, express confidence and optimism wherever you go."

That optimism was somewhat difficult, especially because of the rumors my former colleagues were spreading around the industry with the ongoing investigation.

During this time, I received a call from my longtime friend and colleague, Richard Granzella, president of Richmond Sanitary Services in Richmond, California. He said that his cousin and my friend, Benny Anselmo, had told him that I had been terminated and was looking for employment. I had known Richie since I was six years old. He was one of the people I had traveled the world with, seeking the black box to solve the world's solid-waste disposal problems. He knew and respected my capabilities.

Richie said that he, Concord Disposal, and Pleasant Hills Bayshore Disposal had formed a joint venture of sorts and were in the preliminary stage of developing a regional sanitary landfill in Contra Costa County. They needed someone to coordinate the development of the project, and he felt that I had the proper credentials and reputation. I told him that my former company was in the process of conducting an investigation of my affairs for the past five years, and that I didn't want that fact to come out after I began work with the joint venture.

His response was: "I don't care. We want you to come to work for us."

I agreed to go to work for the consortium after meeting with the other two partners, Silvio Garaventa Sr. and Boyd Only Jr. They offered me a starting salary of $50,000, plus benefits, an expense account, and a company vehicle, which I accepted—just four weeks after my termination.

I worked out of Pleasant Hills Disposal's small office off of

Highway 4 and shared a small office and desk with Boyd Only's pet cat, who had free roam of the office and was always sleeping on my chair or desk when I arrived. Plus, the cat's litterbox was nearby. This was surely a great step-down from my large Sunset office and the conveniences and authority I had become accustomed to. But it was a job, an ego saver. I did not have to request unemployment benefits, but instead had a place to work just four weeks after Leo Conte appeared before the grievance committee and stabbed me in the back.

During my tenure with this group, I participated in the design and development of Concord Disposal's pending Lovelace solid-waste transfer station and materials recovery facility.

Prior to my termination from Sunset Scavenger, the City of San Jose had issued a request for proposals (RFP) for a competitive bid for waste-collection services, under an exclusive-terms-and-conditions contract concept, a contract that was currently held by Browning-Ferris Industries (BFI). During my time with the consortium, the landfill project was in a sort of limbo, and the San Jose City Council awarded the contract to Waste Management Inc. (WMI). Out of the blue, Louis Garcia, the city manager of San Jose, contacted me. He wanted me to assist him and the city with the transfer of services between the two publicly held companies. His rationale was simple: "I need you and your talents to make sure the transition of services is accomplished without controversy or interruption and with the ultimate goal of making the city council not look bad—make them look like heroes."

Louis Garcia went on to offer me a $10,000 per month consulting fee for a guaranteed six-month period, and I readily agreed. That was double what I had been compensated as president at Sunset Scavenger Company.

I was able to convince BFI's senior management that it would benefit BFI's long-term public image and interest to make sure that the transition of service went as smoothly as possible. I reminded them that they were still doing business with the City of San Jose, and that it was in their best interest to maintain a good working relationship and not express any anger or a vindictive attitude for losing the contract to Waste Management.

I met with the transition team from Waste Management, headed by John Slocom, the vice president. I introduced myself as an agent for the City of San Jose and suggested that WMI provide me with a wish list of data that they would like to have to make assuming the waste collection responsibilities as easy as possible. I detected a bit of pessimism, so I said, "Tell me everything you would request given the best-case scenario, and I will see what I can do."

In two days, they provided me with a WMI wish list. In less than four days, BFI provided me a summary of sorts of all the questions asked by WMI, and I submitted it to John Slocom, who was directly in charge of organizing the implementation of the new service.

He reviewed the information and could not believe that BFI would provide that much confidential data, customer lists, routing, pricing, and even more, adding, "Did you put a gun in their face? BFI has never done this before when we took a contract from them."

As part of my consulting agreement, I was required to make monthly progress reports to the City of San Jose. It became apparent that the transition was farther ahead of schedule than expected, much to the pleasure of the city. Equipment was being delivered on schedule; truck maintenance facilities and administrative offices were established; and rates, billing addresses, and routes were set up for the commencement of services. All of this was completed well in advance because of the information I was able to acquire from BFI and provide to WMI.

The fact was that this was one of the biggest municipal contracts to be won from BFI, Waste Management's primary rival in the solid-waste industry. During my presentation, as per my commitment to BFI, I made sure that the San Jose City Council was aware of the extraordinary cooperation from BFI in providing the information necessary to make the transition as smooth and successful as possible.

As far as I was concerned, it was a win-win situation for everyone. Waste Management Inc. won the contract; Browning-Ferris Inc. maintained and perpetuated a fine reputation with the city; and the city received a new service at a competitive rate.

The services commenced on the first of the month. Other than a few minor problems, to be expected for a startup of that magnitude, the transition was an extraordinary success. The main reason it was so successful was that I had obtained pertinent information and data from BFI and provided it to Waste Management. I earned the money I was paid for the service.

As a result of my efforts during this significant transition between parties, Waste Management offered me a position as vice president of market development, at three times what I was paid as president of Envirocal/Sunset Scavenger. Finally, someone respected my talents and experience, and I did not have to answer why I drove a Cadillaca car!

Stepping Back in Time

When I became president of Sunset Scavenger in 1965, we did business only in San Francisco, our elected officials numbered less than fifteen, and a political contribution at that time hardly exceeded $100.

As time went by, we began to acquire companies outside of San Francisco and found that we had to learn more about local and state politics. In 1972, we formed an Oregon corporation with the help of our attorneys and accountants. Not only was a political action committee (PAC) legal in Oregon, but the tax liabilities were substantially lower than in California. We called the entity Westencon Inc. (for Western Connections).

Income was derived for the Sunset Scavenger, Golden Gate Disposal, and all the operating divisions. Contributions were determined on a percentage of monthly revenues, billed to and paid by the participating entities. When any of the divisions required or applied for a contribution that was duly approved by Leo Conte (for Golden Gate) or me (for Sunset Scavenger), a check from Westencon was issued and paid directly to the committee or candidate seeking office.

Attached with the check would be the business card of the executive of the company requesting the check. In the case of San Francisco and all state candidates, Leo and I would attach both our business cards.

If the candidate did not recognize Westencon, he or she would recognize the name and company on the card(s) attached to the check. The law required that the recipient of this type of check record where it came from, but the candidate had the option (legally) to include only the name of the company issuing the check, although with the attachment of the individual business card(s), the recipient would know who requested the contribution.

This not only proved to be a convenience for us, but also a totally legal and ethical means of opening doors to the political rat race. Over the years, I can recall at least six times that local papers called to find out what Westencon did, looking to expose something unsavory. After I explained what Westencon was, who ran it, and what its purpose was, nothing more came of the queries.

I include Westencon information at this point to provide insight into a critical error made by the person who took my place at Sunset Scavenger and opened the door for the FBI to get involved.

Livio Cristinelli, the person who helped organize my termination at Sunset Scavenger Company, took over the Westencon entity. At one point, he made a $1,000 contribution to California Governor Deukmejian. For whatever reason, the *Stockton Record* called Cristinelli and asked him what Westencon Inc. was. Rather than take the time to explain what it was and its purpose, he immediately denied any knowledge of the corporation. Even with his clearly legible signature on the check, he further denied having any knowledge of Westencon.

The newspaper put an investigative reporter on the story and dragged Sunset and its companies into a dark hole of political controversy, alleging that the companies were involved in a clandestine practice of paying off politicians and buying influence. This was not the case as far as Westencon was concerned, but the FBI came into the picture.

In fact, a skeleton of sorts hovered in the company's closet that I intimately knew about. This involved a prominent state politician that Golden Gate Disposal and Sunset Scavenger had legitimately contacted to seek an amendment to certain California Environmental Quality Act (CEQA) laws.

We were in the process of developing a major regional sanitary landfill, known as Lynch Canyon in Solano County. We were confident that we could meet the environmental assessment to get it permitted, but there were already moves being made to place the matter on the local ballot. After we presented the argument for an amendment to include all solid-waste permitting into the same category as water-pollution-control plants, we were optimistic that our project would pass the environmental assessment to get the site permitted, but that it would be rejected if it were faced with a voter referendum.

We left the meeting with a commitment from the legislator to study the issue and get back to us with some thoughts. Several days later, we received a call from the legislator's attorney, indicating that his client was prepared to go ahead with our requests. Since the legislator could not officially represent us, his law firm would. He suggested that we retain this firm to help pursue the project. He suggested that we pay an upfront retainer of $75,000 to the law firm, with a monthly fee of $7,500 to assure the legislation would be expedited.

When we asked how long they thought it would take for the legislation to be implemented and signed by the governor, we were told, "Possibly up to two years."

That's $7,500 x 24 = $180,000, plus the upfront retainer of $75,000, totaling at least $250,000.

We weren't naïve; these legal fees were a charade, but evidently this was the way things were to be done. If it got the legislation passed and eliminated the threat of a voter referendum, the $250,000 would just be added to the development of the entire project, which was already forecasted to be in excess of $7.5 million. (This was chump change, for a lack of a better term, and another lesson on how things were done in that era.)

Well, two years came and went. In the interim, a voter referendum was held and approved to challenge citing of the landfill. Not one piece of legislation was ever introduced to amend the Legislative Code. For all practical purposes, "we had been had." With no results from the law firm, the Solano County landfill project was terminated. We informed the law firm that we no longer needed their services and that the monthly retainer would terminate immediately.

We received a call—not a letter—from the attorney saying, "Everyone understands that the lack of progress was unfortunate, but you may want to consider retaining our law firm for your needs. It was respectfully brought to our attention that, at our last rate hearing, one of the three members of the Garbage Rate Setting Committee voted against the rate increase and that person who voted against the rate increase was now the chairman of the Garbage Rate Control Board."

The attorney added that if we continued to retain his law firm, we could rest assured that this person would always register a "yes" vote in future rate proceedings.

Clearly, no one had to be hearing- or reading-impaired to comprehend what was going on. Retaining the firm on the assumption we could get the necessary legislation to eliminate the voter referendum made some sense, but this suggestion was an outright extortion move. I made the decision to refuse it.

Leo Conte, on the other hand, went ballistic. "Damn it, Lenny, we have to pay this money. Golden Gate Disposal has all these commercial accounts and does not need any delays—worse yet, no rate increases."

I refused to participate because it was nothing more than extortion, and I advised Leo that if he wanted to continue to pay the law firm, he was on his own. This was 1984. Leo Conte, to the best of my knowledge, continued the monthly retainer payments through 1990, for an estimated $324,000. Adding the $250,000 paid early on, it represented well over a half million dollars paid to the law firm, which did nothing to justify the expense or fees for legal services.

In 1988, Cristinelli signed that check from Westencon and then denied any knowledge of Westencon. This one childish error, typical of his business style, caused the *Stockton Record* to embark on an investigation and expose the records and Westencon itself. It also resulted in the FBI knocking on my door at 8 PM

When they rang the bell, my wife went to the door and asked who they were. When she looked through an observation window, the investigators flashed their official ID cards and asked her to open the door. She refused, asking what they wanted.

"We are looking for Leonard Stefanelli. Is he home?" answered one investigator.

She said, "He's not here. If you see him first, tell him he's late for dinner." Then she turned off the porch light and went back to the kitchen.

After the FBI agents and I became better acquainted, they told me that they had *never* been treated like that. My wife became sort of "legendary" among the ranks of the FBI, given that everyone typically gets intimidated when the badge is flashed.

At the time, though, I had no idea what the FBI wanted me for. During my initial interview with the agents, I told them the primary purpose of Westencon, and that we did not do anything illegal with the funds. Because I had no allegiance to the company(ies), especially to the people who did me in, I was hesitant to provide the FBI with any specifics other than to justify the creation, purpose, and existence of Westencon.

Thanks to the inexperienced move by Livio Cristinelli, he and others did not address, nor consider any potential consequences of, their efforts to discredit me. They were evidently confident that they would find some proof that I was embezzling money from the company, and that my credibility could come into question if I challenged them sometime in the future.

The really funny part of the allegations that I was stealing money from the company was that many members of the new board and many Boss Scavengers believed the lie.

After several weeks, the FBI agents contacted me again. To my surprise, they asked specific questions regarding substantial payments made to a prominent politician. I had no reason to deny those payments. After all, you don't lie to the federal government, and I certainly had no allegiance to Conte and his people to consider doing so.

I had a valid reason to challenge the company, but this situation was something that I did not anticipate and was not necessarily ready to take advantage of.

The FBI Inquiry

Unbeknownst to me, the FBI was gathering data from many sources. Some weeks later, the FBI applied for and received search warrants for the office of Norcal Waste Systems in San Francisco. The FBI targeted many of the Norcal officers during the process. The FBI raids became public, and the names of these individuals were published in the local news media.

Talk about conspiracies! From the very beginning, the goal was to eliminate me from the presidency and then to merge the companies through the employee stock ownership program that Norcal conceived. Obviously, it was not feasible for Sunset Scavenger Company to consider such a program under the current rate-making formulas in the city. Sunset would never be allowed, either legally or ethically, to include ESOP debt and related interest expense to appear in the rates, whereas Golden Gate was not regulated as such and could include those expenses in the rates with no recourse from the city.

During the process to merge and create the Envirocal Sunset ESOP and then merge that into the Norcal ESOP, Waste Management asked to appear before the Envirocal board of directors to offer an $85 million purchase of the company, just one day before scheduling a shareholders meeting to present the Norcal offer.

The Envirocal board, as the record shows, canceled their normally scheduled meeting "because there was nothing of significance on the agenda. . ."

In either case, Waste Management was denied the ability to formally submit the offer to the board, but they developed a summary of the offer at my urging. Others and I made sure that it was distributed to as many shareholders as possible prior to the scheduled shareholders meeting, where they were to vote on the Norcal ESOP proposal. As the meeting came to order and the Waste Management offer was informally presented on the floor, the company attorney, James Meeder, responded, "The Waste Management offer should not be even considered. It was an 'unsolicited offer' and if challenged by your board in a court of law, would be declared invalid. Therefore the only legal proposal before you tonight is the offer from Norcal."

Prior to the FBI controversy, my sources who were still on the board of Envirocal told me that Mike Sangiacomo, my former chief financial officer, was making all the decisions for Sunset Scavenger Company because Livio Cristinelli was incapable of doing so. When the company completed the merger with the Norcal ESOP, Mike was assigned a prominent role with the senior management of Norcal, along with Leo Conte, Peter Gardella, Fiore Garbarino, and others. The former senior management of Envirocal/Sunset Scavenger Company was reduced to middle management or less, having nothing to say regarding the NORCAL ESOP affairs.

When the FBI controversy became public in 1989, and the company experienced severe financial (as I predicted years earlier) and political setbacks, the ESOP board, led by Justice Molinari, made a bold move and terminated virtually all of the senior management of the Norcal ESOP. This radical but necessary change stabilized the company. Even though Mike Sangiacomo had been with the company(ies) since 1982, his professional background and the fact that his hands were clean, so to speak, made him the most logical person to assume control of the company and the Norcal ESOP board. Sangiacomo was nominated to serve as president, and he sought and retained the services of competent people outside of the former rank and file of the company. Under his leadership, financial stability within the company was eventually restored.

Sometime later, a new Waste Management western regional vice president was assigned, and he brought in his own people, as is typical in large public companies. Many of the personnel at my level were replaced, and I was one of the casualties. Once again, I was seeking employment.

My Third Career Change

I was not out of work long—one week to be exact—when Richard Granzella, president of Richmond Sanitary Services, asked me to come to work for him in Richmond, California. My responsibilities were mostly centered on public affairs, business development acquisitions, and some operational requirements.

Richmond Sanitary Services, like Sunset Scavenger Company, consisted of nine partners, one of whom was the woman whose father had started the company in 1918. She was the oldest partner in the company. When her father died, she assumed the company's administrative functions, although her background was in education in Contra Costa County. All of the other partners at one time or another had worked on the trucks, and all of them assumed some form of management position as the communities they served grew in population.

During the course of business, the shareholders and partners of Richmond Sanitary were facing a situation similar to the one at Sunset and Golden Gate Disposal: their "real" equity in the company was worth far more than they could get with their limited market (i.e., another employee or a relative). The problem was compounded by their advanced age; in fact, the female partner turned ninety-one in 2000. The company clearly had to modify its outdated means of transferring or selling its equity if shareholders were ever to realize its real dollar value.

Part of my role in the company was to provide advice, and I was asked for suggestions on how to address this problem. In my professional and experienced opinion, there were only three options for them to consider:

1. Transfer Equity to Siblings. This was not feasible because several partners had more than one sibling, and many of them were incapable of assuming the responsibility of management. Also, this option did nothing for those who did not have siblings.
2. Purchase of the Company with Venture Capital. I explored this possibility with a venture capitalist in San Francisco, but ran into problems regarding the perpetual liability of maintaining the Post-Closure Fund

for the Class 1 (hazardous waste) disposal site the company once
operated and closed, which involved millions of dollars. Further, the
venture capitalist could not justify the values necessary to create an
offer that would maximize the equity value to the partners.
3. Outright Sale. Create a package that would be attractive to a publicly
held company.

Some five years after I became associated with Richmond Sanitary Services, the third option came to pass. The Richmond partnership eventually created a committee of three (made up of the
company's chief financial officer, the company's attorney, and me),
independent of the nine partners, to create a package offer to potential suitors. Our committee brought in representatives of Merrill
Lynch to review, consider, and meet with virtually every company
that might be interested in and have the financial resources to
make such an offer. The group of qualified companies included
Norcal Waste Systems.

During the five years since Mike Sangiacomo had become president of Norcal, he had changed the direction of the company and
slowly brought it back to financial soundness. The company now
could conceivably finance the acquisition of Richmond Sanitary,
so we scheduled a meeting with Norcal.

The night at the North Beach Restaurant when we met with
Mike Sangiacomo and his senior staff to discuss their possible interest in and capability of acquiring Richmond Sanitary Services
was interesting. To say there was a chill in the air would be an
understatement, especially since it was the first face-to-face meeting, or any other form of communication, I'd had with Mike in at
least nine years. Although we made a sincere effort to offer Norcal
the opportunity to purchase Richmond Sanitary, it was concluded
that Norcal did not have the financial resources necessary to pay
the Richmond Sanitary Company for their potential or real value.

Eventually the committee narrowed down the list of potential
suitors to three and then to one; we concluded that Republic Services could offer the most beneficial package, financially and legally. As a matter of professional courtesy and ethics, I will not
disclose the final dollar value the nine equal partners received, but
it was substantial.

Another significant incentive for the nine partners to consider a
sale to Republic Services was a full indemnification to the partners

for any future liabilities on the Class 1 hazardous waste site Richmond had formally operated. The other companies being considered refused to consider that incentive as a part of the final sale.

After the deal was completed in 2004, Richard Granzella (president), Lloyd Bonfante, Eddie Menosse, and I were provided three-year employment agreements. We were led to believe that we would manage the affairs of the company for that period of time under the auspices of Republic Services, which was headquartered in Florida, with western regional offices in Las Vegas. Much to our surprise, Republic Services compensated the four of us well, but we had nothing whatsoever to do with managing the company. Our primary purpose for three years was to take care of the local and state politics, attend fundraisers, kiss babies, entertain people, play golf, and the like.

That may have been fine for Richie, Lloyd, and Eddie, but I felt that I still had a lot to offer—especially to Republic Services. I personally knew the president, James O'Conner. He had been associated with Waste Management at the same time I was, and the two of us played many games of golf at the Olympic Club. He left Waste Management at about the same time I did, and I introduced him to Richard Granzella prior to the decision to place the company up for sale. When I called him about taking a more active role, rather than just being a playboy, he said to speak to the western regional vice president, Arthur Dudinski, another former Waste Management employee. Discussions with Dudinski went nowhere: After three years, he called me for a separation review, in which he explained how I could seek replacement health insurance, pension payments, and so forth. When everything was said and done, I asked him the inevitable question: "Art, why did you and Republic Services never take advantage of all my talent, experience, and reputation in the industry?"

His response was incredibly frank: "Lenny, in my opinion, your abilities do not conform to the corporate profile that Republic Services is attempting to establish."

"What does that mean?" I asked.

"You figure it out. . ." he responded and then left.

With that, my three-year career with Republic Services fell upon the cutting-room floor, with nothing really productive to show for it except a good time. I felt I had not accomplished anything, and we parted ways.

Life after Richmond Sanitary/Republic Services

Having maintained my contacts with people in the solid-waste industry, people quickly knew when I was no longer associated with Richmond Sanitary/Republic Services. However, I had signed a non-compete agreement that I was tied to for three years.

I was contacted by several small operators of debris-box or roll-off operators in San Francisco and San Mateo Counties, and invited to coordinate, manage, and grow their businesses. This position would, of course, put me in a somewhat complicated spot with Norcal, especially because I would be competing with it. But I concluded still that it could be a promising prospect, one that could provide me with a chance to use my experience, create a source of income, and achieve an equity position in a new venture in time.

As I was in the process of developing that program, I was contacted by two of my close friends and former Boss Scavengers in the Sunset Scavengers: Joseph Pesce, who was a former board member, and Richard Borghello, who was now the manager of all of the debris-box operations under Norcal Waste Systems. They had heard of my pending relationship with the haulers and expressed concern about what I was planning to do. They suggested that I meet with John Legnitto, Norcal's group vice president of San Francisco operations. I knew John Legnitto well.

After I left Sunset Scavenger in 1986, Legnitto left Forbes and went into the insurance business. After Mike Sangiacomo became president, he sought out John Legnitto and, because of John's knowledge of the company and his CPA background, Mike asked him to join Norcal Waste Systems. He agreed to do so.

I was a bit apprehensive meeting with John, primarily because of my past relationships with the company, before and during the FBI investigations. I was sure that I was not on the most-favorite-persons list by any means, but I figured that it was worth the effort to see what John had to say.

I met for lunch with Pesce, Borghello, and Legnitto, and, after the formalities, they made a simple offer: a position as a consultant and not an employee. I asked what Mike Sangiacomo had to say about this offer, and Legnitto said that Mike would support the proposal of my rejoining the company in that capacity.

The offer made sense to me after some consideration. Although I believed I could create a successful venture with my prospective partners, I considered my age as well as the time, risk, and expense of setting up a new entity. As an added incentive, I thought it *might* give me the opportunity to, once again, be associated with the company that I had given my life's blood to. I told John I would accept the offer.

I was provided a consulting agreement that really offered nothing more than the similar employment I'd had with Republic Services, except that I had received medical benefits with Republic. This agreement was not much more than a non-compete agreement. This was a "do-nothing" contract that would, in essence, take me off the street for three years, which I knew full well was Norcal's intent. I knew that Mike Sangiacomo really did not want me around. I believe he thought I might cause some kind of problem for him, but I actually had no intent of challenging him in any way.

On the other hand, it was better for them to have me under control than for me to be outside of the company causing problems. I was prepared to accept those conditions with the hope that, over the next three years, I could demonstrate that I was no longer the enemy, but a person who wanted to become a part of the team again and could contribute to the growth of the company.

As I write this final chapter, I am pleased and proud to report that I am commencing my eighth year of what started as a three-year agreement. My desire to become part of the team came true. During that period, I was allowed to participate in many programs and given many assignments. As one member of the executive management has said, "Give Lenny an assignment and go to sleep with the knowledge that it will be accomplished."

The ultimate compliment came from Mike Sangiacomo when he was interviewed by *San Francisco Business* magazine and asked a series of questions regarding the success of Norcal Waste Systems under his leadership. One of those questions was, "Who was your mentor?" and his response was, "Leonard Stefanelli." Without a doubt, that was my ultimate reward.

As I approached my eighty-third year, I realized that I had been associated with garbage all of my life. I actually got paid to be in the garbage business at nineteen years of age, became a Boss Scavenger at twenty-three, married a garbage man's daughter at twenty-five, and became president of the company at thirty-one.

During my tenure as president, the company came out of its Stone Age and became a respected leader, creating new and innovative programs for solid-waste industry-waste diversion and recovery, transfer stations, transportation, and advanced landfill disposal techniques—setting today's standards for environmental quality control. It included the first commercial system of methane gas recovery processed and used for electrical energy development, a standard and a requirement for today's landfill operations.

As I noted at the beginning, San Francisco generates more than a million tons of waste annually and has no physical or legal place to dispose of it, and yet the services have never stopped. The reason for that is our total solid-waste management program. We have always provided a means to dispose of the waste we have collected. None of this would have been possible were it not for our demonstrated ability to work in liaison with elected officials rather than in competition with them.

All urban communities need to have well-regulated and scheduled waste collection, and once that waste is collected, it must be disposed of on the same day. To make that happen, you must have a dependable and environmentally safe disposal facility or program.

Norcal Waste Systems, under the leadership of Mike Sangiacomo, has enhanced the programs that I helped to create so many years ago. The name *Norcal* was a common term used by many companies. At one point, management made a name change and it is now known as Recology Inc., better reflecting the company's operating philosophy and goals, as well as its deep history.

San Francisco enjoys the most comprehensive, efficient, and cost-effective solid-waste management system in the world—that is fact, not fantasy.

In my humble opinion, such an exemplary system developed under the leadership of Mike Sangiacomo, his executive staff, and a board of directors whose excellent record of success will not only continue but be enhanced. I thank Mike and his board, and I am honored and proud to continue to participate in this great venture.

In closing, I want to recognize and thank the old-timers who had the courage to leave their homeland, travel thousands of miles to an unknown place, meet people who were not necessarily friendly, and work in a business no one else wanted. These men survived and created the foundation as Boss Scavengers, which grew into the great company now known as Recology Inc.

I am sure that they would be extremely proud of our company, as I am today.

About the Author

LEONARD DOMINIC STEFANELLI, a third-generation San Francis-can, still lives there and enjoys the ever-changing faces of that mercurial city where he and his wife Virginia Luisa (Campi) have raised their two children and put down roots. At eighty-three years old, Lenny is still loving life and work as senior advisor and con-sultant for Recology Inc., going on sixty-four years in the gar-bage business, and he is once again a part of the company that he helped create.

Lenny still occasionally drives a completely restored black 1976 Cadillac Fleetwood Brougham, with its very special license plate, "RUMENTA," that at one time was recognized throughout the City of San Francisco.